D0615498

**THE BLACK
SCHOOL SUPERINTENDENT**

DISCARDED

HOWARD
UNIVERSITY
PRESS
Washington, D.C.
1980

THE
BLACK
SCHOOL
SUPERINTENDENT

*Messiah or
Scapegoat?*

HUGH J. SCOTT

Copyright © 1980 by Hugh J. Scott.

All rights reserved. No part of this book may be reproduced or utilized in any form without permission in writing from the publisher. Inquiries should be addressed to Howard University Press, 2900 Van Ness Street, N.W., Washington, D.C. 20008.

Printed in the United States of America.

Library of Congress Cataloging in Publication Data

Scott, Hugh J.
     The black school superintendent.
     Includes index.
     1. Afro-American school superintendents and principals. I. Title.
LC2731.S36   371.2′011   75-33305
ISBN 0-88258-036-1

To the Memory of
Dr. Marcus A. Foster

Marcus Foster possessed an infectious
personality which complemented his
exceptional intellectual resources and down
home practicality. A pragmatist, Dr. Foster
demonstrated unusual skills in recruiting
support for reforms. He had all of the very
special qualities of an outstanding educational
leader. Dr. Foster could have authored the
book on relevancy. He resolutely believed that
a black educator must commit his expertise and
position to the eradication of racism and the
rectification of socioeconomic inequities. He
was a militant black who "had his thing
together" — philosophically and
programmatically.

One cannot replace the Marcus Fosters of this
world. One identifies their contributions and
seeks to profit from their efforts and examples.
While his influence exceeded narrow
categorizations, Dr. Foster was held in
especially high esteem by his fellow black
educators. His pursuits and accomplishments
will provide an invaluable reference for black
educators, present and future.

Marcus Foster believed in both the future of
this nation and the future of black Americans.
He offers a theme to guide our reformative
efforts: "Working together, we are limited only
by our imagination." Therefore, this book is
dedicated to the life and memory of Dr. Marcus
A. Foster.

Preface

Scholars are just beginning to comprehend fully the changes that have grown out of the multiple domestic and international crises that engulfed the country between 1968 and 1974. The appearance of black school superintendents during this period went relatively unnoticed. Yet their emergence has made a drastic impact on the personnel structures of about 100 school systems across the nation. Until the late sixties, black school superintendents held posts mostly in extremely small and predominantly black rural school systems in the South and Southwest. Ironically, segregated school systems provided more promotional opportunities than integrated school systems. Desegregation efforts in the South, however, have produced a reduction in the number of black administrators in their traditional geographical stronghold. Along with the inheritance of school systems that serve large numbers of students with cumulative deficiencies in the basic skills and that are inadequately funded, black superintendents soon learn that textbook theories in school administration are not relevant to challenges of such magnitude.

The study from which this book emanated aimed not only to identify and examine black superintendents and their activities but also to chronicle this unique era in public education. Since most blacks live in urban environments and since many future black educators will be significantly affected by their social and professional experiences in urban communities, the book begins with a chapter on the urban crisis. This chapter examines specific causes of deprivation and deterioration in the urban centers as they directly apply to the growing complexities of the school system. The specific challenges of urban education are investigated. What is equality of educational opportunity, and how does it relate to quality education?

The heart of many inherent obstacles in the urban school system is the budget. This book delves into the politics that affect the fiscal well-being of city schools. Having served a rather tumultuous thirty-six months as superintendent in the District of Columbia, I feel that there are particular qualities that every superintendent should possess in order to fulfill responsibilities and maintain individuality. A chapter devoted to the superintendency as it affects the person will clarify, it is hoped, many ambiguities about the job. The particular plight of the black superintendent deserves to be examined. The burden and the dilemma of the influence of black consciousness is discussed as it relates to the intergroup and intragroup struggle of black Americans. This new emphasis has had a profound impact on policies and procedures in school systems across the nation.

I have selected seven school systems which have been headed by blacks to provide a deeper look at specific areas from which problems have arisen: the demography, the fiscal picture, the school board and its relationship to the superintendent, and the community. The seven systems were chosen because they represent a cross section of the problems and experiences that bind together the rather amorphous American education system.

Finally, I speculate on the future of the school superintendency, the future of black educators in the position, and the future of public education. From an historical viewpoint, a look at the black school superintendent is also a glimpse into the history of black leadership. Acknowledging the precarious nature of the superintendency, with its tendency toward rapid turnover, I provide a personal look at each of the seven superintendents with the hope that the aspiring educator will gain a sense of their motivations and style. The appendices contain their personal profiles.

This book has a single author, but its completion represents the combined input of a great number of people. I am indebted to those individuals who contributed to the effort: the seven superintendents, executive officers, staff assistants, secretaries and clerks in each of the systems, and the members of the school boards who gave assistance. The cooperation of the mayors and other city officials provided valuable input.

My wife, daughter, and son granted me the needed periods of isolation. I am grateful for their support.

Contents

Tables

THE BLACK
SCHOOL SUPERINTENDENT

1

The Urban Crisis

Between 1965 and 1970 about one quarter of a million blacks migrated from the South to central cities in the North and West; about one half of them were from nonmetropolitan areas of the South. The migration was indicative of the whole American population: This once agrarian nation had shifted to one under-girded by technology and science. The transformation increased the complexities of our social institutions and changed many social distinctions. These phenomena of modern American life were most visible in the metropolitan areas that had begun to replace the isolated rural areas and the small towns. For many Americans, urbanization produced serious social and ecological problems. Social displacement created grave problems of read-justment.

The whole of society is affected by urban deterioration. Check-ing and rectifying deterioration would be less difficult if the finger of guilt could be pointed at select institutions and indi-viduals. Today's social order must be indicted for urban decay, which has produced a colossal form of dysfunctional communal living. Some Americans have suffered more than others. For decades accepted reports depicted the volatile atmosphere of urban centers, but redemptive efforts have been dissipated by the fervor of American life. While society has marveled at the accomplishments of technology and science, the slow but steady deterioration of the quality of American life has been ignored.

The limits of this nation's capacity to absorb the denegration of its basic institutional structures cannot be determined. Many

Americans have elected to escape rather than confront the forces and symptoms of deterioration. They have sought to escape the clutches of decline through flight to the suburbs. This evasion has only succeeded in expanding farther the boundaries of deterioration and disorganization. This society must face the reality that it cannot permit the deterioration of the central city while encouraging suburban development or everyone will fall victim to this shortsightedness.

Today, the urban centers are the reservoirs of the consequences of humankind's inability to control its self-destructiveness. Statistics tend to substantiate this theory of urban self-destruction. A survey indicated that in 1972, Atlanta, one of the progressive cities of the South, had one murder or nonnegligent manslaughter for every 1,951 residents. Statistics suggested that one out of every five females living in Washington, D.C. would be raped during a normal lifespan, if the rate prevailed. The Environmental Protection Agency noted that Pittsburg had as much as 127 micrograms of particulate matter per cubic meter of air filtering throughout the metropolitan area.

Effect of Deterioration and Deprivation on Urban Life

When there is a major breakdown in the delivery of essential institutional supports, the hard times that accompany such deficiencies are acutely felt by the disadvantaged. Recent unemployment figures show that racial minorities, who make up the overriding majority of the disadvantaged, experience twice as much unemployment as whites. But all segments of the society are critically dependent on basic institutions and essential institutional services. When these basic institutions are experiencing internal conflict, and when gaps exist in providing institutional support services, the ramifications are widespread.

The following statistics indicate, to some extent, how certain segments of urban life had been affected by societal disorganization and/or deterioration by the early seventies:

> *Family Life:* The family unit and role relationships within it had undergone profound changes. In 1973

about three-fifths of all black families were husband-wife families. About 35 percent of black families were headed by women; this was an increase over the comparable proportion five years earlier. Between 1967 and 1972, the proportion of black children living with both biological parents decreased from 68 percent to 61 percent. Divorce, separation and desertion were on the increase. The relevance of marriage had come under great scrutiny by many young people. The family unit had begun to lose its influence on both its individual members and society at large.

Housing: Blacks paid a larger proportion of their income for rent than did whites in 1970 — about 45 percent of black households and 35 percent of white households expended at least one-fourth of their income for gross rent. About 63 percent of the black-owned households were mortgaged properties. The annual housing cost was at least one-fourth the income for 30 percent of these black households, compared to 18 percent for the comparable group of white households in 1970. Nearly 6 percent of all housing units in Newark lacked some or all plumbing facilities; over 14 percent of the housing units in Newark held 1.01 or more persons per room, making Newark the city with the worst housing problem of the fifty largest American cities. Black-owned homes tended to be more dilapidated than white-owned homes. Fifty-nine percent of the black-owned homes had been built before 1950, compared to 45 percent of the white-owned homes. Yet insufficient housing was a problem of not only the poor. Studies show that middle- and lower-middle-class families had found financing increasingly difficult to obtain and were living in apartment units longer than ever before. Racial discrimination still prohibited free access to available housing.

Churches: Churches struggle for existence in a society beset by value conflict. The church's influence had begun to decline more rapidly. A growing number of people viewed churches as pillars of materialism rather than shrines of spiritualism. The upheaval among the clergy continued over the question: How will the church change to conform to the changing contemporary society? An Episcopal priest was brought to trial on a charge of violating church law because he allowed a woman to celebrate holy communion at his church. In general, most of the churches with the strongest economic foundations had moved from the urban center. Washington, D.C.'s oldest Baptist congregation had moved from its historical church to an abandoned synagogue in an area far less accessible to the less affluent parishioners.

Food: Budgetary rather than dietary constraints cause many Americans to miss meals. Between January 1974 and January 1975 food prices rose 11.1 percent in the United States. Foods that were once considered the staples of the poor were becoming too expensive for them to purchase. Even though the basic costs of food for the rich and the poor were the same, item by item, the poor paid more.

Health Services: No nation in the world exceeds America in the exceptional quality of its health services; these services, however, are not distributed equitably. Detroit had a ratio of 545 people to 1 medical practitioner; Los Angeles had allocated only 41 hospital beds per 10,000 residents. In many cities, those citizens who lived nearest comprehensive medical centers and who had the greatest need received the least amount of health services. The cost of adequate health services had risen at such an inflationary rate that it was beyond the reach of the poor. Because of the inaccessibility of diagnostic

services, many young people continued to be hand-
icapped by curable physical and mental impair-
ments.

Employment: The nation's economy appears geared to
a specified number of Americans remaining unemployed. This economic course hits hardest those in
the most desperate need of employment. Workers
had been displaced because of automation or major
shifts in national spending priorities. Schools continued to prepare students inadequately for the
world of work. Career-oriented education had made
an earnest, though fledgling, effort to eradicate this
posture. Inequality in employment opportunities for
minorities, women, and the poor continued to be one
of the nation's flagrant violations of civil rights.

Recreation: If the entire population of Newark were to
have spilled into the city's parks one day, each resident would have had to confine himself to a 4 x 4 foot
area. Needless to say, such a space limitation would
not have allowed much spirited exercise. The National Park Association stated that there were only 4
acres of park and recreational land per 10,000 residents in Newark and only 10 acres in Washington,
D.C. Because of the lack of recreational space in large
cities, television had become the major form of enter-
tainment.

Safety: The poor and the affluent share a common concern about the rise in crime. Crime had become the
paramount concern of many city dwellers, regardless of race. According to FBI records, in 1972 Atlanta had the worst homicide rate among the 50
largest cities in America. There were 255 murders
and nonnegligent manslaughter cases reported.
Newark was the scene of 4,788 robberies. At that rate,
the odds were that a person who spent a lifetime in
Newark would be robbed at least once. Security and

protective services had become increasingly popular with the modern urban dweller. Homes had become fortresses, and correctional institutions had become larger. Despite street crime, organized crime continued to grow throughout every phase of American life.

Education: Public education in many urban communities serves a clientele that is predominantly poor and black. Many urban schools had been confronted with imminent bankruptcy. Public education was increasingly being viewed by the poor as inescapable, while middle-class black and white parents looked for alternative schooling.

Socioeconomic Influences on Learning

A child's school behavior is contingent on both school and home environments. No child learns his mores, social drives, and values from books alone. The child learns his particular culture from those around him. These rather circumscribed personal interactions contribute to the development of social classes.

All societies have a core of values that represent what the dominant groups within the society hold as the ideal norms and standards for human behavior. Individuals are often stimulated to act or to refrain from acting by the anticipated reaction of their most intimate associates to the particular act. But peoples' wishes are not always consistent with what has been declared to be good and proper. No group within a society is ever totally free from demonstrative disregard for some of the established standards of propriety. This inclination toward nonconformity is always inherent in social life itself. The strength of such tendencies toward nonconformity varies in relationship to the extent of social disorganization and alienation.

The root causes of the inadequacies of students which have been attributed to deficiencies in public education and to the existence of callousness and ineptness within the education

profession have been misjudged. The causes of the dispropor-
tionally higher dropout rate and distribution of lower achievement test scores among blacks and the poor go far deeper than
those effects produced by shortcomings within the education
profession and the limitations imposed by the boundaries of
knowledge in the behavioral sciences.

Campaigning feverishly for reform in public education while
ignoring or giving insufficient attention to the root causes of
societal deterioration and socioeconomic deprivation, then, is
an exercise in futility. A number of unfulfilled educational
needs of not only the disadvantaged but also other segments of
the American population cannot be resolved solely or primarily
by maximizing access to equal educational opportunity or by
implementing a rational and workable system of educational
accountability.

"A child from any circumstance who has been deprived of a
substantial portion of the variety of stimuli to which he is mat-
urationally capable of responding is likely to be deficient in the
equipment required for learning."[1] In America a normal child is
defined as an individual who is born with the appropriate distribution of the intellectual and physical capacities that are needed
for effective participation in a highly technological and scientific pluralistic democracy. Nature has not denied America's
poor white and black citizens innate intellectual potentialities.
For each child, free access to an environment that stimulates his
innate capacities is a fundamental prerequisite to adequacy in
communal living.

Any reform movement, therefore, must encompass improvements in employment opportunities, housing conditions,
health services, welfare assistance, and family life as well as in
public education. Without such concurrent reforms, the positive
benefits of a one-dimensional reformation would never be felt.

2

Urban Education: Challenges and Deficiencies

Crisis in Urban Education

The crisis in the inner city dramatically documents the consequences of societal deterioration in its advanced stages. The public schools in these depressed areas reflect the most pronounced inadequacies of public education; urban education carries with it the connotation of failure; few black parents have been willing to defend urban education. Whatever the explanations, one cannot refute the fact that urban students are not achieving at the same levels as their suburban counterparts.

A large number of school personnel believe the public's criticism of them is too harsh. Many educators see the problems confronted by urban schools as derivatives of problems students bring to school. Some educators claim that urban schools are not inferior to suburban schools. Nevertheless, urban schools appear to be incapacitated by the challenges of the disadvantaged. "The schools of the urban crisis, as they now exist, perpetuate the cycle of poverty, the merry-go-round of despair and frustration. They consciously or inadvertently discriminate against the poor and the powerless."[1] The cancerous nature of racial and socioeconomic discrimination and the resiliency of deprivation are reflected in the inadequacies of public education in ghetto schools.

The rapid expansion of knowledge, the emergence of a commitment to equal educational opportunity, the increase in educational costs, the burgeoning problems of the urban centers, and the growing concern for more efficient and effective use of financial and other resources have underlined the national concern for educational reform. The urban crisis and the glaring deficiencies of urban schools have illustrated that the problems of society are the problems of the school. Luvern Cunningham, former dean of the College of Education, Ohio State University, stated:

> The last half decade has been marked by frustration, tension, and great hopes dashed on the hard surface of despair. It has been a period when the educational excitement and prospects generated out of the early and mid-sixties have fallen on hard times. It has been an age when the society and its institutions have had to reexamine themselves — reappraisal focusing upon the extent to which the schools, for example, are serving the very purposes for which they were created. It was an era when the schools were called upon to negotiate for the society itself some of its deepest, most severe problems — racism, prejudice, intolerance, inequity. It was a time when the junior and senior high schools became the stages where the nation's most basic agonies were on display — where we expected teachers, principals, students, and parents to solve problems that have resisted solution in all other institutional settings. And it was a period when the richest nation in the world ran out of money — for education and other domestic needs.[2]

Quality Education Defined

Public education should be administered with a set of principles and social values geared to enhance the critical role of democratic public education. Education has to be viewed as more than a process of dispensing information and weeding out slow achievers. "Both of these approaches are futile. They are not only a disservice in a democratic society; they are contrary to the realities of growth and development."[3] Education must be more than mere training and preparation for adjustment to life. The truly educated person is one who is prepared to take part in remaking his or her world by making adjustments and decisions essential for creative living. Students should be encouraged to manipulate their environments rather than have their environments manipulate them. Equal educational opportunity is a concept without meaning unless it means equal access to quality education.

Quality education in a democracy requires that schools dedicate themselves to the goal of helping people live together constructively. The schools must stress the attainment of skills while demonstrating an equal concern for the individual's capacity to work and play with other members of the society. Integrating the purposes of education with the theory of the educational process, Frederic C. Neff made the following comment:

> Democratic education requires a resolute faith in the infinite possibilities of humankind for moral and social betterment. It means a recognition of the inviolability of human personality, of the practical aspects of Christianity, of the brotherhood of man. On the negative side, it means the rejection of the authoritarianism of fixed standards and dogma, and of the license of any person, state, or institution to prescribe what an individual must believe.[4]

What are treasured and supported as the essential elements of quality education are indicative of what are considered the fundamental needs and rights of the individual in the society. The schools must reform as well as perpetuate society. Ernest Melby, former distinguished professor at Michigan State University, presents a very fundamental question about education in America: " . . . Is American education, now as it is organized and conducted in our country, the kind of education that can save American freedom? That can give stability to our society?"[5] The schools should be identifying and resolving societal problems as they appear on local, state, and national levels. While the schools should not be permitted to promote partisan politics, they should explore contemporary issues and ideologies to help create an informed public. The schools have an obligation to assist citizens in realizing the principles of the Constitution. The schools should espouse and facilitate democratic principles in the context of day-to-day school experiences. If the schools are relegated to the role of passive observers of social injustice and inequities, they cease to serve the interests of all Americans.

Raymond H. Muessig provided the following comment on the role of the school:

> . . . The school should be a place where individual students and groups of learners sharing common needs and interests can reflectively examine problems, frustrations, aspirations, proposals, and values associated with change. . . . The school should be an open, honest, flexible, permissive, relevant, dynamic, human, and humane laboratory which helps pupils to become increasingly autonomous, self-directing, self-actualizing individuals capable of identifying and pursuing their own aims within a living societal context.[6]

Quality education comes from those educational institutions that contribute significantly to the intellectual and psychological preparation of their students. Only the potential of the individual student should limit opportunities provided by quality education. Quality education means altering elements of the social structure to produce equal opportunity.

Equal Educational Opportunity

Education is a form of social policy — a means by which the society distributes power and privilege. "American public school systems support the values and the dominant social class of their constituents' communities."[7] The public schools are the most proficient social institutions in adhering to the dictates of the dominant power structure. This proficiency is carried out through organization and the manner in which various racial, religious, and socioeconomic groups are received. "Social-class research demonstrates that our educational systems perform the dual role of aiding social mobility and, at the same time, working effectively to hinder it."[8]

"Any society which is to remain viable and dynamic must exploit and use constructively high intellectual potential wherever it is to be found."[9] A democracy needs an educated population. This democracy must look to its schools to move the poor up the social and economic ladder. Public education has an undeniable responsibility to direct its efforts to solving problems of community welfare. "The schools have been judged, once again, to be the primary vehicle for the improvement of undesirable social and economic conditions. America can no longer afford to show its poor a different face from the one it shows to the majority of its citizens."[10]

For almost the entire history of public education, the focus of the school has been directed to providing free and equal instruction for all children regardless of background. The exceptions were black Americans and a few other ethnic groups. However, a major breakthrough in upgrading equal educational opportunity was the historic May 17, 1954 decision of the U.S. Supreme Court in *Brown* v. *The Board of Education*. The Court took into account the sociological and psychological aspects of unequal education. In part the Court stated the following:

> Today, education is perhaps the most important function of the state and local governments. Compulsory school attendance laws and the great expenditures for education both demonstrate our recognition of the importance of education to our democratic society. It is required in the performance of our most basic public responsibilities, even service in the armed forces. It is a principle instrument in awakening the child to cultural values, in preparing him for later professional training, and helping him to adjust normally to his environment. In these days, it is doubtful that any child may reasonably be expected to succeed in life if he is denied the opportunity to an

education. Such an opportunity, where the state has undertaken to provide it, is a right which must be available to all on equal terms.[11]

Even though the 1954 decision did not provide the nonnegotiable elements of equal educational opportunity, it did establish the concept as a fundamental right of all children in states with publicly supported schools. The decision provoked much discussion on the purpose of education and the meaning of quality education. James Olsen provided a good summation of this point:

> We are at the threshold of a revolution in our educational thinking in this country. The major part of this revolution lies in our realization that all children in the United States do not have the same opportunities to develop and exploit their capacities and talents. Since cultural and economic differences among groups profoundly influence how a child sees himself as a person and as a learner, what he hopes to get out of school and what he wants to do — or not do — after he leaves school, the people he values and models to be emulated, and perhaps even how he learns, educators need to study class differences and then translate the insights they gain from that study into curricular and organizational modification.[12]

The Constitution projects a commitment to the premise that there are extraordinary possibilities in ordinary people. As long as the states remain in the business of providing publicly supported programs of instruction, equal educational opportunity is a right that cannot legally be abridged or denied because a child is poor, black, female, or poorly motivated. Each child is entitled to an education that stands to develop his potential. An education system without this kind of commitment denies citizens their equal educational opportunity. Even though past decisions of the Supreme Court have advanced equal educational opportunity, there is a possibility that the Court will become more conservative; past decisions could be modified.

Many black Americans have never experienced equal educational opportunity or been the beneficiaries of quality education. The entire social order seems to create and perpetuate the extreme socioeconomic disparities that produce massive inequalities among groups of Americans. While the public schools alone cannot make the difference for all the disadvantaged, they can make some difference. Schools are not the problem, but they are an integral part of the problem. If schools contribute to the cycle of deprivation and despair, one would assume that improvements in the educational structure would better the lives of the disadvantaged.

In separate articles Bayard Rustin and Charles A. Asbury have presented provocative statements on the relationship between good schools and quality living. They state, respectively:

> The course of a person's life may revolve, as Jencks says, on such subjective favors as luck and personality. But education and specialized training are issues of consequence. Even if a college degree meant little in terms of lifetime earnings, or proceeding further, even were we to succeed in achieving a society in which all incomes were equal, education would play an important role in determining the quality of one's life. A scientist can become a laborer if he is so inclined; the reverse is certainly not true.[13]

> Jencks is right when he says that the worst schools with the least able students would still not be as good as the better ones even with a disproportionate amount of resources. It is a sin of omission not to say, however, that these schools and their pupils could and would become better than they now are if the disproportionality of resources existed. They still might not be equal, but everything and everybody would be better off. Is Jencks trying to convince us that anything less than perfection is not to be allowed at all?[14]

"The American people have a sublime faith in the school. They have traditionally viewed education as the one unfailing remedy for every ill to which man is subject."[15] A number of Americans, especially among the poor and the black, still hope that tax-supported compulsory schools can ameliorate social and economic differences. But equal educational opportunity and quality education do not produce themselves. They are the products of the resolute will of a society or a community that commits its resources and efforts to such objectives. Earl C. Kelley stated:

> I have heard people who are earnest, good friends of youth say that we simply cannot afford the burden of good schools. This is nonsense. The people of the richest country in the world buy what they want. It is only a question as to what they value. I believe that we in education should not concede that the American people cannot afford a well-educated teacher and an attractive classroom for each twenty-five or so of our own young. We just have to care more about that than something else.[16]

Financing Urban Schools

The schools of the urban crisis are confronted with a financial crisis. The financial predicament is so severe that many school systems are being forced to reduce basic programs and services. Most of the school districts that have large numbers of blacks have financial problems brought on by inadequate funding. Limited funds have not only eliminated the expansion of ongoing programs and the initiation of new programs, they have also deterred the continuation of already underfinanced programs. To resolve the financial problem, many programs and services have been reduced. Those programs and services usually found to be most expendable are those which make school life most appealing.

Taxpayers are revolting against the current status of urban education. "Expenditures are rising very rapidly with little or no demonstrated increase in educational outcomes. Local taxpayers are revolting and state coffers are stretched, but costs continue to rise while little educational progress is being made."[17] Some taxpayers tend to apply a "production line" assessment to evaluating the public schools. Such an approach tends to dismiss all variables other than the number of students, the number of personnel, and their combined costs. The taxpayer concludes that most schools are more often than not irrelevant, inefficient, and prohibitively expensive. Even those who strongly object to the "production line" approach tend to agree that the cost is high and that the schools have not met the needs of a significant percentage of their clientele.

The public is not inclined to support public education at its present rate of expenditure. That the primary source of school revenues comes from property taxes is unquestionably a factor in the public's reluctance. The public's ability to support education adequately, however, is as much a matter of the public's will as it is a matter of resource capacity:

> The costs of quality and equality in education — calculated, as they usually are, in dollars and cents — invariably turn out to be higher than expected. Not infrequently, the public is unwilling to pay the price, and even when it does so, it is often with reluctance, pain, and resentment toward both those who impose the payment and those who receive the benefits.[18]

Public education, like all other institutional services extended to large segments of the nation's population, is expensive. It is the most comprehensive service that the public makes available to itself. Education is costly, and the costs will increase in future years in direct proportion to the number of students, the scope and complexity of the tasks, and the inflationary rate of the economy.

Some assume that the larger the expenditures, the better the educational services. School districts with large concentrations of blacks and disadvantaged students require proportionately higher expenditures, however, to be comparable with districts with large concentrations of nonblack, advantaged children. If public education is ever to compensate for the adverse conditions stemming from deprivation and discrimination, personnel and financial resources must be allocated appropriately. The commitment should be to providing resources for those students whose needs vary from the norm. The quality and quantity of the school's resources should be in direct proportion to specific student needs.

The term "equalization of educational opportunity" has merit, but should not be construed to mean sameness of programs, per-pupil expenditure, or the number of tax dollars to be paid by each taxpayer. Equalization should mean that educational opportunity is tailored to each child's needs and potentialities. Given students of unequal supportive backgrounds and/or significant variances in readiness or abilities, equal educational opportunity should require the equitable distribution of a system's resources.

"While there is virtually universal agreement that the costs of government should be distributed equitably among taxpayers, the question of what constitutes equitable treatment is far from resolved, as is the question of what criteria and procedures should be employed to assess equity."[19] Unless the equity factor is predicated on need, equalization formulas are not only inequitable but detrimental. Realistic implementation of individualized instruction cannot take place without a complementary funding rationale. Individualized instructional programs are more expensive. The schools have to direct their primary resources toward creating a setting in which the right to read may be translated into the productive and satisfying act of reading. Such a goal can be accomplished only when there is an appropriate degree of individualized instruction, when instructional techniques are demonstrably viable, when school personnel are in effective command of their techniques, when materials and media for instruction are readily available in sufficient amounts, when financial support is adequate, and when resources are distributed equitably. The peculiarities of the educational needs of the disadvantaged literally cry out for financial resources above those in response to which educators dole out resources to the mass of students.

The Potomac Institute sponsored a school-finance-reform report that should be mandatory reading for those who doubt the validity of the pleas for equity in the financial support for urban schools. The report states:

> Contrary to the general assumption at the beginning of the equalization litigation that inner cities naturally would benefit, there are now strong doubts on that score and even suggestions that inner cities may be worse off after equalization. For instance, if a simplistic remedial approach is taken to the 'Serrano' principle and all public education money throughout the state is distributed on an equal-dollar-per-child basis, 'few' major urban education systems in the nation would receive more money for their schools, and some actually would get 'less.' Moreover, because of other municipal services costs, most major cities are below the median in their states in the property-tax rates they apply to education. . . .
>
> Accordingly, we here recommend for legislative and judicial consideration a standard of school-funds distribution within the state that seeks to achieve 'equal educational offering' in each school district. We demonstrate that the 'equal protection' clause of the Fourteenth Amendment requires states to use a school-funds-distribution formula which directly relates money expenditures to educational costs and resources, and that such an equal-educational-offering standard is amenable to objective definition and measurement. Only an equal-educational-offering standard would begin to do justice to cost-burdened inner-city school districts.[20]

The costs are greater to educate appropriately those students whose needs vary widely from the norms. The costs are also greater to provide comparability in educational programs and services to students in some school districts than they are for students in other districts. The State Department of Education in Missouri has declared: "The challenge, which must be met, is to develop and maintain a structure or structures for education which will assure access to equitable educational opportunities for youth and adults wherever they may live within the state and regardless of their socioeconomic status."[21] More funds are needed in urban schools to finance massive programs of staff development, to expand the programs and services for exceptional children, to increase the coverage and quality of programs of compensatory education, to support reductions in class size, to enlarge the coverage of programs in early childhood and adult education, to bring antiquated school facilities more in line with the contemporary requirements of educational facilities, and to keep pace with inflation.

In many ways public education has become the whipping boy for society's ills. No other subject in a community escalates this reaction more than the declining achievement of students and rising educational costs. Educators simply are not developing well-educated men and women in adequate numbers from the mass of disadvantaged students.

The Education Profession

The education profession has yet to develop a systematic measurement to explain the progress of a child. The education profession has not perfected the teaching-learning process. The profession is plagued by too many practitioners who lack the preparation needed to provide satisfactory instructional services. Whatever the extent of the shortcomings of the profession, it does not justify the widely held belief that the quality of instruction can be assessed without taking into account all the external variables.

Teaching is plagued by the many problems inherent in a discipline that is grounded in the behavioral sciences. The diversity of human behavior does not lend itself readily to categorization. Moreover, many concepts regarding human behavior are speculative. Variables combine to contribute to the formation of an identifiable pattern of human behavior. In each individual situation, the variables tend to differ in their mixture and to fluctuate in their dominance. These fluctuations and inconsistencies produce difficulties in predicting, shaping, and assessing patterns of human behavior.

Such problems are not unique to the education profession. However, these problems, in combination with professional ineptness and indifference, do present obstacles to the full acceptance of the teaching profession. Educators must convince the public that they have developed standards of performance not unlike those of other professions. Many shortcomings of both the profession and its practitioners make it difficult, if not impossible, to determine the true capacity of public education to deliver quality services. Realistically, a large percentage of students' academic inadequacies stem from inept instruction and/or inadequately financed programs.

Those who claim that the public schools that serve the poor are worse than they used to be are wrong. These individuals either have faulty memories or utter this nonsense to rationalize their lack of support for urban education. The public schools that serve the urban disadvantaged have never been adequate. The notion that once America had good schools for the poor but has since let them deteriorate is inaccurate.

The public schools cannot pick and choose like nonpublic schools. No viable alternative to public schooling is available to the disadvantaged and large numbers of other Americans. For most Americans, quality education must be delivered through the channels of public education. Black leadership has to commit itself to the awesome task of making education a viable concept while moving simultaneously to improve the quality of life for black Americans. Such a commitment requires a confrontation with the mediocrity in the education profession and with the protectors of this mediocrity. Black leaders cannot afford to lose sight of the root cause for most of black America's ills — racism. America has a racist culture that is incapable of regulating its hostilities.

3

The Superintendency

Life has an explosive quality today. One feels that individuals and groups are antagonistic. Leadership roles, particularly those in the public sector are constantly changing. The school superintendent's role reflects this change perhaps more characteristically than any other leadership position. Most superintendents must deal with crisis situations abounding in conflict and confrontation.

Dan Dodson, sociologist, explored the positive consequences of conflict and confrontation:

> Without conflict and tension, there is very little opportunity for growth. The problem is to deal with the tensions so that they do not produce overwhelming and paralyzing anxieties or erupt into destructive conflict, but so that these tensions restructure society in order that more people are served in a better way. The average school person is not equipped to work with conflict situations of this sort.[1]

Few other executive positions are more complex and demanding than the superintendency. The superintendent must establish the leadership climate for the entire system. Numerous anxieties, tensions, frustrations, conflicts, and confrontations affect the superintendent's capacity to lead. Several years ago in Detroit, I along with other black school administrators invited the newly appointed superintendent Dr. Norman Drachler to dinner. In the discussion period, Drachler was asked why he wanted to be a superintendent. He replied: "If you have to suffer, you might as well suffer at the top." The full meaning of his response was not completely understood by many at the dinner.

As a system's chief executive officer, the superintendent is expected to provide leadership for both the community and the school system. The contemporary superintendent must not only possess the necessary technical and managerial skills but must also be able to handle controversial issues. The American public has always looked to its schools to provide resolutions for many of the social ills of the society. As the societal problems have increased, so have demands for better educational programs and support services. Demands made upon the school superintendent are not well understood by those either within or outside of the school system. The following statement provides a very perceptive view of the multi-dimensional role of the contemporary school superintendent:

> He interprets the purposes and performance of the schools. . . . He often becomes a target for those who are discontent; he is the community social lightning rod; he negotiates competing special interests; he protects the public interest from the encroachment of subversives; he stimulates and leads his professional colleagues; he is alert to promising new educational ideas — sorting out those with promise and those without.
>
> The superintendent is a manager of conflict. In our intensely pluralized social environment he must possess a sense of society's complexity, of the needs, of its meaning for one of its most basic and primary institutions — the schools. He must be an interpreter and translator of social events into public policy. And in our times he must feel — he must feel the agonies of the poor; their frustrations, their confusions. He must sense and understand hosts of community forces. But he must not be immobilized by them.[2]

Duties and Responsibilities

Generally, superintendents are responsible for the orderly and effective administration of the schools in accordance with the policies established by the school board. Most of the superintendents interviewed in this study expressed concern about the vagueness of their responsibilities and authority. Superintendents and school boards constantly bicker over power boundaries. The superintendent's power is determined by the statutory designation of authority established by the board; the undesignated authority permitted by the board; and the authority the superintendent maintains despite the board's objections.

The following are a fair cross section of the general duties and responsibilities of a superintendent:

> Develop and present policy recommendations to the board of education for the purpose of initiating new policies or for effecting changes and clarifications in existing policies.

> Provide the board of education with regular and accurate information related to the overall conduct of school affairs, in general, and the implementation of specific policy directives of the board of education, in particular.

> Establish and administer an organizational structure that effectively facilitates the achievement of the system's goals and objectives.

> Define and clarify the purposes and direction of the schools in accordance with solid educational concepts, goals, and practices and with the policies of the board of education.

> Effect the maximum efficiency and effectiveness through the application of the system's personnel and financial resources.

> Generate community support (parent, professional, business, and industry) for cooperative involvement in the system's educational processes.

The superintendent's prestige and influence has declined over the past years. But this decline has not left the office bare of some inherent pluses. Superintendents are accorded special treatment as customers in restaurants and stores; they are usually treated with deference by government employees, other than elected officials; they are known in the community and are usually treated amicably; in most systems they are provided with some form of financial subsidy for transportation and miscellaneous expenses. Nevertheless, today's superintendent is confronted by unprecedented challenges from the board, the superintendent's own employees, students, parents, and other people in the community.

Basically, the superintendency is what the superintendent can make it or what others will permit it to be. The superintendent must develop wide public support for his or her administrative and leadership goals. In meetings and in other contacts with members of the board, the superintendent must identify, promote, and defend his or her programs and practices. With staff members, the superintendent must identify and assess problems and needs, plan new endeavors, evaluate ongoing programs, and establish general procedures for the day-to-day activities of the school system. The superintendent must articulate his or her educational philosophy and programmatic impact to a broad spectrum of audiences and judges.

The competent superintendent encourages new ideas and promotes successful instructional techniques and materials; makes judicious use of the media; and uses appearances at schools and other sites as a means of assessing programs and community needs. Even though he or she must assume the ultimate responsibility, the superintendent must delegate most tasks to staff members. Although frequently burdened with numerous distractions, the superintendent should concentrate on the most critical role, that of initiator-evaluator of sound policies, programs, and services. This role offers the greatest potential for professional satisfaction and community-life improvement.

Some superintendents will readily admit that they spend less time as initiators-evaluators and more time as managers.

Whether by personal inclination or by imposed priorities, superintendents in the larger school systems devote more energy to managerial rather than to educational matters. Dr. James Redmond, former superintendent of schools in Chicago, spoke of this concern:

> I spend a major portion of my time in the broad field of finance. I do not mean that I am the comptroller or the business manager, but more of those decisions are being made in my office. I also spend a great amount of time building the budget and negotiating the approval of the budget with my board and with the legislature.
>
> Collective bargaining has also changed the role of the superintendent. You are not just bargaining with the teacher organization. There are other employee organizations. The teacher organization has captured the public's fancy. I have better than 3,000 members of the building services. They can lock me up just as fast as the teachers. I am spending a good deal of my time in dealing with the bargaining units. I see this as a general superintendent's job, not a delegation for his personnel expert. I have to have him, but when that president of that union and I get together once a month, it is not the number two guy with whom he wants to talk, and he should not be.[3]

Boards and communities pressure superintendents to become personally involved with a number of day-to-day details of administration. Based on the input received from more than one-half of the superintendents who are members of the Council of the Great Cities School Systems, the following are typical responses about this pressure:

> I have had board members say: 'You ought to be out there.' And I would reply: 'If I rush out there without the facts, I run the unnecessary risk of making a poor administrative decision with no administrative channel left open for a review.'[4]

Today, with so many crises arising daily, the
superintendent is being called upon to put out so many
fires that he loses his effectiveness in terms of the board
leadership — which may in the long run help to prevent
some of these little fires which arise.[5]

Because of contemporary demands on the position, the
superintendency has probably tainted or stymied more professional reputations than any other job. Some very dedicated,
highly competent, and widely respected educators have been
literally consumed by the pressures and frustrations of the
superintendency; some have met with failure because their aspirations exceeded their competency; some have been temporarily
blinded by the alleged prestige of a superintendency; some
survive because they do not "rock the boat"; some are removed
because of their administrative inertia. A large number of
superintendents manage to survive termination, but the number
who not only survive but provide assertive leadership is small.
Failure, success, and competency are factors that are not always
determined by the superintendent's shortcomings and merits.
Very little objectivity is applied to judgments about the superintendent's strengths and shortcomings. Also, few persons, in any
given community, have full access to information needed to give
an unbiased judgment about the superintendent's performance.

Even with a supportive board, the expectations are sufficient
to discourage all but the most hardy and optimistic school administrators. Barbara Sizemore, at one time the only female
superintendent in a large, city school system, experienced what
all new superintendents must. "One disadvantage of being new
is that you have to read everything that went on before you as
well as what is going on now. You practically had to do it at the
same time."

Few school superintendents are ever presented performance
criteria. Often, judgments about the superintendent's performance are based on the particular concerns of individual board
members. This "gut-reaction" approach to judging the superintendent's performance serves as a persistent source of friction
between superintendents and boards. Superintendents are irri-

tated because they often do not know what they are expected to do or by what criteria they will be assessed. Nevertheless, superintendents reluctantly tolerate this unfortunate aspect of the job. Since the situation has existed for years without resolution, superintendents feel virtually powerless and usually concede to the boards.

Gene Geisert and Marcus Foster, provided insights concerning accountability:

> The concept of the superintendent who comes in and who is going to reform the system has died. It ought to be buried because it is obvious that no one man is going to make that much difference.[6]

> It is easy to hold somebody else accountable while you sit in judgment, but it's a little more difficult when you step out into the same arena and subject yourself to the same accountability.[7]

What are the necessary qualities needed for a good superintendent? Richard Gousha, Gene Geisert, and E.L. Whigham offered the following comments:

> The superintendent has to be a person who lives comfortably with himself. I think that he has to be a person who recognizes that there are both positive and negative factors impacting on him. He has to be open, in the sense that he will at least review and give consideration to all points of view.[8]

> The superintendent has to be able to work with people. I think that is probably the most important skill that a superintendent can possess.[9]

> Does the performance of this person give you any understanding that he really has the knowledge and personal qualities to manage what is a very complex operation? I am still a believer that it is important. I do not mean in authoritarian terms.[10]

The superintendency is unique in its complexities and the ambiguity of expectations. Regardless of the individual's attributes, no guarantee for success can be prescribed. Of the

superintendents interviewed, those with the most successful
tenures possess many of the following qualities:

Intelligence: The information that flows through the
superintendent's office is both voluminous and
complex. The position requires an intelligence that
is quick and comprehensive. Serious intellectual inadequacies spell disaster for the superintendent and
chaos for the schools.

Integrity: The superintendent is the educational leader
for the entire community. The public, the board, and
the superintendent's staff must be able to look to the
superintendent for objectivity and consistency. The
superintendent must place issues above personality
conflicts and what is right above what is simply
expedient. The absence of integrity would make it
virtually impossible for a superintendent to earn the
respect of the community in general and of his or her
colleagues in particular.

Perception: The superintendent must be able to identify and assess a situation; he or she must be able to
read people. The superintendent must be able to
discern quickly the meaning of proposals and actions of the board, community groups, school personnel, and students. He or she must be able to decide when to be conciliatory and when to forego
compromise. In spite of the manner in which grievances are registered, the superintendent must be able
to hear what people are trying to say as well as what
they are saying.

Dedication: In the midst of many conflicting demands,
excessive requirements, and undue hostilities, the
superintendent must demonstrate commitment to
equal educational opportunity. The superintendent
must be able to convince the board, staff, and community that he or she is thoroughly dedicated to
transforming his or her commitment into programs
and principles geared to delivering quality educa-

tional services. Among supporters and nonsupporters, the matter of the superintendent's dedication as an educator should never be doubted.

Decisiveness: People who are reluctant or incapable of making critical and often controversial decisions need not be superintendents. Decisiveness is an important quality for successful educational leadership. Procrastination would debilitate the entire organizational structure.

Stamina: The work load is heavy and the work week is long. A superintendent must be able to withstand a rigorous work schedule and a relentless series of crises. Mentally and physically, the superintendent should project the competent and assured image.

Patience: Unless a superintendent is patient, each day becomes a chronicle of minor incidents that develop into major battles. In meetings, especially with aroused community representatives and temperamental board members, the superintendent's patience often serves to calm less disciplined heads. The absence of patience tends to aggravate unpleasant situations. The superintendent's comments are well-remembered. Statements by the superintendent that are motivated by petulance or anger are generally nonproductive.

Organization: The superintendent must be systematic. The superintendent must manage his or her time. Time is a resource that, once wasted, remains lost. The superintendent needs time for long-range planning.

Authority and Responsibility

States vary in the amount of authority and responsibility given to the superintendent. Most state legislatures and state boards help determine responsibilities and authority. Local boards usually set responsibility and authority guidelines. The greater dimensions of the superintendent's authority are generally implicit. As the chief executive officer of the schools, the superintendent is administratively accountable only to his or her board. Exercise of authority on a day-to-day basis is subject primarily to the board's monitoring. Norman Drachler stated that the superintendent obviously has the authority, but the question is how he or she can use it.

School superintendents often complain that they do not have sufficient authority to carry out many of their assigned responsibilities. A smaller number dispute the belief that they are not vested with sufficient authority to match their responsibilities. Two superintendents from large urban school systems, Thomas Goodman of San Diego, California and E.L. Whigham of Dade County, Florida commented on the authority versus responsibility problem:

> I would say there is not the authority available to a superintendent to go along with the responsibilities imposed upon him.
> I think that a superintendent ought to have sufficient authority to put together a management team of his choice. He ought to have authority to assign or to reassign personnel without limitation. And if he is not doing a good job, the board can take appropriate action.[11]
> I think that school superintendents in the public school systems of the United States have ample authority. It is a matter of mobilizing that authority and knowing when and how to use it. I think that there is considerable misconception about this. The common public misconception is that the superintendent has absolute authority. Many staff persons think the superintendent has absolute authority. I say thank God that he does not. I think that superintendents of schools, particularly in the larger systems, have a very considerable amount of authority.[12]

Board-Superintendent Relationship

In order to conduct school affairs in an orderly manner and insure the effectiveness of both parties, the board and the superintendent must have a good working relationship. The school superintendent should not perceive the board as his or her rubber stamp, and the board should not view the superintendent as its robot. Historically, the relationship between the two has fluctuated between harmony and discord. All superintendents and boards must determine how to establish a mutually acceptable working relationship.

Traditionally, the school board has been given legislative and judicial powers as citizen representatives with the authority to set educational goals and policies. Difficulties are manifested in making clear-cut distinctions between those functions of the board and those of the superintendent. School boards have the responsibility to function as units. Legally, a single member has no authority outside the formal structure of the school board. The school board should not undermine the superintendent's position by making unreasonable demands on his or her time.

The contractual relationship between the superintendent and the board symbolizes both trust and hope. The trust is founded in the board's acceptance of the superintendent's credentials and previous professional experience. The hope is that the credentials and experience will result in effective leadership for the school system. His or her formal appointment means the board is committed to support the superintendent as he or she administers the personnel, financial, and physical resources of the school system. The efforts of the board and the superintendent are highly interrelated and interdependent. The effectiveness of one depends on the efforts of the other. A good operational school system maintains a balance between the superintendent and the board.

Gene Geisert views the board-superintendent relationship in the following manner:

> The board's responsibility is to hire a good
> administrator and give him adequate backing. He needs
> both direction and support. If he is successful in

carrying out what the board and community feel is
right, he should be given the appropriate credit, salary,
and all of the other benefits that go with the job. If he
does not produce, then the board should relieve him of
his duties. The responsibility of the board is to find a
superintendent who can do the job right. Boards should
not hire a strong superintendent and encourage him to
build a strong management team and then become
threatened and try to cut him down because of his
strength.[13]

The board that seeks to reduce the superintendent's administrative authority destroys the integrity and vitality of the administrative structure. Any superintendent who works to negate or limit the policies of the board violates his or her contract, and seriously erodes this necessary citizen involvement. Boards and superintendents cannot be expected to agree on all issues, but discussions and debates should focus on issues and situations rather than on personality conflicts. Each party should recognize the prerogatives of the other while simultaneously emphasizing their mutual purpose.

Goodman, Geisert, and Roland Patterson offered the following commentary on the board-superintendent relationship:

In the 'good old days' the typical board of education
consisted of the leading businessmen of the community
or the leading farmers. They had other 'axes to grind.'
They concentrated on really making key policy decisions. They looked to the educational experts, the
superintendent and his staff. Now everybody thinks he
is an expert on everything. Your typical board member,
today, wants to go beyond just policy determination.

The fine line between administration and policymaking just does not exist. If it is there, board members
quickly forget it. They always acknowledge it in
speeches and so forth, but they do not observe it. They
want to be in on appointments; they want to be in on
discipline policies in the schools; they want to be in on
everything.

There is distrust between superintendents and boards of education. Some board members feel that educators think they are a little above the board members because they have more education. Some board members feel that the administration is really not telling the truth; that we are holding things back; that we don't trust them. Some board members feel that we don't really feel that they should be involved and that we just tolerate them because of the structure of public education.[14]

Some board members perceive their election as a mandate to run the school system. A strong administration will bother that type of board member. It takes a strong board member to understand that one of his major contributions is the hiring of a good administrator who is capable of carrying out the concerns of the board. Unfortunately, there are board members who take the opposite approach — that is, 'I am not getting all of the limelight that I ought to receive, therefore we have to put the superintendent down and get the board members out there in front.' This, of course, if carried to extremes, makes the superintendent's role as a leader very difficult to perform.[15]

The superintendent's prerogatives are cloudy, but with the kinds of changes occurring in public education and the kinds of problems, I don't know if I would want it any differently. I feel if it were highly structured, it would hamper me from acting. Now with it being unclear, I can always act and then say that I didn't understand it that way.[16]

In the late sixties, for the first time in the history of public education, boards began reflecting a better cross section of the nation's population. School boards now have more ethnic representation than ever before. The average age of a board member has been lowered significantly. Some boards have student members with full or partial rights. Some school boards have members who are from the lower rungs of the socioeconomic ladder. Black representation has increased sharply. Because of this transformation, more citizens are being heard.

Members vary considerably in their preparation for membership on the board. Some come well-prepared intellectually and some come ill-prepared intellectually. School superintendents and other school officers believe that school boards are rejecting many of the traditional relationships between board members and school officers in their quest for reform. Life is rarely uneventful at either the closed or the public sessions of the board.

School board members often encroach on the administrative authority of the superintendent. Most of the board members interviewed either implied or said quite explicitly that they cannot do their jobs as they perceive it without getting involved in so-called administrative matters. Superintendents often refer to the need to "educate" their boards, while the boards are quick to "straighten out" the superintendent. Some superintendents are able to take a more philosophical view in explaining why board members desire to be involved directly in the administration of the schools. But most superintendents are highly irritated by what they consider a usurpation of an essential right of the superintendent.

Some school officers are contemptuous of this "meddling." A staff person in one of the seven school systems highlighted in this study commented on this "meddling." These comments are probably indicative of the general feeling of a large number of school administrators. In reference to the active involvement of board members in what is interpreted by school officers as the administrative domain, the staff person stated: "The board members who do such are little people placed in a big position without sufficient capabilities and an adequate temperament."

Whigham and Redmond are less negative in their commentary on the overly involved school board member. They commented:

> It is a constant temptation for a citizen who is elected to a board by the political process for various motives — very proper motives or they may be improper motives — to want to get involved in administrative matters. We

have to prepare for this and view it as an expected
phenomenon.[17]

Board members in all good conscience want to put
their fingers into the actual administration of the
schools. If you call them on it, they will swear that they
were not intending to do such. The desire of many
board members to play a role other than policy determination is one of a superintendent's major problems.
How do you deal with it? You try to make the situation
work. We have a lot of board committees, and everybody has a job on a board committee. The chairman of
each committee sees himself as having to produce
something that is significant. I'm sure the story is the
same or similar in other situations.[18]

As a professional, the superintendent cannot ignore the problems that beset a board in its intrapersonal relationships. Con-
versely, a school board should not ignore the needs of the
superintendent. A school board member accepts a nonnegotiable responsibility to contribute to the improvement of the quality of educational programs and services. Such a responsibility
extends well beyond the mere declaration of a system's alleged
inadequacies.

No policymaking body in a highly troubled school system can
logically disclaim partial fault for the inadequacies and needs.
Election or appointment to a board of education automatically
removes the member from the position of external critic. Membership on a school board, while offering many opportunities for
constructive service to a community, also makes the member a
part of the establishment. On this point Norman Drachler says:

A board member must be careful to recognize that
whatever he says at a meeting becomes a chain of events
which eventually creates a certain image in the community. This image influences some major decisions. A
board member must be critical of the quality of education, always challenging for better schools. He must
also keep in mind what he is saying and how that

influences the community. How will they react to requests for funds and so forth?

One's criticism must be constructive and not give the
impression that the board member and superintendent
have completely negative feelings. The skill of the
board member and superintendent is in maintaining
that fine balance. If the board member does not feel
totally negative about the school system, he ought to
make sure that positive things are said about the school
system and not say only those things which continue to
build the image of negativism in the community.[19]

Despite the shortcomings of some school board members, few
public servants contribute as much to a community and receive
such inadequate recognition and low or no monetary compensa-
tion. Many board members put in longer work hours on behalf of
board business than do some well-paid school personnel. Community control of public education in America is an essential
component of a democratic society. School board members are
the major vehicle through which the community may control
public education. Dr. Charles Wolfe, superintendent of schools
in Detroit, Michigan, stated:

If you are going to say that we believe in community
involvement and community control, you better really
mean it. And when you really have it and see how
different it is from how most people conceptualized it,
you do not turn against it. You try to work out the
frictions that inevitably begin to appear.[20]

Reform or Obsolescence

School superintendents have many traits in common, but they
are by no means carbon copies of each other. Their professional
problems and needs are more similar than the superintendents
themselves. Success in two different urban school systems
might come from two different kinds of people. Because of the
diversity and complex dissimilarity among school districts, that
which is successful in one might bring total failure in another.

Therefore, predicting success for a newly appointed superintendent is impossible. The superintendent who leans toward autocracy survives in one system and perishes in another. Forcefulness is assessed as leadership by some boards and viewed as antagonism by other boards.

An urban school superintendent is confronted daily by a host of problems and a diverse cast of characters. Not all of the difficulties that superintendents face are the result of the actions of an overly zealous board of education or of major philosophical differences between the superintendent and the board. Some superintendents plant the seeds of their own destruction or dismissal. Every superintendent who quits in anger or who is dismissed cannot legitimately blame an ill-defined role, personality differences, or a board that is inappropriately involved in school administration as the cause of his or her departure. Some superintendents quit or are dismissed because they are simply incompetent.

Many superintendents would probably contend that the major rift between themselves and the school board is the dilemma of expectation vs. authority. The contradictions and inadequacies in the board-superintendent relationship contribute more to crises than do the various mixtures of personalities of members of school boards. The ill-defined relationship stimulates personality conflicts and role confrontations.

Neither a part-time nor a full-time board of education can administer efficiently or effectively a school system. A superintendent who is unreasonably restricted by the efforts of the board or by the board's lack of appropriate policy cannot provide efficient or effective leadership. The executive officer of a school system should not be a confused administrator who is uncertain of his or her prerogatives and of the support to be rightly expected from the board of education. The confrontations and conflicts between boards and superintendents often become so heated and so complicated that neither party is able to initiate a resolution short of the resignation or dismissal of the superintendent.

School systems are, in part, a business. School systems, like other businesses require executive leadership. That leadership in the private sector is usually entrusted to a single person who is held accountable for administrative matters. Seemingly, boards and superintendents cannot live with or without each other. Reform in the management of public education is long overdue. The time has come to either upgrade or downgrade the superintendency. Either the superintendent is provided with sufficient leverage to administer the schools or the expectations should be sharply reduced.

Any major reform in urban life must involve the public schools. Any significant improvements in public education must involve adjustments in the board-superintendent relationship. In 1970, when I accepted the appointment as superintendent in Washington, D.C., there were twenty-four superintendents serving as members of the Council of the Great City School Systems. Three years later, I, along with thirteen other school superintendents, had left. Three of the superintendents served a period shorter than the tenure of their contracts. The citizenry must prod the various state legislatures to effect legislation that provides an equitable balance between school boards and superintendents. Presently, school boards and superintendents are stepping on each other's toes.

School boards and superintendents will become obsolete if they are rendered inoperative by structural deficiencies that prevent the orderly operation of public education. Communities should insist that the board-superintendent relationship be reformed and that this reform include clear and feasible regulatory guidelines that separate functions and distribute authority. Such input from the public should produce clear indications of what it deems to be the appropriate separation of the administrative and policy determining prerogatives between the school board and the superintendent.

4

Black
School
Superintendents

This nation has more than 2 million public school teachers and approximately 16,700 superintendents. Despite the difficulties and the high rate of turnover, many educators apply for the vacant superintendencies. Women, blacks, and browns are the major groups most discriminated against in recruiting and selecting a superintendent. In 1974 women held 86 superintendencies or approximately 0.5 percent. The 44 black superintendents constituted about 0.25 percent. The number of brown superintendents during that period is not available, but was considered to be much less than the number of black superintendents.

The American Association of School Administrators (AASA), the nation's largest and most influential organization of superintendents and other upper-echelon school administrators, does not collect or disseminate the names and locations of black superintendents. The National Alliance of Black School Educators (NABSE), is the only organization with a list of black superintendents.

In 1970 Charles Moody wrote a doctoral dissertation at Northwestern University on black superintendents and identified twenty-one systems with black superintendents. Four of the twenty-one were acting superintendents. Moody commented that he could find no source to consult in collecting his roster of superintendents.

Black superintendents operated in almost total obscurity until they became heads of large urban systems. Ersel Watson, appointed superintendent in Trenton, New Jersey in 1969, was the first black appointed to a prominent urban system. The late Marcus Foster was appointed in July 1970 to the Oakland, California position, and I became superintendent in Washington, D.C. in October, 1970. Upon being appointed in October 1971 to the Baltimore, Maryland superintendency, Roland Patterson administered the largest system. In July 1973 Alonzo Crim left a superintendency in Compton, California for the position in Atlanta, Georgia, and became the first black superintendent in a major deep South city. Two blacks became chief state school officers: John Porter, appointed state superintendent of education in Michigan in 1969, and Wilson Riles, elected state superintendent of instruction in California in 1970.

Even though blacks served in superintendencies before the late sixties, the education profession was either unaware of or ignored their existence. In a 1973 survey the Alliance identified the following blacks as the forerunners of current black superintendents: Lillard Ashley, Boley, Oklahoma, 1956; Lorenzo R. Smith, Hopkins Park, Illinois, 1956; E. W. Warrior, Taft, Oklahoma, 1958; and Arthur Shropshire, Kinloch, Missouri, 1963.

In February 1974, I sent forty-one black superintendents a questionnaire seeking basic information about their school systems. The questionnaire also sought background information on each of the black superintendents.

Background Information

Table 1 lists those black educators who were superintendents in March 1974. (Subsequent to this survey additional blacks were appointed to superintendencies.)

TABLE 1
Black School Superintendents
March 1974

State	City and/or District	Superintendent
Alabama	Greene County	Robert Brown
	Macon County	Ulysses Byas
Arizona	Roosevelt No. 66, Phoenix	Russell Jackson
Arkansas	Wabbaseka	Eddie Collins
	Moscow	Peter Daniels
	Menifee	Peter Faison
	Magnolia	W. B. Moss
	Rosston	Mitchell Roland
California	Del Paso Heights, Sacramento	Charles Townsel
	Ravenswood, East Palo Alto	Warren Hayman
	Sacramento	Edward Fort
	Berkeley	Laval Wilson†
Delaware	Wilmington	Earl C. Jackson
District of Columbia	Washington, D.C.	Barbara Sizemore
Georgia	Sparta	Marvin Lewis
	Atlanta	Alonzo Crim
Illinois	Lovejoy	James Barker
	Hopkins Park No. 259	Lorenzo Smith
	Harvey No. 147	Leslie Crumble
	East Chicago Heights No. 169	Samuel Shepard
	East St. Louis No. 189	William Mason
	North Chicago No. 64	Charles R. Thomas†
Maryland	Baltimore	Roland N. Patterson
Massachusetts	Cambridge	Alflorence Cheatam
Michigan	Ecorse	James Johnson
	Muskegon Heights	John Sydnor
	Highland Park	Charles Mitchell
	Inkster	Albert Ward
Missouri	Kinloch	John Wright
New Jersey	Plainsfield	Russell Carpenter
	East Orange	Ortha Porter
	New Brunswick	Charles Durant
	Essex County	Simeon Moss
	Newark	Stanley Taylor
	Lawnside	William C. Boyd†

TABLE 1 (continued)

State	City and/or District	Superintendent
Ohio	Youngstown	Robert Pegues
	Jefferson Township, Dayton	Herman Brown*
Oklahoma	Boley	Lillard Ashley
	Taft	E. W. Warrior
	Tullahassee	Elmer Jones
South Carolina	Ridgeland	Solomon E. Bonds, Jr.
	Yonges Island	J. L. Brockington
	Summerton	B. S. Butler
Virgin Islands	Charlotte Amalie	Harold Haizlip

State Superintendents
John Porter, State Superintendent of Education, Michigan
Wilson Riles, State Superintendent of Public Instruction, California

Source: Information collected from various documents of the National Alliance of Black School Educators and the author's consultation with officers of the Alliance.

*Mr. Brown was replaced by Roger Snead.

†Survey conducted prior to these appointments.

Table 2 provides some interesting comparisons among twenty-one of the school systems. One should note the ratio of regular funds to the number of students and the number of blacks compared to the total school population.

The average age of these twenty-one superintendents was 40; the oldest was 62 and the youngest 28. Three were in their second superintendencies; 8 were elected from within the systems they served. Nine had served as assistant superintendents or the equivalent, and 9 were former principals. Four had been in office less than one year; only 4 for four years or more; and 13 for two years or less.

All but one possessed a master's degree; 8 had doctorates. Most were issued three- or four-year contracts. One worked under no contract. The highest salary was $50,000; the lowest was $10,200. Four earned at least $40,000; 9, at least $30,000; and 19, at least $20,000. Upon their appointments, 4 received salary increases of at least $3,000; 2 had salary reductions.

TABLE 2
Pertinent Information Regarding Participants in Survey of Black Superintendents

Superintendent	System	Total Students	Black Students	Regular Funds
Roland N. Patterson	Baltimore	182,981	129,173	$181,874,620
Barbara Sizemore	Washington, D.C.	136,133	130,321	167,807,500
Alonzo Crim	Atlanta	88,114	72,800	107,031,856
Stanley Taylor	Newark	75,787	54,756	104,161,662
Edward Fort	Sacramento	47,426	8,389	44,506,153
Robert Pegues	Youngstown	23,402	10,658	16,222,723
Earl C. Jackson	Wilmington	14,688	12,144	19,600,000*
Ortha Porter	East Orange	11,555	10,821	16,200,000
Russell Jackson	Roosevelt No. 66, Phoenix	11,068	4,001	8,841,250
Charles Mitchell	Highland Park	7,230	6,656	10,295,919
Albert Ward	Inkster	5,542	4,088	4,440,432
Ulysses Byas	Macon County	4,909	4,633	2,137,621
John Sydnor	Muskegon Heights	3,874	3,205	1,600,000
Robert Brown	Greene County	3,222	3,200	2,000,000
Marvin Lewis	Sparta No. 1	2,500	2,477	294,400†
Herman Brown	Jefferson Township	2,444	1,885	1,990,968
Charles Townsel	Del Paso Heights	1,534	1,074	1,828,051
Eddie Collins	Wabbaseka	454	437	348,190
Peter Faison	Menifee	347	322	230,733
Peter Daniels	Moscow	329	315	302,957
W. B. Moss	Magnolia	275	275	N. A.‡

Source: Data collected from completed questionnaires received from each of the superintendents in March and April 1974.

*Figure represents funds requested.

†Figure represents funds from local sources only.

‡Figure was not available.

The twenty-one superintendents reported to predominantly black and male school boards: 16 boards had a black majority and 19 had a male majority. In 16 school systems, blacks constituted a majority of the community's population.

The superintendents had a combined student population of 623,814, of whom 460,600 were black. In all but two systems, black students constituted the overwhelming majority of the population. Deficiency in reading achievement was a severe problem in all but two of the twenty-one systems. Table 3 shows the scope of reading achievement.

TABLE 3
Estimates of Percentages of Students in Grades One-Six Testing Below National Norms On Reading Achievement Tests in Select School Systems With Black Superintendents

System	Grade One	Grade Two	Grade Three	Grade Four	Grade Five	Grade Six
Baltimore	N.T.*	NT	73	73	72	80
Washington, D.C.	59.3	68.5	79.7	81	83.4	84.1
Atlanta	65	72	74	77	82	83
Newark	69	73	86	90	88	89
Sacramento	38	45	48	52	NA	NA
Youngstown	N.A.†	NA	NA	47	NA	46
Wilmington	N.A.	NA	80	80	80	80
East Orange	59	66	74	79	81	83
Roosevelt No. 66, Phoenix	72	78	82	84	88	88
Highland Park	N.A.	48.5	65.6	62.8	67.8	81
Inkster	N.T.	75	75	75	80	80
Macon County	90	90	90	91	91	84
Muskegon Heights	35	40	45	50	50	65
Greene County	10	30	70	92	95	97
Sparta No. 10	90	90	90	90	94	96
Jefferson Township	40	40	50	40	63	61
Del Paso Heights	81	67	83	84	89	88

Source: Data collected from completed questionnaires received from each of the twenty-one systems surveyed.

*N.T.: Not Tested

†N.A.: Not Available

In twelve of the twenty-one systems, white employees paid from regular funds outnumbered black employees. Eleven systems employed 500 or fewer persons; five systems employed fewer than 100 persons, and four systems had 5,000 or more employees. Eight systems employed fewer than 100 blacks. Six systems offered a minimum salary of less than $7,000 for teachers with a bachelor's degree, and four systems offered a minimum salary below $8,000 for teachers with a master's degree. Table 4 provides figures on salary schedules for teachers within the systems.

TABLE 4
Ranges of Salary Schedules for Teachers in Select School Systems with Black Superintendents

Salary Range	Number of Systems
Minimum Salary — with Bachelor's Degree	
$5,000-$ 6,000	6
$7,000-$ 8,000	13
$9,000-$10,000	2
Maximum Salary — with Bachelor's Degree	
$ 6,000-$ 7,000	4
$ 8,000-$ 9,000	4
$10,000-$11,000	2
$12,000-$13,000	6
$14,000-$15,000	5
Minimum Salary — with Master's Degree	
Below $7,000	4
$7,000-$ 9,000	8
$9,000-$10,000	9
Maximum Salary — with Master's Degree	
Below $8,000	4
$ 9,000-$10,000	3
$11,000-$12,000	3
$13,000-$14,000	6
$15,000-$16,000	4
$17,000-$18,000	1

Source: Data collected from completed questionnaires received from each of the twenty-one systems surveyed.

Major Problems

All systems present certain difficulties to superintendents, but some are far more difficult than others. The large urban system poses the most challenges. The black superintendent's efforts are affected by multifaceted impositions and barriers that are uniquely linked to society's treatment of blacks and black leadership. The recognition of such obstacles is apparent in some black superintendent's observations about the systems they headed in the early seventies.

When Marcus Foster became Oakland's superintendent, the public had little confidence in the school system. Foster's leadership contributed to major improvements in the school system and renewed public confidence. He felt that the schools were the center of the storm, their situation stemming from the breakdown in the American economy, political system, and concern for human rights. In a speech before his staff he said, "No other institution has promised so much, yet the chasm between our promise and our performances, particularly for the urban poor and minority groups, is there for all to see."

In his research, Moody, a former superintendent, stated that, in terms of their responsibility, black superintendents are not allowed to concentrate on the instructional aspects of the system. He wrote that the superintendent is "expected to be a miracle man who can undo in a few days conditions that years of neglect, and in some cases, mismanagement have created." Moody's dissertation substantiates the following hypotheses:

> There is a decline in the financial conditions of the school system manifesting itself in a deficit prior to the appointment of a black superintendent.
>
> There is an increase in the amount of Title I funds received by the school districts.
>
> The nonwhite student population was in the majority at the time of the appointment of the black superintendent.

The nonwhite population of the community is in the majority or projections indicate it soon will be.

There is a majority nonwhite school board at the time of the appointment of a black superintendent.

The nonwhite teaching staff increased significantly prior to the appointment of the black superintendent.

There is a significant increase in the percentage of black administrators.[1]

In 1967 Edward Fort became Michigan's first black superintendent. In 1971, Fort left the Inkster, Michigan position and became deputy superintendent in Sacramento, California. He was appointed Sacramento's superintendent in 1972. He identified negative attitudes of teachers as a major problem. In a speech he stated:

> Perhaps one of the greatest prevailing forces which the superintendent of schools must effectively deal with, particularly in the large urban complex with large numbers of black kids, is that concerned with the teacher or principal who is somehow convinced that 'these kids cannot learn.'
>
> This attitudinal force, if deep-rooted enough in the staff of the district, offers the severest of challenges to the superintendent, particularly when held together by a thread of black as well as white teachers. For it obviates some thrusts designed, by the superintendent, to prove that minority kids can learn. And yet, rather than allowing the system to continue perpetuating the myth that these kids cannot learn, the educational leader, as superintendent, is going to have to launch the kind of massively contrived effort necessary to reverse this attitudinal force.[2]

Charles Durant, superintendent in New Brunswick, New Jersey, and John Minor, former superintendent in Ravenswood,

California, and later an associate superintendent in Atlanta, both viewed making the bureaucracy relevant and responsive as an urgent problem. Durant commented on the role of the superintendent as a change agent:

> The lack of innovation in city school systems, except as periodically stimulated by outside funding, is indicative of this status quo orientation. Over the last sixty years, city school systems have experienced a high degree of professionalization combined with extensive centralization of the educational bureaucracy. In every large city, an inbred bureaucratic supervisory staff sits at headquarters offices holding a tight rein on educational policy. Their vested interests are clear: any major shift in educational policy might well challenge their control of the system. Perhaps the only new agent to enter the domain of school affairs in recent years is the teacher organization or union. Unfortunately, these groups have concentrated their attention on salary and related issues; on all other questions, they have supported establishment policies. Additionally, we have seen the abdication of responsibility for education by civic groups, businessmen, labor unions, and parents. The result is a closed political system, which, if measured against the need for public information and public participation, falls far short of any standards for a pluralistic society.[3]

Minor, in a critique of presentations made by representatives of the National Education Association and the American Federation of Teachers at a "Politics and Education" conference sponsored by black school superintendents, commented on the need of black superintendents to challenge such organizations:

> I take it for granted that we educators are all implicated in the actions of the professional associations to which we belong, whether we have taken a direct hand in their decision-making processes or not. With this thought in mind, I

contend that we are all co-defendants in a
nationwide trial; we have been charged with conflict
of interest and mismanagement of resources. I
contend that the American system of education may
very well depend upon the verdict.[4]

The twenty-one superintendents were requested to identify
the five most significant needs of their systems and the five most
significant problems confronting them. (Complete responses are
found in Appendix B.) The most common responses are presented in the following list:

Needs

Improved academic achievement.

Reorganization of the system.

Educational accountability.

Expanded community participation.

Staff development.

Staff unity.

Management improvements.

Long-range planning.

Problems

Low academic achievement.

Recruitment of staff.

Keeping public informed.

Insufficient funds.

Reorganization of system.

Board-superintendent relations.

Teacher accountability.

Teacher attitudes.

Image of system.

The public's image of a school system contributes heavily to
its assessment of the superintendent. Invariably, superintendents placed in communities beset by social disorganization and
deterioration will have their job security and reputations

threatened. Most black superintendents operate under circumstances that demand exemplary educational leadership and extensive community resources.

Blackness and the Superintendency

Black consciousness and professionalism are not incompatible. Without a satisfactory blend of the two, each is diminished in content and productivity. Professionalism enjoins a commitment to the inauguration of systems of education in which all students are accorded equitable opportunities to attain a quality education. Professionalism is the revelation of a defensible philosophical foundation undergirding programmatic thrusts and administrative actions. Professionals must oppose those policies, practices, and programs that are detrimental to any group of students.

In 1974, Alonzo Crim of Atlanta offered his perception of the black consciousness movement and his position:

> I have my own brand of black consciousness. I really see it in the sense of children. The neediest children tend to be black and brown. When I was in California, I saw the Chicanos suffering to a greater degree than most of the black children that I know. I quickly identified with the Chicano group, and I tried to do as much as I could to alleviate some of the desperate conditions under which they lived. I think that an educator has to have an abiding interest in children. If you are in a needy situation anywhere, regardless of race and ethnicity, then you should give a good account of yourself. I do not see black superintendents. I see good superintendents. We have to be damn good — better than most.[5]

Does the public respond differently to a black superintendent? Black superintendents interviewed believe they are treated differently. Most of the superintendents contacted agree that white superintendents encounter fewer difficulties. Rarely is race incidental to the assessment of the black superintendent's expertise and performance.

John Dobbs, special assistant to the state superintendent for public instruction in Michigan, commented on the uniqueness of the role of the black superintendent:

> The black superintendent, more than his counterparts of other backgrounds, is generally one of the highest-level, most visible public officials. This means that he serves as a role model for the entire black community and is expected to play a much broader leadership role in addressing the longstanding concerns of heretofore unrepresented black and poor people who have been historically least served by the public schools.[6]

Solomon E. Bonds, Jr., superintendent of schools in Ridgeland, South Carolina, provided the following comments about the unique aspects of being a black superintendent:

> ... The black superintendent's response to his responsibilities is uniquely affected by the fact that people — black and white — respond to him differently because he is black.
>
> The school superintendency is one of the most crucial and perhaps most difficult positions in American life today. The black superintendency is doubly difficult and complex because this type of leadership is at the center of virtually all the current social revolutions of educational leadership.
>
> A black superintendent finds prestigious leaders, indifferent masses, officials, committees, newspapers, and traditions perennially at odds regarding his total responsibility and the development of policies essential to the long-range quality of public education.
>
> It is true but unfair that a black superintendent must be far better at handling the demands and fulfillment of the role of superintendent and the

> solution of day-to-day problems in a meaningful
> framework. As a result, there exists, though
> infrequently, considerable potential for
> intraorganizational conflict. It is also true that black
> superintendents are showing evidence of goals being
> achieved and not merely promised.[7]

One superintendent from a district in which blacks do not constitute a majority commented on how blackness affected him:

> The very fact that he is black renders it probable
> that the urban area's response to him will be
> uniquely different from the response to his
> Caucasian counterpart. If, for example, the black
> superintendent is responsible for the administration
> of an urban school district which is ethnically
> heterogeneous and which contains fewer than 20
> percent black students, and Chicano citizens are
> demanding instantaneous response to their demands
> for more brown teachers, one may rest assured of the
> fact that the brown citizenry views with suspicion
> the commitment of a black superintendent to any
> presumed intent of compliance with their entreaties.
> The white power structure will similarly view my
> movement in the direction of 'equity' for black,
> brown and Asian students as ethnic favoritism
> because I am a black superintendent. For a white
> superintendent, similar attempts would be viewed as
> the actions of a 'liberal.'[*]

Albert A. Ward, superintendent of schools in Inkster, Michigan, highlighted the difficulties that a black superintendent encounters from some blacks:

> ... There do seem to be distinguishable
> commonalities among the problems experienced by

*Superintendent requested anonymity.

black and white superintendents. However, there are differences in the responses of black persons to black superintendents. One difference is the 'walk-on-water' quality of expectations that students, parents, and staff have of the black superintendent. You're expected to solve immediately problems that stem from decades of economic, social, and racial injustice. For example, how can you have a quality educational program with current and historical grossly inadequate levels of funding?

A second problem is the persisting 'test-of-fire' quality of interaction with black peers, staff, and students. Many don't seem to be satisfied unless there is a constant pass-fail kind of confrontation with the superintendent. It reminds me of the adolescent game, 'playing the dozens.'

Another impression is that many blacks seem to object to taking direction or orders from a black leader. It's the 'you're-just-another-nigger' phenomenon. Perhaps the union president verbalized the problem best when this newly appointed superintendent tried to correct some staff abuses: 'You will not tell us [the teachers] what to do.'[8]

Many black superintendents are reluctant to admit that blacks impose greater demands on them than on their white predecessors. Black superintendents are placed in the awkward position of understanding both sides of the question. They know what their position demands and they also understand why blacks are suspicious of the school system. Charles Townsel, superintendent of schools in Del Paso Heights, California, reflects this anguish in his statement: "This syndrome of 'blackness' permeates not only the superintendency but all positions of authority where blacks are in charge. Have you ever had a black community person call you a 'nigger' in a community meeting? This lack of respect is indicative of responses heaped upon black superintendents because they are black."[9]

In 1972 Russell Jackson left the superintendency in East Orange, New Jersey, for the same position in Roosevelt School District in Pheonix, Arizona. Jackson provided detailed commentary on the special demands placed upon black superintendents. He stated:

> There is the demand from the people that you be highly accessible to them. This demand for accessibility comes from not only the established power structure of a community, it also comes from other levels of the community which more readily identify with you because of your blackness. These would be people from low-income families who are themselves black. They expect you to be immediately accessible to them. They expect you to respond to their demands and their petitions in a way in which they have not expected other superintendents who are white to respond. These people are very often parents. They expect you to be available by phone when they call. They expect you to return their calls. I find that they call me as a black superintendent much more readily than they would call a white superintendent. I have found this to be uniquely true, and it has been reported to me by other employees who have worked for many years in the superintendent's office — both white and black personnel.
>
> There is a tendency for people to respond with a lack of trust. The mistrust varies in many ways. It may be a lack of trust in your ability or as they perceive your ability to perform a job. There is a lack of trust that you will respond any differently than the white superintendent who may have preceded you. The expectation quite often is that you will not respond and that you will simply ignore their demands and petitions. The whole lack of trust exists in the white community as well as the black community. There is a fear in the white community

that you will hire all black personnel in administrative positions or that the district is moving to an employment policy which will preclude the hiring of white personnel. Many of the things which deal with the whole matter of trust are preconceived notions of what you might do as a black superintendent.

When you come into a superintendency as a black, you are expected to perform at a level of excellence that is usually unreal. You are expected to perform miracles. These miracles may be removing all of the problems which have existed in the district, in a short period of time.

The conflicts which exist in the black community create problems for the black superintendent. Very often these conflicts are among the black leadership. Demands are made from the various conflicting groups to identify with their particular group. You are often torn between the various conflicting groups. These groups will seek to get your allegiance or your participation. At times, you are used by one or more of the contending groups.[10]

Blacks are demanding that *all* school personnel help resolve the problems of black people in a racist society. Black superintendents are a direct consequence of increased minority militancy. The relationship black superintendents have with other blacks and many whites is a manifestation of the sociological forces and psychological pressures of contemporary racial attitudes in America. Urban education has been a dreadful failure for the mass of black Americans. "Establishment" representatives in urban education, be they black or white, receive little empathy from the various constitutencies in urban communities. The black superintendent must temper black-on-black hostility and distrust — and simultaneously provide leadership in the formulation of cooperative and constructive ventures in the reformation of urban life and urban schools.

5

A Capsule Examination of Seven School Systems

These seven school systems were chosen because they were reasonably representative of the problems that the more than forty black superintendents encountered in 1974. Two systems in the South are examined; both large and small school systems are included. The superintendents in each of the seven systems expressed an interest in the study and a willingness to cooperate.

The seven superintendents were asked the following questions:

What was the status of public education in the school district prior to the appointment of a black superintendent?

What are the major goals and objectives that you have established?

What are the administrative efforts that you have made to effect improvements in the delivery of educational programs and related support services?

What are the dominant internal and external factors impacting for and against your efforts and those of your school board to effect improvements in the delivery of educational programs and related support services?

Data were gathered from the superintendents and key members of their staffs and the president and other members of the respective school boards. Along with other city officials, three black mayors were interviewed. The living conditions in the communities were examined. Court opinions were reviewed. Although this documentation is not offered as an adequate substitute for a comprehensive examination of the critical factors that shape education, it will provide insights into the problems and needs of seven systems and the motivations and views of many persons in the systems' critical leadership positions.

Macon County, Alabama

The County

In 1974 Macon County ranked among the most economically depressed areas in a state beset with economic woes. Poverty and deprivation were readily visible in most sections of the county. In many respects, Macon County was the rural counterpart of an urban ghetto. Macon County has a long history of economic difficulties. Most residents of this predominantly black community had never known many of the conveniences most Americans took for granted.

The demographic information that follows was extracted from the Blue Ribbon Citizens' Committee study of the public schools.

> According to the U.S. Bureau of the Census, Macon County, in 1970, had a total population of 24,841, of which four-fifths (20,147) were black or Negro. Slightly more than half of the population was classified as rural, but only 7 percent were engaged in farming. The age distribution revealed 2,008 under five years of age, 7,812 between ages five and nineteen, and 2,866 sixty-five years of age and over. There were 5,072 families. In white families, there were 2.85 persons per household; in black families 3.9 persons per household.

In 1970, the median school years completed by the population twenty-five years and over was about one year higher for females than for males, with the median being higher for whites than blacks.

In 1969, the per-family income for the total population was $5,058, but that of black families was only $3,940. Of the total families, 37.4 percent were below the national poverty level. Of all black families, 42.9 percent were below the poverty level.[1]

Tuskegee Institute, a veterans' hospital, and the Macon County public schools were the major employers. Job opportunities were limited. Fewer and fewer farmers were able to earn an adequate living; most were engaged in submarginal farm operations. The county provided few job opportunities for skilled, unskilled, or professional workers. Young people left the county to look for employment in other parts of the state or country.

The Blue Ribbon Citizens' Committee observed the following about the governmental structure and social relations:

The major governmental structure of Macon County consists of a county commission of five members and two municipalities, Notasulga and Tuskegee, each governed by a mayor and city council. In the county several federal programs are operating, two of which (Community Action Agency and Model Cities) have helped the poor in the county as well as the citizens in Tuskegee.

In political, civic, and community welfare there is some interracial interaction and cooperation, but the social and religious structures and practices have experienced the least change. In the homes, social clubs, and churches there is little interracial social interaction. The existing interaction involves mainly persons employed at Tuskegee Institute.

Most of the white children of school age attend the racially segregated private Macon Academy, or go to school in adjoining counties, so there is little practical opportunity for black and white children to grow to understand, respect, and cooperate with one another.[2]

The most valuable resource in Macon County is its leadership, which is dedicated and black. In 1974 the county had a black majority on the county commission and a black sheriff; four of the five members of the county board of education were black. In 1970 the board had appointed a black superintendent with a predominantly black administrative and instructional staff. The executive officers of the veterans' hospital and the Tuskegee Institute were black. The city of Tuskegee, the principal community, was headed by a black mayor. Despite awesome problems, the leadership emphasized that life in the county would continue to improve.

The black leadership discouraged unfavorable judgments of the future. Regardless of the leaders' high hopes for economic growth, the county is unalterably dependent on external sources for substantial increases in economic aid and technical assistance. Macon County does not have the untapped resources required to produce a forward economic thrust. For a number of reasons — e.g., that the county is predominantly black and the state is poor — the state of Alabama cannot be expected to do much for Macon County. Nevertheless, the black leadership believed that the steady decline in the economic base — an economic base that has never been adequate — had been halted.

Mayor Johnny Ford was unrivaled as a spokesman for the people of Macon County. When interviewed, Ford expressed these views of the county's problems and leaders:

> The basic problem is the need for money. Macon County does not have adequate local financial support for its public schools. There is also a need for centralization of many of the educational services.
>
> The various heads of the key agencies in the county have been able to coordinate their efforts. We exemplify unity and the capacity to work together. We have come a long way in Macon County — not necessarily because the leadership is black, but I

think that we now have the kind of leadership that is responsive to the total community. It is responsive, in particular, to those who are poor and disadvantaged.

I think that I have a particular responsibility to see that those people who are black and who are poor and disadvantaged have their needs met. Their needs have been traditionally overlooked in the past. The leadership in the past was not responsive to their needs. The leadership has to recognize that it must make a greater effort to meet the needs of lower-income people. You have to go that extra mile. I have the sensitivity that it takes to serve a constituency that is black, poor, and disadvantaged. Tuskegee has rich whites and poor whites, and it has rich blacks and poor blacks. You have to deal with poor folks, rich folks, conservative people, liberal people, and racist people.[3]

The School Board

The Macon County Board of Education members are elected to six-year terms. Shortly after the appointment of Ulysses Byas in 1970, the two white board members resigned. The board's three black members appointed one white individual, Allen Adams, who was later elected to a full six-year term. With the full support of his black colleagues, Adams defeated his two black opponents by a 5 to 1 majority.

In March 1974, the following persons constituted the Macon County Board of Education:

> P.K. Biswas (chairman) — faculty member at Tuskegee Institute and local businessman (black).
>
> J.H.M. Henderson (vice-chairman) — director of the Carver Research Foundation at Tuskegee Institute and local businessman (black).
>
> Allen Adams — retired from the armed service, and local businessman (white).

Ellis Hall — director of clinics of the School of Veterinary Medicine, Tuskegee Institute, and local businessman (black).

Consuella Harper — director of OIC in Montgomery, Alabama, and former teacher in the Macon County public schools (black).

The board members established a wholesome working relationship. The most controversial issue centered around the consolidation of two high schools — one with a good number of white students and the other with no white students. The problem was resolved by transferring all high school students to the predominantly black high school in Tuskegee. Adams opposed the consolidation. He contended that a high school in the predominantly white section of the county would encourage more whites to return to the public schools. He was convinced by a prominent citizens' committee that his rationale was unsound, and he voted for consolidation.

During an informal interview, the board members unanimously agreed that there had been improvements under Byas. Members who had served during the tenure of Byas' predecessor indicated that they had reluctantly become involved in matters that were purely administrative. Henderson stated:

> Before Mr. Byas came, this board had the problem of being involved in the administration of the schools. This was done because the board had no choice but to become involved rather than let the system collapse. The superintendent was not carrying out the policies of the board in a manner consistent with the policies established by the board. When Mr. Byas was appointed, a clear and mutual understanding was developed. He has been completely able to carry out the board's policies. We completely put things in his hands.

Hall stated that the board wanted a strong superintendent: a person who could implement the policies of the board without having to come to the board for every detail after policy was set.

In its search for a superintendent the board had sought an educator with experience and the capacity to make decisions. Henderson emphasized that the board wanted a "professional and not a politician."

Mrs. Harper, once a teacher in the system, was an activist who vigorously advocated resolving the needs of students and the community. Of all the board members, she most identified with the grass roots population. Mrs. Harper had taught in a rural school; she lived in that community and sent her child to the neighborhood school. The most militant board member, she wanted to see more community involvement and more input from the "little man."

Biswas avoided being an autocrat. Though soft-spoken, Biswas had developed firm views about public education. He had been elected president by his colleagues for two consecutive terms. Biswas' educational philosophy had been strongly influenced by the British system of public education. While he maintained a nonaggressive relationship with his colleagues and the superintendent, Biswas promoted the better aspect of British education.

The board found the school system to have the following needs:

> Significant improvements in academic achievement.
>
> Additional financial supports for education.
>
> New school construction and remodeling of existing facilities.
>
> Some form of consolidation in the use of the existing education facilities.
>
> Accreditation of all schools by the regional accreditation commission.

The School System

The system's nine schools are scattered across the county. One of the elementary schools is located twenty miles from the central administration office. Of the system's 5,049 students, only 318 were white. Academic achievement was a major problem; as

Table 5 indicates, achievement test results in reading were very low. In grades one through six, nearly 9 out of every 10 students tested below the national norms. The system employed 644 persons from all operating funds in school year 1973-74; 581 employees were black. The salary schedule for teachers was not attractive: Table 7 shows that maximums at all levels were low, and the various minimum and maximum differentials did not exceed $400.

TABLE 5
Estimates of Percentages of Students in Grades One-Six Testing Below National Norms in Reading Achievement: Macon County Public Schools

		Grades			
One	Two	Three	Four	Five	Six
90	90	90	91	91	84

Source: Questionnaire completed by Macon County public schools, March 1974.

TABLE 6
Breakdown of Select Professional Staff Funded from Regular Funds, School Year 1973-74: Macon County Public Schools

Teachers	Principals	Professionals on Superintendent's Staff
227	9	5

Source: Questionnaire completed by Macon County public schools, March 1974.

TABLE 7
Minimum and Maximum Ranges of Salary Schedules for Teachers by Degree: Macon County Public Schools

Range	B.A.	M.A.	M.A. + 30
Minimum	$7,885	$9,210	$ 9,910
Maximum	8,285	9,610	10,210

Source: Questionnaire completed by Macon County public schools, March 1974.

TABLE 8
Breakdown of Student Population by Race, School Years 1971-72 to 1973-74:
Macon County Public Schools

School Year	Black	White	Total
1973-74	4,731	318	5,049
1972-73	4,696	316	5,012
1971-72	4,815	262	5,077

Source: Questionnaire completed by Macon County public schools, March 1974.

TABLE 9
Financial Support from Regular Funds, School Years 1970-71 to 1972-73: Macon
County Public Schools

School Year	Amounts
1972-73	$2,137,621
1971-72	2,024,538
1970-71	1,986,535

Source: Macon County public schools, July 1974.

Superintendent Byas identified the following as the most significant needs and problems of the school system:

Significant Needs

Financial support for the schools.

Funds for the recruitment of specialized personnel.

Massive improvements in the physical conditions of
the schools.

Construction of a vocational education and continuing
education facility.

Significant Problems

Improving student achievement.

Effecting the superintendent's role as that of a change
agent.

Motivating key personnel to produce improvements and to do such with enthusiasm.

Keeping the public informed of the system's problems and needs.

Improving the management of the system's resources.

Developing more adequate school facilities.

Developing proposals.

On August 29, 1972, with the recommendation of Byas, the board voted unanimously to form a Blue Ribbon Committee to examine the system and to present recommendations for improving the delivery of services.

The seven-month Committee study was the most comprehensive citizen-staff evaluation that had ever been attempted in Macon County. The Committee noted:

> There is no substitute for overdue schoolwide improvements in education except constructive change within the framework of what is practical and possible. This has been the rationale of the Blue Ribbon Citizens' Committee as it sought the facts in nine important components of the Macon County school system. In each of these components the Committee found strengths. In each, too, it found problems and needs that undermine existing strengths. There are problems of upkeep of all school plants, each requiring maintenance that requires budgetary support. There are problems of providing adequate instructional staff for each of the elementary and high schools, when units permitted by ADA standards make equitable offerings a financial impossibility. There are problems of duplications of facilities and staffing, administrative and instructional, that cannot be justified in terms of the number and distribution of student population. These grave problems are on us now and cannot wait for answers that, though needed for the ideal, are beyond the financial resources now available.

In its initial charge, the board challenged the Blue
Ribbon Citizens' Committee to 'dream': to go
beyond changes for urgent improvements to the
long-term goal of 'excellence.' The danger of
immediate adjustments is always that we may lose
our sensitivity to greater possibilities. The
Committee has not lost its conception of what,
ideally, is excellence for the public school system of
Macon County. The current norms of achievement
do not represent the learning potentials of our
children. It may be that for many children, even
national norms are low ceilings to which teachers
should aspire. The proposed short-term
consolidations must not be a satisfactory answer to
the dream of one countywide high school in a new,
modern, versatile plant, and several relocated,
modern elementary schools — all staffed with
teachers highly competent to perform their
professional responsibilities within a curriculum that
is comprehensive enough to provide for the diversity
of abilities, interests, and future goals of the student
population. Supportive services must be more
adequately staffed to provide and maintain improved
facilities. Local sources of finance must be identified
and developed to their fullest capacity. Citizens
must be encouraged to contribute their moral and
financial support and their ideas and talents to
extending educational opportunities to a
twelve-month school term. The summer programs
should be designed to complement the academic
with recreational and creative offerings that are
important avenues to full living throughout a
lifetime.

Our faith in such a future possibility must be a
strong one; and that faith must be supported with
willingness to work in our various ways to bring to
fruition an education system for Macon County that
will be a model for other systems in the state, and

>   beyond. This *is* a possibility toward which our
>   schools and school communities *must* work,
>   cooperatively and enthusiastically.[4]

The inadequacies of the physical facilities used for instruction reflected a long standing program of neglect. The superintendent and the board had given top priority to remodeling and repairing existing facilities, constructing new units, and adding to some existing structures. The board had been diverting funds to school facility improvement since 1970. The conditions documented in 1968 by the Macon County Education Study Committee had improved. Yet much remained to be done.

Mayor Ford attended the Macon County public schools when they were racially segregated. He assessed the improvements in the system:

>   A number of people said that when you got a
>   black school superintendent the school system
>   would really go down, that the appointment of a
>   black superintendent would be the end of public
>   education in Macon County. Most of the whites fled
>   to the private academy, but over the past several
>   years there has been a slight increase in whites
>   coming back. I think that one of the reasons they are
>   coming back is that under the leadership of the
>   superintendent and his staff there have been
>   improvements in the educational system. There have
>   been revisions and updating of the curriculum.
>   There is a more innovative approach to instruction
>   and curriculum. There have been improvements in
>   the physical facilities. The free lunch program has
>   been expanded significantly. Having grown up in
>   Macon County, I can see the differences.
>
>   We still have a long way to go not only in the
>   school system but in city government. But by and
>   large that is attributable to the fact that additional
>   money and resources are needed. Everyone talks
>   about what they are going to do, but I am a very
>   practical man. Money is needed.[5]

With regard to his relationship with the school system and his perception of the role of the superintendent, Mayor Ford stated:

> As Mayor, I do not dabble in education business per se because I am perfectly comfortable with the leadership that we have. We get together and try to help each other with various common problems in which the expertise of one or the other is needed. The city administration serves Tuskegee and the County Board of Education serves all of Macon County. The fact that the school system serves Tuskegee gives us a reason for dabbling in school affairs, but the quality of leadership and cooperation makes this unnecessary. Under the former superintendent, this would not have been the case.[6]

Superintendent Byas did not underplay the importance of the improvements that had occurred during his administration. He highlighted many unresolved problems. He observed that, given the proper conditions of the mind and the willingness to work hard, deprivation in any form could be overcome.

Future gains in Macon County, however, will be shaped without the influence of Byas. He has departed Macon County. Circumstances placed Byas in the tenuous position of being able to depend only on the support of three of the five board members. The lone white board member was identified by Byas as a racist who believed that the superintendent was moving too rapidly in the desegregation of the teaching staff. The opposition of this board member had been expected. But Byas unexpectedly lost the support of another board member. This board member had been employed in the system as a Head Start teacher previous to her election to the school board. Upon her election she continued in this employment. Her colleagues on the board interpreted this dual role as a conflict of interest and voted 4 to 1 to suspend her. Byas, who also served as the secretary to the board, was required, on the board's behalf, to write the letter that notified her of her suspension as an employee of the school system. Byas indicated that from the day the board member received the letter of suspension under his signature, he lost the support of that board member.

Byas's two nonsupporters on the board gave their support to a candidate in the school board election who had announced opposition to Byas. In anticipation that the school board election would produce results that would remove Byas's majority support on the board, the school board offered him a four-year contract. Byas chose not to accept the board's offer. He suggested that the board offer him a two-year contract and retain an option to renew the second year. If the board decided not to renew the second year, Byas had to be informed by no later than January 31, 1977 and had to be paid as superintendent until July 31, 1977. The board also was obligated to retain Byas as a consultant for 80 consecutive working days commencing on July 31, 1977.

The school board election did produce a new board member who aligned with Byas's two nonsupporters on the board to form a majority against Byas. Not wanting to remain in a superintendency in which his opposition constituted a majority of the board's membership, Byas sought to implement his insurance plan. He suggested that the board cancel the second year of his contract. On November 26, 1976, the board, meeting in executive session, asked the superintendent to leave the meeting in order that they might discuss his contract. Byas cited Title 52 of the Alabama Code, which authorized his presence at such a meeting, and remained for the session.

In executive session the board voted 3 to 2 to cancel the second year of Byas's contract. But the board did not want him to remain in the superintendency until July 31, 1977. The motion to cancel was rescinded. A motion was offered to terminate Byas's contract as of the close of the work day on December 17, 1976. Speaking on the motion, Byas reminded the board of the provisions of his contract and indicated that he would contemplate securing legal assistance if the board did not honor his contract in full.

After a lengthy discussion, the board and Byas reached agreement. The following motion was passed by three votes: the board requests the resignation of the superintendent; the superintendent be paid his regular salary through June 30, 1977;

and Byas be paid as an advisor to the board for 95 consecutive working days beginning on July 1, 1977.[7] Byas and the board signed an agreement which stipulated that each party agreed not to bring lawsuits, litigation or claims against the other and that the relationship of employer and employee that previously existed between Byas and the board was totally concluded.

Byas decided against continuing an awkward and ineffective working relationship with his board. He opted for compromise rather than confrontation. His commitment to the belief that a board ought to have confidence in its superintendent directed his decision to seek a mutually acceptable resolution of an unsatisfactory situation.

The state of Alabama is not noted for responding to the problems and needs of black Americans. Yet Macon County's black leadership has been able to secure increased assistance from the state. The scope of economic assistance that the county can receive from the state is constrained by two significant factors: the state is among the most economically disadvantaged states in the union, and the state's policymaking bodies are still strongly influenced by racists. Hopes for a better tomorrow must be predicated on the county's ability to attract economic assistance from private investors and the federal government.

Nevertheless, citizens are involved in school affairs. Innovative programs have been initiated to prevent and correct academic retardation. Teachers and administrators are actively engaged in staff development programs geared to improving their skills. Public education in Macon County has advanced since 1970. Yet the calamitous inheritance that blacks in Macon County received from a racist white power structure has made the advancements relatively minor in comparison to what remains to be accomplished.

Atlanta, Georgia

The City

The city of Atlanta is frequently described with superlatives. Maynard Jackson, Atlanta's black mayor, declares that Atlanta is the best city in America for black people to live in. Julian Bond, the nationally known Georgia State Respresentative, once stated that Atlanta was the best place for blacks in the United States — if they are middle-class and have a college degree; but if they are poor, it is much like Birmingham, Jackson, or any other place. Atlanta has been in a boom period since the 1960s. Many Atlantans are convinced it is the world's next great city.

Blacks have participated significantly in determining the direction of the city. The city has an involved white business community, which has invested heavily in numerous business ventures, especially in downtown Atlanta. Atlanta has an extremely potent black political force, which exercised its power in the election of a black mayor in 1973 and which influenced a majority white board of education to accede to the appointment of a black superintendent. For blacks and whites, Atlanta is an improvement over most urban centers; but, like other urban centers, the city has had serious problems. Atlanta is " . . . a city with an amazing success story and a winning mystique but a whole lot of social problems, most of them bound up in the racial dilemma."[8]

A number of factors have contributed to Atlanta's economic growth and the city's rather positive black-white community relations. The white business power structure has invested a good amount of both time and money in the promotion of Atlanta's economic growth. For years Atlanta has had an influential black middle-class whose representatives have made meaningful contributions to the city's destiny. Most of the people that were interviewed concurred that, while not perfect, race relations in Atlanta are the best of any large urban community. Confrontations between black and white leaders have, for the most part, produced constructive results. The Atlanta University complex provides a base of black intellectuals who have participated in identifying and redressing black Atlantan's problems and needs. In the sixties, during the administration of former Mayor Ivan Allen, Jr., Atlanta prospered economically and developed black-white relations that were often cited as models for the nation to emulate.

Edgar and Patricia Cheatham, in an article in *Mainliner* magazine, highlighted the important personalities who shaped the movement at a time when many other cities were retrogressing socially and economically:

> The city's promise has been enhanced by such towering contemporary figures as the late Ralph McGill, Pulitizer Prize-winning publisher of the *Constitution*, and Dr. Martin Luther King, Jr., Nobel laureate, who challenged not just the conscience of this city and the South but of the nation. Mayor William M. Hartsfield, who coined the phrase 'Atlanta is too busy to hate.' Ivan Allen, under whose guidance Atlanta led the South and much of the nation in race relations during the crucial sixties, and his successor, Sam Massell, a plucky, self-avowed liberal who was the city's first Jewish mayor. In a hard-fought election last fall, Massell was defeated by vice-mayor Maynard Jackson, articulate, dynamic, and black. Voting in the runoff was somewhat along racial lines, with Jackson getting a massive black vote and picking up some 20 percent of the white vote. Jackson, scion of one of the South's most accomplished and notable black families, is vehement in his determination that racial differences here, which have so far been minimized, cannot and will not polarize the city at this late date.[9]

Much of the economic growth of Atlanta has been directed by downtown investments. In 1973, Atlanta issued $226.7 million in building permits. Plans were under way for the construction of two hotels with a total of 100,000 rooms. Approximately 430 of the nation's 500 corporations have branch offices in Atlanta. The city has an impressive new civic and convention center, and a world-trade center. This economic growth has not solved the employment needs of all black Atlantans, but the boom has been beneficial to most and has encouraged other blacks to move to Atlanta. An *Ebony* magazine article on the top ten cities in the nation for blacks stated:

As the financial, manufacturing, and communication center of the Southeast, Atlanta offers to blacks, who constitute 51.3 percent of its population, an opportunity for advancement on many fronts. The Atlanta metropolitan area has about 1,650 manufacturers, who employ a fifth of the areas workers in the production of aircraft, automobiles, chemicals, furniture, iron and steel products, soft drinks, and textiles. In addition, the more than 3,000 wholesale firms in the city sell about $8.5 billion worth of goods yearly. Presently, about 15.7 percent of Atlanta's black wage-earners have been defined by the U.S. Labor Department as high-salaried, as against 52.0 percent of whites. This disparity arises partially because many blacks do not have marketable skills in such booming occupational areas as accounting, engineering, marketing, retail selling, and the skilled crafts. On the other hand, some blacks are still working below their ability because of job discrimination. The Atlanta Urban League is among those agencies waging a continuing battle to reduce the ranks both of the underemployed and of the unemployed.[10]

During the sixties, the city's white population declined by 60,084 and the black population increased by 69,602. Estimates indicated that in 1980 the city's black population would increase to 61 percent. By 1974 the black unemployment rate was still relatively high, and the crime rate was steadily increasing. The future of Atlanta looked promising and it appeared that blacks would benefit from the prosperity:

The median income for families in the metropolitian Atlanta region was four hundred dollars below the national urban median in 1960, but by 1970 it was five hundred dollars above it. Retail sales in the region went from one billion four hundred million to three billion one hundred million dollars between 1960 and 1971, and the annual expenditure on

private construction increased from two hundred
and seven million to seven hundred and seventy
million dollars. ... In 1972, Atlanta became the
eleventh most prosperous city in the nation in terms
of retail sales volume. The unemployment rate for
the nation as a whole in 1972 was 5.6 percent but
for metropolitan Atlanta it was 3.3 percent.[11]

On October 6, 1973, Maynard Jackson was elected mayor. For
years, a small group of white businessmen had ruled the city's
economic and political life. In his campaign, Jackson challenged
both the white and black elite. Eventually the black, old guard
gave its support to him in his runoff election against incumbent
mayor Sam Massell. Jackson won 59 percent of the 125,000 votes
cast. He received about 22 percent of the white vote. In the same
election, nine blacks and nine whites were elected to the city
council. Also, four whites and five blacks were elected to the
board of education. The election results indicated that Atlanta
would be reshaped with black input.

In 1973, Atlanta's black power made its greatest impact. The
election forced the formulation of a new power coalition. "Generally the leaders of Atlanta have put their trust in the old
coalition of moderate black leadership and pragmatic white
businessmen."[12] The prevailing view among black leaders was
that too many white dollars had been invested in Atlanta for the
white business power structure to desert the city in protest
against emerging black power. The importance of black votes
and white dollars in the future of Atlanta is critical to the city's
continued economic and social growth.

The School Board

In October 1973, the board election culminated in two historic
firsts: a black majority and a female majority. The elected board
members beginning their four-year terms in January 1974 included five incumbents and four newcomers. The new election
process brought in six members elected by districts and three
members elected at large.

The following persons began four-year terms in January 1974:

Benjamin Mays (at-large member and president) — President Emeritus of Morehouse College (black).

June Cofer (at-large member and vice-president) — graduate of Anniston Business College in Alabama and public relations advisor with the 4-C program in Atlanta (white).

Ann Woodward (at-large member) — has a record of extensive involvement in civic affairs (white).

Margaret R. Griggs — housewife, mother of five children, and volunteer worker (black).

John Albert Middleton — former president of Morris Brown College (black).

Angella C. Ioannides — housewife and active PTA worker (white).

Richard E. Raymer — lawyer; served as chairman of the Educational Task Force of the Chamber of Commerce (white).

Asa C. Yancey — medical director of Grady Memorial Hospital in Atlanta and associate dean at Emory University, School of Medicine (black).

Carolyn Crowder — employed as a stenographer by the U.S. Department of Agriculture and mother of six children (black).

Mays is one of the nation's most distinguished educators. For twenty-seven years, he was president of Morehouse College. He has influenced more outstanding black male Americans than perhaps any single individual in the nation's history. His reputation as an educator and a humanitarian has been acclaimed internationally. Mays has not let his age reduce his professional and civic activities.

In 1969, at the urging of his supporters, Mays became a candidate for membership on the board. When interviewed in May 1974, Mays was serving his fifth year on the board. He was an overwhelming choice of the voters in 1969 and 1973. In each of his years on the board, Mays has been selected by his colleagues as school-board president. His major goals are to maintain a unified board and to establish quality education throughout the public schools. Mays observed that the history of the past is that [educators] tend to neglect things which are predominantly black; he does not think that this must be.

As a former school administrator, Mays seeks to maintain the board as a policymaking, not management, unit for the system. He believes that the board should determine policy and make sure that the superintendent implements it. Mays emphasized that it takes "eternal vigilance" to maintain an effective board and a satisfactory relationship between the board and the superintendent:

> I do not believe that members of the board of education can do their job if they are scrapping at each other. If the board is scrapping among themselves, then some members are also scrapping at the superintendent. You cannot have a divided board and also have a superintendent dealing with a unified school board. If you have a divided board, some of the board members will be with the superintendent and others will be against him. I want to keep the board together and to keep the board and the superintendent from fighting each other. I think that if I have made any real contribution as president it has been due to the fact that the board has not been torn asunder.[13]

Mays has established a foundation aimed at achieving some of his own personal objectives for the public schools. He wants to establish quality education for both whites and blacks, to preserve a well-integrated system, and to improve the basic learning skills in reading and mathematics.

Previous school boards have used litigation to delay desegregation and to reduce desegregation mandates. The Atlanta public schools did not begin to desegregate until 1961. A plan called for school desegregation at the rate of one grade per school year. In 1972, the Fifth Circuit Court of Appeals notified the board that the plan was unacceptable. The court gave the board six weeks to submit a new desegregation proposal.

The school board, through negotiations with several citizens' groups, effected a plan known as the Atlanta Compromise of 1973. Lonnie King, then local president of the NAACP, played a critical role in shaping the compromise. King yielded on the strict pupil ratios for integration, but he took a firm posture in support of giving blacks the decisive voice in administering the schools. He explained that the NAACP had battled all over the South with racists — the boards and the administrators — on those points (pupil desegregation and maximum faculty desegregation) and had won in court. But those same boards and administrators had maintained control of those systems.

The compromise provided for the creation of several new high-level administrative positions and specified that nine of the seventeen positions on the superintendent's cabinet — including the superintendency — be filled by blacks. Other key positions just below cabinet rank were also designated to be filled by blacks. The following criteria were presented to the court as desegregation guidelines:

> No school would contain fewer than 30 percent black students.
>
> No exceptions unless a school was shown to be stable and integrated 20 percent or more black.
>
> White students would be transferred only into schools where the resulting enrollment would be 30 percent white.
>
> All black schools unaffected or left "untouched" would be determined according to agreed upon objective criteria such as condition of the building, classroom space, distance to other schools, and phasing out.
>
> The preceding requirements would be applied in all efforts to maximize integration of all students.[14]

The School System

Compared to most other large urban school systems, the Atlanta public schools have been well-administered. Superintendent Alonzo Crim was elected on July 1, 1973, and of the seven superintendents interviewed, he alone still holds his position. He did not inherit a system with obsolete or poorly maintained facilities. His predecessor had efficiently managed the schools' financial and physical resources. Crim's paramount challenge was that most students tested below the national norms in reading achievement. Table 10 indicates that more than two-thirds of all students in grades one through six tested below national norms in reading achievement.

TABLE 10
Estimates of Percentages of Students in Grades One-Six Testing Below National Norms in Reading Achievement: Atlanta Public Schools

		Grades			
One	Two	Three	Four	Five	Six
65	72	74	77	82	83

Source: Questionnaire completed by the Atlanta public schools, March 1974.

TABLE 11
Breakdown of Student Population By Race, School Years 1971-72 to 1973-74: Atlanta Public Schools

School Year	Black	White	Other	Totals
1973-74	72,800	15,961	353	89,114
1972-73	74,186	21,857	405	96,448
1971-72	74,152	27,796	246	102,194

Source: Questionnaire completed by the Atlanta public schools, March 1974.

In school year 1973-74, 89,114 students were enrolled in the schools. At least 8 out of every 10 students in the system were black. Table 11 reveals that the student population was declining. For school year 1972-73, 1,350 students were recorded as dropouts. Slightly more than one half of the student population received free lunch during school year 1973-74.

TABLE 12
Minimum and Maximum Ranges of Salary Schedules for Teachers by Degree: Atlanta Public Schools

Range	B.A.	M.A.	M.A. +30
Minimum	$ 7,950.00	$ 8,770.00	$ 9,550.00
Maximum	12,421.88	13,671.88	14,921.88

Source: Questionnaire completed by the Atlanta public schools, March 1974.

Some 4,359 teachers were employed from regular funds in school year 1973-74. Of this total, 2,967 teachers were black. Unlike teachers in almost all large school systems, Atlanta teachers did not operate under a collective bargaining agreement with the board; at that time the teachers had not petitioned the board for collective bargaining. The school system had a more extensive in-service education program for teachers than those found in most systems. A teacher competency test in reading and language arts instruction was administered to teachers in the related subject areas. Staff development programs were prescribed for those teachers whose performance on the tests were assessed as unsatisfactory in one or more skill areas.

TABLE 13
Financial Support from Regular Funds, School Years 1971-72 to 1973-74: Atlanta Public Schools

School Year	Amounts
1973-74	$107,031,856
1972-73	104,379,580
1971-72	97,123,223

Source: Questionnaire completed by the Atlanta public schools, March 1974.

While the financial support for the Atlanta public schools was sufficient, increases did not keep pace with the inflationary rate of the economy. With a per-pupil expenditure of $1,290 in school year 1973-74, the system was in a position comparable to most large urban school systems — and in a better position than most school systems in the South. In December 1973 Research Atlanta, an independent, nonprofit organization that studies public policy issues affecting the metropolitan Atlanta area, issued its review of the financial support the system had received between 1963 and 1973. The report also commented on the future financial needs of the school system. Research Atlanta cited as significant the following points about the financial status of the Atlanta public schools:

Based on our analysis of Atlanta school finance, Research Atlanta finds the following four points particularly significant:

The Atlanta public school system has been and is now on a sound footing due to a growing economy, past public support, and a declining enrollment.

Continued increases in the number of "high-need" pupils in the future will require not only higher per-pupil educational expenditures but a more rational, need-oriented system of allocating resources to schools.

Georgia's school-financing methods have often penalized independent school systems such as that in Atlanta because of their urban status and have only recently been amended to ameliorate this situation.

Federal grants-in-aid for special education programs in Atlanta have only partially filled the financial gaps left by inadequate state and local funding arrangements but nevertheless remain a potentially powerful force for promoting equality of educational opportunity.[15]

In 1973, Crim saw the following as needs and problems:

Significant Needs

Improved student achievement in basic skills.

Organization of appropriate staff-development programs on systemwide basis.

Stabilization of student mobility — particularly white students.

Increased community involvement.

Organized management program.

Significant Problems

Public distrust of the public schools.

Communication channels not yet established.

Change of leadership style — not yet understood by staff and community.

Management team not yet moving by design.

My own impatience.[16]

Crim believes that the board and personnel have sufficient resources and the will to improve educational services. Teachers and administrators perform in the schools with adequate to excellent environments for instruction and learning. Teachers and administrators receive salaries that are the best in the South and that compare favorably to many urban school systems in the North. Crim is satisfied that the public schools have the ingredients to develop an excellent system. His primary objective is to establish an organizational structure that brings the various positive ingredients together and that most effectively provides a means for making prompt and accurate judgments about ineffective programs and services.

A comprehensive plan for public education in Atlanta is being developed. This plan seeks to provide the critical resources needed to allocate resources and utilize personnel more effectively. Crim is preparing his administrative and instructional staffs to assume leadership in effecting a reconstituted system of public education. Under the plan all school administrators participate in an extensive program of management training designed to improve educational leadership.

All teachers participate in staff development programs. These programs are intended to expand the skills of teachers and to broaden the base of their professional experiences by placing them in leadership positions other than the classroom. Crim is aware that reorganizing and revitalizing the public schools in Atlanta will not be easy. He is committed to doing what needs to be done to "earn his role of leadership."

Superintendent Crim must manage to preserve his integrity while seeking to provide leadership to all segments of the population. His administrative style lends itself to cooperative ventures rather than to alienation. Crim has experienced relatively smooth sailing in his superintendency. Benjamin Mays has been the only board president he has served. His relationship with Mayor Jackson remains close. Turnover on the board has been minimal. Crim and the board function in an atmosphere of mutual respect. The response of teachers and administrators has been positive. He has access to key black and white leaders in the community.

Crim stressed that good relations with his board and a 10 percent improvement in achievement test results contribute to his stability and survival. He offered the following comment on his approach to board-superintendent relations:

> I try to find ways to communicate effectively with each board member. I try to identify those things which are the most pertinent to each board member. The members of the board have brought great commitment to their tasks. Benjamin Mays has been an outstanding board president who has served as president throughout my tenure as superintendent. He has stated publicly on many occasions that he thinks well of my work, and with that kind of support, it has helped pave the way for my being able to relate to the board in a very easy and informal way.[17]

Commenting further on his relationship with members of the board, Crim noted that he had a close and friendly relationship with each board member and that the board functioned as a unit rather than as a collection of various groups. He states: "Contrary to some of the boards in the nation in which the superintendent becomes a tennis ball and the board members are the players, seeking a chance to hit the ball, board members in Atlanta have not had that kind of friction between themselves and the superintendent or among board members. There are differences of opinion, but these differences are resolved in an orderly and cooperative manner."[18]

Crim believes that a superintendent must realize that he or she is appointed by the board and serves at the pleasure of the board. "I try to make certain that the Board of Education receives the respect and dignity that it deserves as a major elected body that is responsible for the conduct of an institution that spends close the $125 million per year."[19] Crim knows that the life of a superintendent has its ups and downs, but he hopes that the good atmosphere will prevail and that he will be permitted to remain in the superintendency in Atlanta for several more years. He sees the constant turnover among urban school superintendents as an impediment to the establishment of quality educational programs. "The job is so hard, so difficult that in order to realize the kind of progress that students deserve, it takes eight to ten years to get a comprehensive instructional program installed."[20]

Atlanta is a paradox. While the great majority of the urban centers are engaged in a seemingly losing effort to regain their economic vitality, Atlanta is experiencing an economic surge that could very well culminate in the city's becoming one of the major cities of the world. If money alone were the element needed to reverse the onslaught of urban deterioration, Atlanta's salvation would be reasonably assured. The city is confronted with nearly all of the problems and needs of other large urban centers. Although Atlanta is making more progress than most other communities, the city is far from declaring that it provides adequately for the fundamental as well as the varied cultural and recreational needs of all segments of the city.

Can whites and blacks in Atlanta effect a commonality of purpose and a cooperative existence with equality and justice governing the partnership? Will middle- and upper-income blacks and whites preserve the status quo while lower-income blacks and whites remain entrapped in a woefully inadequate existence? Can Atlanta become a great city while academic achievement in the public schools remains at the bottom levels? The answers to these questions will be shaped by Atlanta's black and white leadership.

Washington, D.C.

The City

The first home rule legislation for the District of Columbia in over 100 years was enacted by Congress in 1973. Basically the bill provides for an elected city council; an elected mayor; judges for the Superior Court and the District of Columbia Court of Appeals appointed by the President and confirmed by the Senate; elected advisory neighborhood councils; and five independent D.C. government agencies. Under the home rule bill, the District's annual operating budget must be approved by Congress. Congress retains veto powers over any legislation passed by the city council. The partnership between the District and Congress has been modified, but District voters remain the displeased silent partner.

In 1970 the District had a population of more than 756,000, of whom approximately 71 percent were black. Among America's major cities, Washington has the highest percentage of blacks. For blacks, life in the District is a mixture of contrasts and contradictions. Large numbers of blacks live very well and large numbers do not. Affluent blacks in Washington have for years maintained highly elegant patterns of social activities. Few other communities can match the elaborate homes and fine furnishings of Washington's black middle-class. Yet lower-income blacks are as disorganized and disadvantaged as blacks in other urban communities. While blessed with extraordinarily attractive residential areas, the District is beset with slums that are eyesores and reminders of the serious gaps between the classes.

Poverty in the nation's capital, except for the elderly, is confined almost exclusively to blacks. Poverty affected 17 percent of

the District's population in the early seventies.[21] One out of
every five families earned less than $5,000. Fifty-seven percent
of all families living in poverty were headed by women. Four out
of every ten persons living in poverty were children. Almost
21,000 families, slightly more than 1 out of every 10, were
identified as low-income families. The District's median family
income was $9,583 and mean family income was $12,189. In a
1973 demographic report the Office of Planning and Management of the District government stated:

> It is estimated . . . that approximately 5 percent of
> the District's population had incomes 25 percent
> above the poverty threshold for particular family-size
> units. In that case, an additional minimum of 37,000
> marginally poor persons could be added to the
> 123,000 classified as in poverty as the potential base
> for Medicaid eligibility.[22]

The District's labor force was almost 50 percent female. Government was the chief employer. Twenty-nine percent or 95,600
persons were employed in clerical positions. Former superintendent of schools Sizemore provided the following comments
on unemployment and underemployment in the District in relation to the city's overall picture:

> In 1971 Washington had the lowest
> unemployment rate of fifteen central cities for which
> monthly data were available. Further investigation
> has, however, brought out the fact that a major
> problem in the District with respect to employment
> is not unemployment but subemployment — a large
> population of workers employed in on-again,
> off-again jobs offering little or no advancement. The
> 1970 census figures show that of the 40 percent of
> all D.C. residents employed at the date of the census
> 158,000 out of 397,000 were out of work during part
> of the preceding year. Moreover, the low, reported
> unemployment rate does not reflect the 49,000
> adults who are classified as 'not in the labor force'

for 'no apparent reasons' but who, upon closer study, are not looking for work because of poor health and lack of skill, experience, or education.[23]

Washington was once among the most thoroughly racially segregated cities in the nation. Today, blacks live in all sections of the city, but whites are concentrated primarily in the far northwest section and Georgetown. Property in the District is expensive: "The District is a city of renting householders. With the exception of Boston, it has the smallest percentage, 26 percent, of its households, in owner-occupied units."[24]

Many families with incomes well above the poverty level are not able to afford adequate housing. The high cost of housing affects both low- and middle-income families: "The annual mean gross rent is higher than in most cities, except San Francisco and Boston, and takes a larger percentage of the combined mean income of families and individuals."[25] Lower grade government workers are the hardest hit by the high cost of housing in the District. If they do not purchase or rent housing in depressed sections, their alternatives are either to move to high-priced apartments or to investigate equally as expensive homes in Maryland and Virginia.

Walter Washington was the District's first mayor and the first black to head the District government. First appointed by President Lyndon Johnson and reappointed by President Richard Nixon, he was later elected to the position. Washington was criticized by some blacks as being too passive and too compatible with Congress. He was also praised by many for stabilizing relations between whites and blacks. Washington repeatedly emphasized that he preferred to resolve differences with Congress in behind-the-scenes efforts away from the public spotlight.

Washington, an outgoing man, rendered crowd-pleasing speeches in the manner of a Southern Baptist preacher. He had to cope with a government dominated by congressional influence and with the provisions of the home rule bill of 1973. Washingtonians were skeptical about the alleged benefits produced by the bill. But the government provided the residents with elected

officials through whom they could exert political pressure on
Congress.

The School Board

The school board consisted of the following members:

> Virginia Morris (president) — program director with a
> local antipoverty agency (black).
> Julius Hobson, Jr. (vice-president) — research assistant
> at Howard University (black).
> Bettie Benjamin — lawyer (black).
> Therman Evans — physican employed by a community
> health program (black).
> Elizabeth Kane — employed by the Folger Shakespeare
> Library (white).
> Raymond Kemp — minister (white).
> Hilda Mason — housewife and former teacher (black).
> Carol Schwartz — housewife and former teacher
> (white).
> Barbara Lett Simmons — consultant (black).
> William Treanor — former teacher and project coor-
> dinator for a youth advocate organization (white).
> John Warren — legislative aide for the House Commit-
> tee on Education and Labor (black).

Morris came to the board with a reputation as a fair person
who acts independent of pressure groups. Upon being elected
president, she issued her policy statement. The following excerpts are indicative of that policy:

> Every member of this board also brought his
> individual concerns and commitment to the board of
> education. However, it becomes immediately
> apparent that while the individual is important, the
> power and strength of the board are embodied in the
> unity of the board.
> It is imperative that the board develop a unity of

purpose which is not shallow and superficial but which emerges from the difficult process of confrontation and resolution. The process will force the board to face the issues squarely, establish priorities, and make the difficult decisions necessary to redirect and reshape the school system.

The board develops educational policy for the school system. The superintendent is our chief administrator. While the board must be aware of administrative affairs and constantly raise questions relevant to the problems facing the school system, we are not able nor were we selected by our constituency to administer the school system. We have chosen a superintendent, who without question is capable of meeting the challenges of the schools of the District of Columbia and administering the system to ensure that it meets the educational needs of our community. The board must provide the intellectual and institutional support to enable the superintendent to meet the challenge, but that support is only meaningful within the context of a critical and hard-thinking board. One which grapples with and confronts the problems in our schools. The board must identify its strengths and direct those strengths to the resolution of the educational dilemma in which we find ourselves.[26]

As president, Morris did not want to lobby her colleagues to gain votes. She stated that board members ought to vote on an issue based on the facts and their personal commitment to students. She hoped that members would move away from the past practice of dealing with personalities rather than issues. Mrs. Morris indicated that she wanted the superintendent to succeed; she wanted the superintendent to reach out to teachers and administrators. As a board member, Mrs. Morris directed her efforts to developing a school system in which students were able to compete academically and were able to assume functional positions in the economy.

The School System

Washington was the first major school system to serve a predominantly black student population. Many opponents of racial desegregation referred to Washington schools as an example of the consequences of integration. Although the system has the unique problem of congressional interference, Washington is still better off than most urban systems. But the system shares many of the same problems of all urban schools — declining achievement, violence in the schools, vandalism, insufficient funds, business-management difficulties, and teacher militancy.

The track system, a form of ability grouping, was the most controversial aspect of public education in the District in the mid-sixties. Many black parents complained that the track system was a form of segregation. A group of black parents sought redress in the courts. Citing the discriminatory elements inherent in the track system, Judge J. Skelly Wright, in June 1967, ordered its termination. He also ordered the systematic integration of school faculties and programs and the development of an equitable formula for grouping students. The white superintendent expressed his objections to the Wright decree by submitting his resignation.

Later, in 1971, Judge Wright informed a predominantly black board and its black superintendent that the system had not adequately responded to his June 1967 decree. In a later decree, Judge Wright stated that the school system expended greater funds for instructional services in those schools that had a white majority. Although the system had less than 8,000 white students, out of a total of 140,000, the court ordered the system to equalize expenditures with respect to the assignment of teachers to elementary schools. The system was prohibited from deviating in each elementary school more than plus or minus 5 percent of the citywide mean for expenditures for teachers in elementary schools.

The D.C. public schools served 136,133 students in school year 1973-74. While whites in the District constituted about 30 percent of the population, the school system registered 5,812 white students in school year 1973-74. Table 14 shows the racial composition of the student population for three consecutive school years. In school year 1972-73, the system employed 10,290 persons from regular funds. Figures were not available on the racial composition of school employees. However, the majority of teachers and administrators were black. The salary schedules for teachers were competitive with surrounding school districts. Table 15 provides the 1973-74 salary schedules for teachers; increases granted to teachers in August 1974 are not included in the figures.

TABLE 14
Breakdown of Student Population by Race, School Years 1971-72 to 1973-74: D.C. Public Schools

School Year	Black	White	Total
1973-74	130,321	5,812	136,133
1972-73	133,651	6,349	140,000
1971-72	136,256	7,155	143,411

Source: Questionnaire completed by the D.C. public schools, March 1974.

TABLE 15
Minimum and Maximum Ranges of Salary Schedules for Teachers by Degree: D.C. Public Schools

Range	B.A.	M.A.	M.A. +30
Minimum	$ 8,770	$ 9,650	$10,090
Maximum	13,615	15,675	16,120

Source: Questionnaire completed by the D.C. public schools, March 1974.

On October 1, 1973, Barbara Sizemore became the system's second black superintendent and its first woman superintendent. She entered a system in which the board and previous superintendent frequently disagreed on how the system should be administered. While progress had been made in reducing some of the major difficulties, Sizemore inherited a position demanding immediate decisions concerning ongoing reforms and improvements delayed by the change in leadership.

Six months after her appointment, Sizemore identified the following as the system's most significant needs and problems:

> *Significant Needs*
> Reorganization of prekindergarten-to-grade-twelve multi-age, multi-level group practice.
> Decentralization mechanism.
> Allocation-of-resources formula.
> Special-education-services continuum.
> Staff development.
> *Significant Problems*
> Moving staff where needed.
> Changing structure.
> Board relations.
> Student and community involvement expansion.

She provided the following commentary on instituting change:

> If you wanted to retool a factory, you'd close it down. But you can't send the kids home for six months while you change the schools. So we have to be very careful about our short-range goals. The schools are very rigid institutions to which we legislate entry and exit, like the Army and the prisons. We want to restructure the system to have multi-age, multi-level groupings that are more compatible with human growth and development. Our major goal is to decentralize so that the distance between the making of policy and its implementation at the classroom level is shorter, so that the system becomes more responsive to the clients — the parents and the students.[27]

Table 16 indicates the decline in reading test scores.

TABLE 16
Estimates of Percentages of Students in Grades One-Six Testing Below
National Norms in Reading Achievement: DC. Public Schools

		Grades			
One	Two	Three	Four	Five	Six
59	68.5	79.7	81	83.4	84.1

Source: Questionnaire completed by D.C. public schools, March 1974.

Fiscal decisions must run the bureaucratic gauntlet through not only staff, school board, community, but also the mayor, city council and Congress. Congress has repeatedly inserted the priority judgments of its members above those established by the school board. Congress exercises line-item veto authority over budget items. The remains of a nineteenth-century paternalism have denied school officials the degree of autonomy needed to administer efficiently a major school system.

The system requires an 8 percent increase in the budget each fiscal year to cover mandatory increases. When appropriations are not sufficient to cover mandatory increases, reductions have to be effected. Except for salary increases for school personnel and increased funding for special education, as of 1974 no major new programs had been supported by increased appropriations in four fiscal years. New programs approved by Congress had been financed by reducing previously funded programs and services. Table 17 shows the financial support received by the school system from regular funds for three consecutive school years.

TABLE 17
Financial Support from Regular Funds, School Years 1971-72 to 1973-74:
D.C. Public Schools

School Year	Amounts
1973-74	$167,807,500
1972-73	154,682,400
1971-72	142,946,600

Source: Questionnaire completed by the D.C. public schools, March 1974.

Against recommendations made by the mayor for salary increases for teachers, Congress approved legislation granting teachers a salary increase of 13 percent over a two-year period. Former Mayor Washington supported a 10 percent increase for one year. The District government was forced to establish new revenue sources to fund most of the increased costs of the salary increases. In order to meet its mandatory increases and to cover its share of the cost of salary increases, the system had to reduce the budget approximately $6 million. School year 1974-75 commenced with budgetary reductions taking priority over all other activities of the board and superintendent.

On March 8, 1974, Sizemore issued a 120-day report. The report, a response to a contractual obligation, presented what she intended to accomplish in her three-year term and what resources would be needed and adjustments made to implement the objectives. On Thursday, May 30, 1974, the board approved, with some stated reservations, her plans for the reorganization of the school system. The board approved the following:

> Restructuring of the schools so that students of different ages and abilities can be taught in the same classroom.
>
> Decentralizing the school system into six administrative regions with the use of PACTS as the means to accomplish decentralization. (PACTS: Parents, Administrators, Community Residents, and Teachers and Students working together.)
>
> Curricular changes: Multi-lingual instruction; combinations of like disciplines being taught together; emphasis placed on concepts rather than facts; and flexible time sequences.

James Williams, a Sizemore appointee from Chicago, served as her deputy superintendent for management. He abolished eight departments and 650 positions. As a result, he became involved in litigation related to his attempt to remove the system's financial director.

Sizemore had proposed and implemented some sweeping

changes in the conduct of public education in the District. She stated that her intentions were to approach the question of goal setting, planning, organizing, coordinating, communicating, decision-making and evaluation through the collaboration of an administrative team. The superintendent's administrative team or council consisted of the Council of School Officers, principals, and region superintendents. Assessing the efforts of the administrative-team concept, Sizemore stated:

> Based on my initial months as superintendent, I am pleased with the degree of commitment, dedication, willingness to work extremely hard, and readiness to share authority demonstrated by the administrative staff. They are prepared to become members of a team. Crucial, however, to the ultimate success of this new direction is an understanding and acceptance of the team concept by the board of education.[28]

In 1974, three of Sizemore's top executive officers resigned. Her vice-superintendent, who was assigned to oversee decentralization, resigned. The administrator responsible for the day-to-day operations of the school and support instructional units resigned to assume a lesser but higher paying position in a neighboring school system. Sizemore's deputy superintendent for management resigned to return to the Chicago public schools. Sizemore continued her systemwide reforms without the services of three senior members of her executive cabinet while confronting a school board that was increasingly more critical of her performance.

Sizemore's superintendency had begun in a relatively satisfactory climate in board-superintendent relations. Her predecessor, Hugh Scott, had given the board nine months notice of his decision not to seek a renewal of his contract. Scott cited philosophical differences with certain members of the board as a factor in his decision not to pursue a second term as superintendent. During Sizemore's first months as superintendent the board consciously sought to maintain positive relations with the superintendent and between board members.

Superintendents commonly note that the board that hires you is not the board that fires you. During Sizemore's tenure as superintendent, the board underwent numerous changes in membership. Only two of the eleven members of the board that appointed her served on the board at the time of her dismissal. These two members voted for her termination. The board that appointed Sizemore had eight black and three white members. The board that terminated her contract had four white members. All four of the white board members voted for her termination.

The differences between Sizemore and members of the board became more pointed and public during the early days of her second year as superintendent. Some observers trace the beginning of Sizemore's final days as superintendent to a particular board meeting in which Sizemore soundly criticized several members of the board for being more concerned about political aspirations than the educational needs of students. On May 31, 1975, after a meeting of the Committee of the Whole, Sizemore was informed that the board

> proposes to terminate your contract and to remove you from your position of Superintendent of Schools no earlier than 30 days from your receipt of this notice. It is proposed that you be removed for cause affecting your efficiency as Superintendent of Schools, and to thereby terminate the contract dated September 6, 1973 between the Board of Education and Barbara A. Sizemore.
>
> The charge against you is: Neglect of or inattention to your duties as superintendent and failure to comply with directives and policies of the board.[29]

The board held a dismissal hearing to provide an opportunity for Sizemore to respond to the seventeen charges against her. The appointed administrative law judge found that the charges had been improperly constituted, because the full board in public session had not adopted the list of charges. On August 28, 1975 the board of education, in public session, adopted the report of the Committee of the Whole by a vote of 7 to 3 (with one member absent). Sizemore was so notified, and the dismissal hearing, with the public invited, began on September 8, 1975. Herbert O. Reid, Sr., a professor at the Howard University School of Law and its former dean, served as the administrative hearing officer.

Sizemore, who was represented by Attorney DeLong Harris, was required to respond to the following 17 charges:

1. Failure to provide a plan for equalization of schools.
2. Failure to provide quarterly safety reports.
3. Failure to provide and implement adequate personnel hiring controls and failure to maintain hiring within fiscally responsible limits.
4. Failure to fill position as directed by the board.
5. Failure to provide a timely selection procedure for the selection of regional superintendents.
6. Failure to comply with board directives concerning federal grant proposals.
7. Failure to provide a timely annual report.
8. Failure to comply with board directive to appoint administration committee.
9. Failure to provide responses to the board's questions on the FY-1975 financial plan.
10. Failure to comply with board directive to submit status reports on expenditures.
11. Failure to provide quarterly financial reports.
12. Failure to provide quarterly personnel reports.
13. Failure to comply with board directive to provide FY-1975 legislative proposal.
14. Failure to comply with board directive to make recommendations on permanent tenure.
15. Failure to obtain for the board student comments on proposed rules on students' rights and responsibilities and code of conduct.

16. Failure to provide curriculum development in FY-1975.

17. Failure to provide report on declining enrollment.[30]

The dismissal hearing concluded on September 18, 1975 with the presentation of oral arguments. Charges 7 and 14 were dropped by the administrative hearing officer because the "board did not carry its prima facie burden in its case in chief. . . ."[31] Reid examined charges 1 through 6, 8 through 13 and 15 through 17 to determine whether or not the board had successfully discharged its burden of proof. He ruled that the board had substantiated thirteen of the seventeen charges. Reid found that charges 7, 14, 15, and 16 were not sustained by the evidence produced at the hearing. The board adopted the finding of the administrative hearing officer on October 9, 1975, and at the same meeting voted 7 to 4 to terminate Sizemore's contract.

In an editorial dated October 11, 1975, the *Washington Post* declared that Sizemore's dismissal was not the result of petty conflicts in personality and rejected the notion that Sizemore was "a well meaning administrator victimized by chronic problems and outmoded bureaucracy and other circumstances beyond her control."[32] The editorial states that Reid's findings present "a sorry picture of a willfully uncooperative and unreliable administrator who not only failed to do what she should have in many instances, but did so on purpose, in conscious defiance of the board's wishes."[33]

In her defense at the dismissal hearing, Sizemore submitted a 113 page response to the seventeen charges. This document concluded with Sizemore's declaration:

> . . . The Respondent says that no charge is true and no charge, even if true, has or will affect her efficiency as superintendent of schools and that if there be no finding that the board of education has proved not only that a charge is true but also, and more importantly, that her conduct in such an instance rendered her inefficient as superintendent of schools, then in either or both of such events

> Respondent demands a finding and a conclusion
> that the said charges have not established
> inefficiency.[34]

Sizemore obtained a legal evaluation of her dismissal from a law firm based in Washington, D.C. The legal evaluation was initiated by Sizemore to determine what options for legal claims arising out of her dismissal were available to her. The seventy-five-page report was delivered to Sizemore in June 1978. The report takes issue with various aspects of the legal defense accorded Sizemore and challenges many of the conclusions reached by the administrative hearing officer. The report neither advocated nor advised Sizemore to seek redress through the courts.

None of the seventeen charges presented against Sizemore by the board drew attention to the fact that Sizemore and a majority of the board members differed significantly on how racial minorities ought to be educated. Sizemore's philosophical bent as much as her administrative style were rejected by the board. Along with her difficulties with the board, Sizemore received limited support from several of the system's high ranking school officers. The board's charges against Sizemore were focused overwhelmingly on managerial deficiencies. While the superintendent must accept the overall responsibility for general functions not discharged in a satisfactory manner, the charges highlight that if others in key positions had been more efficient and effective, Sizemore's superintendency would have been less vulnerable to charges of inefficiency. Asked what she would do differently, Sizemore responded by saying that she would study more closely the superintendency of her predecessor and would fire several key school officers.

On the day the board voted to terminate Sizemore's contract, it appointed Vincent E. Reed as acting superintendent. He is the current superintendent, and the system's third black superintendent. Sizemore was the fifth school superintendent in a decade to depart the District's school system in a cloud of controversy. She was not the first superintendent to be fired by a school board in Washington, D.C. William Chancellor was terminated as superintendent in 1908 by a unanimous vote of the board. He was white. Chancellor and Sizemore have been the only school superintendents in the nation's capital ever to experience a public dismissal hearing.

Success and survival as school superintendent in the District of Columbia requires support from the Congress and the board. Congress has established a record of interfering in the internal affairs of the school system and has consistently expressed its unwillingness to appropriate increased funding. Ironically, while the level of appropriations has increased each fiscal year, reductions in programs and services have been required to balance the budget. The board, especially since the emergence of the elected board, has demonstrated an inclination toward disharmony.

The provisions of the home-rule bill have stimulated increased public involvement in District affairs. Some school board members are inclined to conduct their business like ward politicians. The school board has served as a starting block for election to the city council. Four former members of the school board have been elected to the city council. (Marion Barry, who served as president of the school board that appointed Sizemore, has advanced from a seat on the city council to the position of mayor.) Increased pressure will be placed on the elected mayor and city council to be more active advocates for the public schools. Jurisdictional disputes between members of the school board and other elected officials appear to be inevitable. School officials confront a mayor and city council that exhibit greater scrutiny on expenditures for public education.

Baltimore, Maryland

The City

Baltimore lies forty miles north of the nation's capital. Baltimore is not as old as such Atlantic seaboard cities as Boston or Philadelphia, or nearby Annapolis, state capital of Maryland. It was not laid out until 1729, eighty-five years after the colony of Maryland was founded by Lord Baltimore. Baltimore is the most northern of America's southern cities. The city is "a polygot place that has attracted many different ethnic groups," but is "also a traditional town where the owners of blocks of look-alike row houses take pride in keeping their front stoops scrubbed."

In 1970, the population was 905,759. Blacks constituted 46.7 percent of the population. People under the age of eighteen (304,261) constituted 33.6 percent of the population; 95,942 people, or 10.6 percent of the population, were sixty-five or older.

Approximately 68.1 percent of the 89,920 black families were headed by a male. The average family size was 3.65 persons. For black families, the average family size was 4.37 persons. In 1969, the median income of all families in Baltimore was $8,814. The median income for black families was $7,287. Slightly more than 23 percent of the families earned less than $5,000; 16.7 percent had incomes of $15,000 or more. Of the 215,833 families in Baltimore, 14 percent, had incomes below the low-income (poverty) level in 1959. Of the 163,700 persons below the low-income level in 1969, 68.4 percent were black; 57.4 percent of the low-income families were headed by a woman. Children under eighteen years of age represented 44.8 percent of all persons below the low-income level.

The largest percentage of workers were employed in manufacturing. Baltimore's labor force numbered 373,122 or 58.8 percent of all persons sixteen years or older.[35] In April 1970 the unemployment rate for the city was 4.6 percent compared to 3.5 for the metropolitan area. Blacks comprised 43.1 percent of the labor force. Of the 160,280 blacks in the labor force, 6.2 percent, or 9,909, were unemployed in 1970. Of the women in the labor force, 8,004, or 5.1 percent, were unemployed. Baltimore, like other urban centers, has felt the crunch produced by escalating governmental costs and a declining revenue base. The city's property-tax assessment rate in 1973 was the highest in Maryland. The increased costs of providing governmental services necessitated increasing the property tax assessment rate. Baltimore's revenues had been growing at a rate of 1 percent annually. The costs of municipal services in Baltimore rose by 10 percent in 1973. Because of the city's constricted tax base and its large tax-consuming population, Baltimore had a higher rate of increase in property tax than any other Maryland community; nevertheless the higher rate served to raise only the same amount of revenue as the other communities.

The city's dilemma is that although property tax increases produce needed revenues they also produce an exodus of middle-class families and businesses. The exodus of stable blue-collar workers and their families contribute to urban disintegration: "Urban disintegration means more police, fire, and sanitation services and higher costs to the city." The state legislature had not responded favorably to the city's financial plight. In 1974 General Assembly delegates warned that they would support a filibuster if Baltimore sought to gain additional aid.

The mayor is white. In 1974, fourteen of the nineteen members of the city council were white. Mayor William Donald Schaefer has been identified as a moderate in race relations who has moved somewhat to the right since taking office. Schaefer is not noted for his temperament and his capacity for work. He is viewed by some as a very stubborn public official who pays little attention to the public-relations consequences of his actions and statements.

In 1974, William Sykes held two major titles in city government, special assistant to the mayor and director of the mayor's office of human resources. Sykes had lived in Baltimore since 1957. Baltimore, according to Sykes, was a city of distinctive neighborhoods rather than a city in which activities centered primarily around a certain section. East and West Baltimore are the residential areas of the largest number of low-income blacks. The central business area divides East and West Baltimore. Sykes indicated that East Baltimore was better organized politically than West Baltimore. West Baltimore had more organizations, but they were less cohesive than those in East Baltimore. Sykes felt that there was a greater degree of militancy in West Baltimore and that West-side groups were generally more inclined toward confrontation tactics.

Skyes asserted that black power in Baltimore was notably weak in economic development; few blacks owned businesses which grossed more than $500,000 per year. He felt that the usual communication gap among blacks was apparent in Baltimore. Sykes believed that the mass of blacks were relatively passive: there were aggressive blacks around, he contended, but the more militant blacks had either gone underground or had dissappeared. He stated that the major reason for the passiveness of most blacks was the constant changes in leadership. Only a few black leaders had been able to maintain a continuous following. Congressman Parren Mitchell, it is believed, continues to have the greatest following. He is looked upon as an uncompromising "tell it like it is" individual. Among the cadre of influential blacks in Baltimore City, he was considered the strongest supporter of Superintendent Patterson.

The Board of School Commissioners

The nine members of the board of school commissioners are appointed by the mayor; each member serves a six-year term. In August 1974, the following persons sat on the board:

John Walton (president) — professor of education at Johns Hopkins University (white).

James M. Griffin (vice-president) — director of Northwest Community Medical Service Center in Baltimore (black).

M. Richmond Farring — manager of M. Richmond Farring Insurance Company (white).

Larry Gibson — attorney with the firm of Mitchell, Gibson and Lee (black).

Sheila Sachs — attorney (white).

Oscar L. Helm — retired from the Baltimore City public schools (white).

Beryl Williams — professor at Morgan State College (black).

W. Eugene Scott — professor at Johns Hopkins University (black).

Robert W. Schaefer — executive vice-president with First National Bank in Baltimore (white).

Like most board members, John Walton had formed a good number of long-standing views on public education. But unlike most school board members, Walton was once a school superintendent. Walton stated:

> I am in somewhat of an unusual position as a board member. I do not know whether it irks Dr. Patterson or not, but it probably irks some people. I am a board member, but I am also a former school superintendent from a small town in Ohio. I have a large educational background. I am now a professor of education. I cannot give up my personality after all of these years.[36]

As board president, Walton believed that his role was to conduct the meetings and to provide opportunities for board members to work with the superintendent. Walton stressed the need for the school system to improve its business-management functions and to provide educational programs and personnel capable of making significant improvements in academic achievement.

Walton expressed support for Superintendent Patterson's plan for reorganization. "The plan has many good ideas, and I think that it will work.[37] He hoped to see a greater emphasis placed on efforts to work directly with teachers to improve their performance and was convinced that students' difficulties could be reduced if teachers possessed greater communicative skills. Commenting on Patterson's appointments to key administrative positions, Walton stated that Patterson had brought in a number of good people from outside the system to fill some of the key administrative positions.

When asked about the tendency of board members to become overly involved in administrative matters, Walton responded: "Don't you think that superintendents have a tendency to take over policy matters?" Walton indicated that Patterson's predecessor did not have a very cordial relationship with the board and that the split in the board's relationship with the previous superintendent was along racial lines. He did not believe that Patterson's board had responded to issues along black-white lines. This view was not shared by some school officials.

Walton indicated that the board had not demonstrated any overt hostility toward Patterson. In expressing his admiration for Patterson's dedication and hard work, Walton suggested that Patterson needed to develop more extensive forms of communication with city officials and some members of the board. Walton assessed Superintendent Patterson as a very private man who should communicate more with the school board.

As a member of the State Board of Education, William Sykes was in a better position than most Baltimoreans to comment on the school system. Sykes prefaced his remarks about the system and Patterson's relationship with the board by noting that board members often had difficulty comprehending their roles. Sykes believed that Baltimore had good schools and bad schools, and he attributed the differences mainly to the variation in the principals' leadership qualities. Sykes felt that the school system's negative image had been, in part, promoted by white-controlled newspapers. The newspapers, he believed, had concentrated disproportionately on negative commentary about the school system.

Sykes indicated that the power structure in the black community supported Superintendent Patterson. According to Sykes, Patterson's greatest strength in the community was among low-income blacks. This group viewed Patterson as its champion. Among middle-class blacks, Sykes felt, Patterson was tolerated but not widely accepted. Old-line black Baltimoreans tended to view Patterson as an outsider and would have liked to have seen him consult with them more. While expressing his admiration for Patterson's integrity, Sykes felt that Patterson ought to have become more of a politician to complement his strengths as an educator and an administrator.

Sykes believed that the public relationship between the superintendent and the school board was satisfactory, but that the private one was unsatisfactory. He viewed Mayor Schaefer and Patterson as two individuals quite similar in personality: "They get along in a distant sort of way."[38] Sykes indicated that Patterson and the president of the city council were at odds. Sykes saw Patterson's poor public relations program and his reluctance to change a position as his greatest shortcomings: "He does not have much tolerance for changing a position unless he is given a great deal of information."[39]

In his commentary on Patterson's future in Baltimore, Sykes stated:

> Patterson's strength is that he is black and that his removal would be offensive to blacks in general.
>
> Patterson can remain as long as he wants to and as long as he can keep the black politicians in a position where they have to support him. His blackness ensures their support.[40]

The School System

In school year 1973-74, Baltimore had the eighth largest school system in America, and the largest school system administered by a black superintendent — 182,981 students. (See Table 18.) The black student population constituted slightly more than 70 percent. As in all large cities, the public-school enrollment decreased in the seventies. An exodus of whites apparently was the major contributing factor to that decrease.

The school system operated 206 schools in school year 1973-74, and employed 12,462 full-time employees, more than 60 percent of whom were black.[41] Public education in Baltimore is big business. The school budget for fiscal year 1974 totaled

TABLE 18
Breakdown of Student Population by Race, School Years 1971-72 to 1973-74: Baltimore City Public Schools

School Year	Black	White	Total
1973-74	129,173	53,808	182,981
1972-73	129,711	57,295	187,006
1971-72	130,464	60,363	190,827

Source: Questionnaire completed by the Baltimore City public schools, March 1974.

TABLE 19
Estimates of Percentages of Students in Grades One-Six Testing Below
National Norms in Reading Achievement: Baltimore City Public Schools

		Grades			
One	Two	Three	Four	Five	Six
N.T.*	N.T.*	73	73	72	80

Source: Questionnaire completed by the Baltimore City public schools, March, 1974.
*Not tested.

$181,874,620 from regular funds and $218,726,330 from all
funding sources. (See Table 20.) The per-pupil expenditures
totaled $974.63 from regular funds and $1,176.77 from all funds
in school year 1973-74. The salary schedules for teachers did not
compare favorably with nearby Washington, nor with most
other large urban school systems in the East. (See Table 21.)

TABLE 20
Financial Support from Regular and All Funds, School Years 1971-72 to
1973-74: Baltimore City Public Schools

School Year	Regular Funds	All Funds
1973-74	$181,874,620	$212,762,330
1972-73	168,850,751	205,027,758
1971-72	162,412,551	196,964,289

Source: Questionnaire completed by the Baltimore City public schools, March 1974.

TABLE 21
Minimum and Maximum Ranges of Salary Schedules for Teachers by Degree:
Baltimore City Public Schools

Range	B.A.	M.A.	M.A. + 30
Minimum	$ 7,750	$ 8,250	$ 8,750
Maximum	13,200	13,900	14,400

Source: Questionnaire completed by the Baltimore City public schools, March 1974.
*Salary schedules do not reflect increases gained from teachers' strike in 1974.

The steady decline of urban economic resources resulted in inadequate funding. In 1973-74, more than 25,000 pupils received Title I assistance and approximately 70,000 pupils received free lunches daily. Absenteeism was a problem; 34,000 students were reported absent from school forty days or more during school year 1970-71. Massive cumulative deficiencies in basic reading skills were recorded. In grades two through six, at least 70 percent of the students tested in 1973 scored below the national norms in reading.

Patterson stated that Baltimore was in a relentless search to improve the basic skills of all children. One of his earliest innovations was the implementation of a massive, citywide teacher training program in reading instruction. He believed every teacher to be a reading teacher; thus, development of reading skills was stressed in every classroom in the system.

He emphasized that in order for meaningful improvements to occur, the school system had to be overhauled and updated. In his first public address in 1971, Patterson stated:

> . . . It is utterly ridiculous to assume that a member of this education team can carry out his responsibility in an efficient and desirable manner if he has no understanding of the nature of the responsibilities of other members, no means of identifying the line between his responsibility and that of others on the team, and no method of determining if he is fulfilling his responsibilities.[42]

Superintendent Patterson provided the following list of significant needs and problems:

Significant Needs

Improve achievement levels in reading, writing, and mathematics.

Continue the necessary planning for greater accountability on the part of all concerned with schools, including students, administrators, and parents.

Improve human relations.

Develop procedures for increased community participation.

Develop programs that improve student-adjustment
behaviors.

Significant Problems

Public image of department of education.

Relationship with city government.

Availability of financial resources.

Integration of public schools.

Retention of a high-quality staff.[43]

Patterson, in large measure, placed the success of his superintendency on the outcome of his reorganization plans. He indicated that reorganization would extend well beyond decen-
tralizing many administrative functions previously handled by
central office staff. The superintendent defined reorganization
in the following manner:

The word is reorganization — not decentralization.
Decentralization is only a small part of a larger
reorganization of the school system. Decentralization
only refers to the diffusion of administrative
authority from a central headquarters to local areas.
Reorganization, therefore, is the most appropriate
word for describing the process of changing — and
improving the school system.[44]

Patterson stated that the need for the reorganization of Baltimore's school system had been apparent for a number of years.
He contended that Baltimore, with one of the oldest public
school systems in the country, had grown into the eighth largest
in the nation without any fundamental change in its structure
ever being instituted. The following basic goals were established in the early stages of planning for reorganization:

To facilitate the continued development of quality instruction and programming.

To bring schools closer to the people they serve.

To create effective communication and better working relationships between the community and the administration.

To establish effective communication and coordination among all divisions, schools, and staff members.

To provide an efficient management system for the Baltimore City public schools.

To distribute appropriately the responsibility for decision-making.

To facilitate the release of the creative energies of both the community and the staff.[45]

In 1973 the school system was divided into nine regions, each administered by a regional superintendent. Each region included elementary, junior-high, senior-high, and special schools. Student enrollment within each of the nine regions ranged from 19,000 to 24,000 students. Reorganization, including decentralization, resulted in moving some staff members from their previous assignments. This reassignment resulted in a change in status for some incumbents. New offices and positions were created and a significant number of persons were recruited from outside the system to fill both new and established positions. Of the nine regional superintendencies, three were filled by persons new to the Baltimore schools. Also, many persons were recruited from outside the city to fill major central office positions.

Incorporated in Patterson's reorganization of the system was the development of a master plan for education. The final master plan would be the culmination of an intensive and extensive analysis of the needs of Baltimore public schools and would reflect the philosophy, goals, and priorities of the system. The completion of the master plan would provide, for the first time, a comprehensive view of public education's direction.

Superintendent Patterson was committed to extending significantly community involvement in school activities. Each of the nine administrative regions was to have a regional advisory council. The regional superintendents were to consult their advisory councils regarding local school administration. The regional advisory councils were designed for community representatives, primarily parents. The councils would have the following functions:

Hold regular, public meetings.

Make recommendations to the regional superintendent.

Establish and maintain communication with groups of parents, teachers, and principals.

Encourage participation of residents and transfer families, through attendance at public meetings and through membership on subcommittees.

Review problems and functions, evaluate programs and processes with the regional superintendent, and recommend solutions or modifications.

Play a significant role in implementing existing educational goals.

Ensure the development of an advisory group of students, elected by students, to assist the councils.

Recognize that the administrative regulations of the Baltimore City public school system will apply in all matters pertaining to personnel.

Recognize that the Board of School Commissioners will remain the final authority in all matters related to programs, budgets, facilities, staffs, operations of the regional schools, and all other such matters which are within the board's authority.

Recognize that the superintendent of public instruction will continue to have final authority in administrative matters. [46]

A strike by teachers in February 1974 produced salary increases that exceeded the city's existing revenues. City officials indicated that the 10.1 percent budget increase requested by the school board was impossible. Baltimore spent $974.63 per pupil in school year 1973-74 compared to $1,202 spent in Washington, D.C., and $1,290 in Atlanta. (Table 20 indicates the system's financial support-level for three consecutive years.)

In February 1974, the school board was jolted by a mandate issued by the Department of Health, Education, and Welfare. The system was ordered to desegregate its staff and student population or face the loss of approximately $23 million in federal grants. The HEW mandate reordered the school's priorities:

> On February 4, 1974, the United States
> Department of Health, Education, and Welfare
> directed the Board of School Commissioners to
> develop a plan which would bring about further
> desegregation of the students and faculties in the
> Baltimore City public schools, which as a result of
> metropolitan housing patterns are 70 percent black
> and 30 percent white. Shortly thereafter, the Board
> of School Commissioners instructed the
> superintendent to establish a task force to study
> means of complying with the HEW guidelines.[47]

The Board of Commissioners reluctantly agreed to comply with HEW's mandate and incorporated many of the superintendent's task force guidelines for desegregation into the plan submitted to HEW. The desegregation plan proposed by school officials required three years for full implementation, but HEW informed school officials that it would not accept any desegregation plan that went beyond two years and that did not involve the entire school system.

Patterson's differences with the board on these and other escalating problems in 1974 heightened his concern that the white majority on the board would seek his dismissal; this concern proved to be substantive. These differences erupted into full public view on August 8, 1974. The Sun reported: "The city school board's white majority tried to vote Roland N. Patterson out of the superintendent's office last night but chaos prevented the vote from being recorded."[48] Board member Robert Schaefer (no relation to the mayor) had proposed that Patterson be suspended immediately with pay pending a removal hearing. Patterson contends that the board voted to dismiss him because of its disagreement with statements he made in a speech at Dunbar High School concerning schools for disruptive children and in a speech at a local church in which he made a reference to elitism in the schools. In the eventual court proceedings the court noted that some board members had taken exception to statements made by Patterson. Board member Schaefer believed that Patterson put too much emphasis on the elimination of elitism in the schools. Board member Scott stated that he thought Patterson lacked good judgment in berating the City Fathers as racists and that Patterson was wrong in claiming that the failures of black youth in the city were entirely the fault of society. When board president Walton called for a vote on Schaefer's motion, the meeting was disrupted by persons in the audience. The *Sun* reported: "An angry crowd briefly surged onto the stage, ripping out microphone cords and slamming papers and books about the meeting table."[49]

Following the meeting Patterson pledged to return to his duties. Board president Walton offered the following response to Patterson's decision not to vacate the superintendency: "If he has to resort to this kind of anarchy to keep his power, it is clear that he has lost.[50] City Solicitor, Benjamin Brown, upon review of the tapes of the Thursday meeting of the board, ruled that the vote was not valid. Brown declared that the school board had violated all forms of proper parlimentary procedures and that the vote had to be taken again in a public meeting.

Schaefer stressed that his vote to oust Patterson was not racially motivated. "It is not a question of having a black superintendent, but if Dr. Patterson is the best black superintendent for the job."[51] Support for retaining Patterson immediately came forward from prominent blacks in Baltimore City. The local chapter of the NAACP joined with other blacks in demanding that Patterson be retained and that the president of the school board be removed. An article in the *Sun* noted: "The city's school system's crisis had become a clear-cut racial issue at a time when Baltimore could ill afford it."[52]

Patterson secured legal counsel and demanded that the board

give him a hearing with charges presented to him in advance. In a letter dated April 30, 1975, the board informed Patterson that his evaluation would take place in executive session and that he would be permitted to appear with counsel of his choice. These evaluation sessions began on May 9 and concluded on May 21, 1975. The sessions consumed approximately thirty hours and produced 700 pages of transcript. Patterson expressed his appreciation to the board for a thorough and fair hearing.[53]

The board prepared a preliminary evaluation report that was hand delivered to Patterson on June 2, 1975, with the notice that the final evaluation report would be prepared by June 4. Patterson was asked by the board to respond to the evaluation report. His attorney informed the board that Patterson had not been accorded sufficient time to respond to the report. The board's report was released to the press by Patterson's attorney, Larry Gibson, a former member of the school board. On June 4, 1975, the board transmitted to Gibson a draft of its resolution calling for the resignation of the superintendent. The board met on June 9, 1975, and adopted the dismissal resolution and established June 20 as the date for the beginning of dismissal hearings. Gibson obtained two court injunctions against the hearing. Judge Marshall, after granting a 24-hour stay, dissolved the stay on July 1, 1975.

Public dismissal hearings were held at the War Memorial Building with approximately 325 persons in attendance at each meeting. Most of the audience were supporters of Patterson. Gibson and C. Curtis Lee were the attorneys for Patterson. The board was represented by Ambrose T. Hartman with Norman Ramsey, board chairman, presiding through most of the sessions. The transcript of the hearings contains approximately 2500 pages in fourteen volumes covering sixty hours of proceedings.

The charges against Patterson numbered more than sixty. District Court Judge Joseph H. Young grouped the charges as follows:[54]

> Charges which concern poor personnel policies.
> Charges which concern inability to get along with the board.

Charges relating to lack of honesty or candor.

Charges which relate to failure to cooperate with other city agencies, particularly the Department of Finance.

The board concluded its presentation on July 13, 1975. Under protest, Patterson's attorneys concluded his defense on July 14, 1975. On July 17, 1975, the board voted to terminate Patterson's contract. Patterson's attorneys sought and were denied a restraining order by Judge Frank Kaufman. Patterson brought action against the board and individual members of the board claiming that his discharge violated his constitutional rights. Judge Young of the U.S. District Court for the District of Maryland ruled against Patterson in a decision rendered on March 29, 1977.[55] Patterson appealed to the U.S. Court of Appeals, Fourth Circuit. The Court of Appeals affirmed the decision of the U.S. District Court and held that "assuming stigmatization, superintendent was given sufficient notice of his deficiencies and afforded amply sufficient opportunities to protest his 'liberty' interest."[56]

Judge Young declared in his opinion that some of the charges against Patterson were not presaged by any discussions at the evaluation sessions and that certain allegations made by the board with respect to Patterson's personal integrity and demeanor were not supported by the evidence presented in either the evaluation sessions or the dismissal hearings. Commenting on the board's power to appoint and remove a superintendent at its pleasure, Judge Young construed the words "at pleasure" to mean "that the board may remove the superintendent for any reason except an unconstitutional reason. The statute plainly omits any requirement that the removal be for good cause or any specific reason."[57]

Patterson stated that he submitted himself to the demanding and expensive due process procedures because he wanted to have his story understood in the community.[58]

Reflecting on his superintendency in Baltimore, Patterson stated that he would do nothing differently. "It makes no difference who the mayor is. Ultimately — whether you are white or black — you must do what the mayor wants done or you got to come into conflict."[59]

Wilmington, Delaware

The City

Wilmington is the oldest and largest city in Delaware. In 1638, an expedition from Sweden landed on the banks of the Christina River and established the settlement from which Wilmington was developed. Approximately 500,000 people live in Delaware: "Nearly one third of all the people in the United States live within 300 miles of Wilmington; yet the Wilmington area itself is relatively uncrowded."[60] With a population slightly more than 80,000, Wilmington serves as the center for a metropolitan area of more than one half million. The city's more than 35,000 blacks constitute about 43 percent of the population.

Wilmington's principal businesses are financial and office-oriented rather than industrial. E.I. du Pont de Nemours and Company is the largest business in the state. The headquarters and executive offices of the Du Pont Company, the world's largest manufacturer of chemical products, are located in Wilmington. The label "company town" is commonly applied to Wilmington because of the alleged dominance of the Du Pont company.

The hustle and bustle of most urban centers is not found in Wilmington. The city does not have the evening recreational sites and activities that attract conventioners. Downtown Wilmington is almost deserted in the evening. The city's only downtown hotel for middle- and upper-income travelers is Hotel Du Pont. Wilmington is conservative in its appearance and in its politics.

In 1974 unemployment was lower in Wilmington than in most urban communities. Blacks and Spanish-surnamed individuals constituted the majority of the poor. The U.S. Bureau of the Census reported that the median family income in 1970 was $8,050. About 16 percent of all families were identified as having incomes below the poverty level. In 1970, approximately 39 percent of the families below the poverty level were receiving public assistance. A number of the persons interviewed believed that as long as the Du Pont Company remained in Wilmington, serious economic recessions would never occur. This belief was reinforced by a conviction that the Du Pont Company is too deeply entrenched financially and traditionally in Wilmington to depart the city.

The state of Delaware has only one daily newspaper, the *Journal*, which is published in Wilmington. The Du Pont Company owns the *Journal*. A commitment to statewide coverage by the *Journal* limits significantly the coverage of events in Wilmington, especially the affairs of a predominantly black school system. The omissions in the coverage of items of interest to blacks in Wilmington by the *Journal* exceed the deficiencies of most white-controlled newspapers in communities with sizable percentages of blacks.

The mayor of Wilmington is a white Democrat. In 1974 the city council had thirteen members. While blacks constituted about 43 percent of the city's population, only two members of the council were black. Wilmington was run almost totally by a white, heavily Catholic base. Robert Mitchell, former member of the school board, said that blacks in Wilmington did not control anything but the school system. He said that the city council showed concern for the school system only when it presented a financial problem or an embarrassment to the city government.

One school official referred to Wilmington as a welfare state for blacks. The same official noted that the city had only two black dentists, two black physicians, and three black attorneys. Middle-class blacks in Wilmington were neither numerous nor active. None of the blacks interviewed believed that the city government in Wilmington had an influential black. One black indicated that most middle-class blacks employed by the Du Pont Company were pressured, directly and indirectly, by city officials and Du Pont to remain nonmilitant. Some blacks felt that paternalizing city officials and Du Pont executives had caused the low political profile and disadvantaged socio-economic status of blacks. Robert Mitchell, a black Republican and former school board member, stated that investors had not made Wilmington a good community for blacks.

The School Board

Prior to 1970, the Wilmington Board of Education consisted of five members — one member appointed by the mayor and four members appointed by the governor. The board was enlarged to seven members, with the governor and mayor assigned the responsibility for the appointment of four and three members respectively. In 1970, the board had its first black majority. In 1971, the school board selected its first black president. State law required that three members of the board be appointed from the minority party in Wilmington. The black majority in 1970 resulted from the appointments made by a Republican governor and mayor. The black majority on the school board was continued in 1974 by the appointments made by a Democrat governor and mayor.

In its assessment report to the Wilmington public schools the Graduate School of Education of Harvard University noted the following about the board's appointment process:

> Presently board members are appointed by the mayor and the governor. Appointments are not staggered evenly, however, opening the possibility of a serious loss of continuity on the board in years when a greater than average number of terms expire.
> The board should endorse a plan for properly staggered terms and should pursue all formal and informal means of communicating that plan to the appropriate legislative sources. Passage should be urged as soon as possible.[61]

On June 30, 1974, the following persons served as the members of the Wilmington Board of Education:

> Robert Mitchell (president) — employed in the personnel department of the Du Pont Company (black).
> Hermenia Garret — director of a nursery school (black).
> John B. Redmond — minister (black).

Saul Sophrin — commercial artist (white).

Helen Balick — attorney (white).

Janet Greenwald — housewife (white).

Allie Holley — retired school teacher (black).

On July 2, 1974, the governor and mayor named four new appointees to the school board:

Wendell Howell — college student (black).

Benjamin M. Amos — employed by the government housing agency (black).

Daniel S. Frawley — attorney with the Du Pont Company (white).

William C. Lewis — in personnel administration with the Hercules Chemical Company (black).

In an attempt to eliminate racially segregated schools in New Castle County and to force the State Board of Education to fulfill its obligations under state and federal constitutions, five black parents and the Wilmington Board of Education filed suit against the Delaware State Board of Education [Evans v. Buchanan]. The board contended that school segregation in New Castle County originated in state law. "There were schools in Delaware completely overlapping black and white school districts. Schools for black children were, in the most instances, built with 100 percent state financing. Segregation was state-controlled and state-directed."[62] A three-judge panel was convened under the U.S. District Court for the District of Delaware. The trial began in December, 1972; presentations were completed in February 1974.

The school board stressed that artifically created school boundaries in Delaware separated black and white students and did not provide reasonable access to the benefits derived from public education. The school board supported the view "that racially separate schools or racially disproportionate schools constitute barriers to achieving balance within the Wilmington public schools, in particular, and within New Castle County, in general." The board stated:

We are seeking a system where one cannot find a
school 80 to 90 percent black, and ten or fifteen
minutes away, another school which is part of the
same economic and social community, 99 to 100
percent white. It may be that the court or the State
Board of Education, in its wisdom, will call for the
actual merger of school districts. The remedy may
not be necessary. All that the court may find
necessary is that pupils, teachers, and educational
resources must be exchanged across existing
boundaries by contract or agreement in a two-way
process, with each existing district maintaining its
own board and its administrative structure. The form
of the remedy is not the major issue. It is the
educational product and the effect on children that
should be our primary concern.[63]

In 1968, the legislature had passed the Education Advancement Act, which redistricted most of the school districts in
Delaware. But the Act did not resolve the problem of racially
isolated schools. "In fact the Act specifically locked black children into existing boundaries of the Wilmington school district."[64] The pattern of racial isolation in the public schools of
New Castle is illustrated by the following information:

In September 1972, school enrollment in New
Castle County was 80.5 percent white, 18.5 percent
black, and 1 percent other. Wilmington schools were
81.1 percent black, 16.2 percent white, and 2.7
percent other. All nearby districts were at least 95
percent white, except De La Warr, whose enrollment
was 53 percent white, 46 percent black, and 1
percent other.[65]

Since 1970, the board, in controversial matters, had voted
consistently along racial lines. Former board president Mitchell
stated that the board was more racially split than ever before and
that there were always hidden agendas. Mitchell was irritated by

the lack of black unity on the board and felt that black board members were overly concerned about being identified as "too black" in their actions. Mitchell lamented that during his tenure on the school board the four black members never voted as a group on crucial issues.

After Earl C. Jackson's appointment as superintendent, the relationship between board and superintendent became less than adequate. Jackson saw the board as too involved in administrative matters. School officers who commented on the board-superintendent relationship cited both parties as contributors to the strained relationship. Jackson was faulted for not dealing more directly with certain matters raised by the board, and the board was blamed for seeking to become administrators and not resolving their own internal differences.

The School System

In academic year 1973-74 blacks made up almost 83 percent of the enrollment in the public schools. The Wilmington public schools enrolled 14,688 students who attended three senior high schools, four middle schools, fourteen elementary schools, and one special education school.[66] Of these schools eight were at least 40 years old, and one school was at least 50 years old. Table 22 provides the enrollment figures for three consecutive years. From regular funds the school system employed 1,634 persons of whom 997 were black.

TABLE 22
Breakdown of Student Population by Race, School Years 1971-72 to 1973-74: Wilmington Public Schools

School Year	Black	White	Other	Total
1973-74	12,141	2,064	483	14,688
1972-73	12,265	2,452	412	15,132
1971-72	12,229	2,860	238	15,327

Source: Questionnaire completed by the Wilmington public schools, April 1974.

TABLE 23
Estimates of Percentages of Students in Grades One-Six Testing below National
Norms in Reading Achievement: Wilmington Public Schools

		Grades			
One	Two	Three	Four	Five	Six
N.T.*	N.T.*	80	80	80	80

Source: Questionnaire completed by the Wilmington public schools, April 1974.

*Not tested.

Academic achievement was cited as a serious problem by
those interviewed. Estimates presented by school officials indicated that in grades three through six about 80 percent of the
students tested below the national norms in reading achievement. Standardized achievement tests for reading were not administered for grades one and two. (See Table 23.) Jackson stated
that most of the teachers in Wilmington were competent and that
the system had a very capable cadre of school administrators.
Jackson would not cite the number of teachers who needed
extensive staff-development assistance to improve their skills,
but he did state that there were a number of teachers who were
not as competent as they should be. A key official on Jackson's
staff indicated that instructional supervision was inadequate
and that the administrative staff was good but not appropriately
coordinated. The same official stated that administrators and
supervisors tended to operate independently of each other.

TABLE 24
Minimum and Maximum Ranges of Salary Schedules for Teachers by Degree:
Wilmington Public Schools

Range	B.A.	M.A.	M.A. + 30
Minimum	$ 9,260	$ 9,922	$10,804
Maximum	14,111	15,737	17,963

Source: Questionnaire completed by the Wilmington public schools, April 1974.

The teachers' salary schedules were competitive. The salaries for teachers and administrators in the system were the highest in the state and compared favorably with most other school systems. (See Table 24.)

TABLE 25
Financial Support from Regular Funds, School Years 1971-72 to 1973-74: Wilmington Public Schools

School Year	Amounts
1973-74	$19,600,000*
1972-73	18,287,630
1971-72	15,438,236

Source: Questionnaire completed by Wilmington public schools, April 1974.
*Figure represents the amount requested.

While the national trend was toward states increasing the percentage of aid to local school districts, Delaware reduced Wilmington's percentage of state aid for public education. Russell Dineen, then assistant superintendent for business management for the school system, estimated that Delaware provided 67 percent of public school funding. Dineen noted that this figure was a sharp decline from previous levels of state support. According to Dineen, Wilmington received about 53 percent funding for its public schools from the state.

In a document that presents the 1973-74 school budget, the school board deplored the constraints imposed in the establishing of funding requests:

> ... The $19.6 million budget for 1973-74 is simply inadequate to meet the needs of Wilmington's children at the level we would like. Those government officials charged with making decisions vital to public education in Wilmington have not seen the need as we have seen it.[67]

The only new programs to receive funding support from school year 1971-72 through school year 1973-74 were programs in reading and guidance. A reading coordinator, eight reading specialists, and four elementary guidance counselors were added. While not elaborating on the specifics, school officials stated that the state's unwillingness to provide adequate financial support was related to the system's being predominantly black and the legislature overwhelmingly white.

Superintendent Jackson identified the following as the most significant needs and problems of the Wilmington public schools:

> *Significant Needs*
>
> Administrative staff to design and implement the middle-school concept.
>
> Adequate funds for staff development and curriculum improvement.
>
> Administrative reorganization and role definition.
>
> Change in staff perception of the worth and dignity of all students.
>
> Articulation between levels of administration and community.[68]
>
> *Significant Problems*
>
> Board members who confuse their role as policymakers with administration.
>
> Local politicians who appear to be in opposition to the identified needs of the school district.
>
> A state department of public instruction that has been identified by the Civil Rights Commission as a party to racism in hiring and establishing state policy.
>
> A board of education that appears to be split along racial lines.
>
> Administrative insecurity among line and staff administrators.[69]

Mark Sheed, former superintendent of schools in Philadelphia and currently the chief state school officer in Connecticut, headed the team of educators from Harvard University that conducted a survey of the Wilmington public schools. To provide a foundation for program improvement for school year 1973-74, the survey team identified areas of need in the Wilmington schools. The following needs were highlighted in the team's report:

The terms of school board members should be adjusted to ensure continuity on the board.

The governing regulations, policies, and communications effort of the Wilmington school board should continue to be reviewed and updated.

The current financial information system should provide more adequate information to users, both inside and outside the school system.

The Delaware state education-finance policies should be reviewed to determine if the Wilmington school system is receiving its fair share of state funds.

Major changes should be made in the organizational structure of the Wilmington schools.

There is a need for management-development programs for both building level and central office administrators.

The school board and administration should continue to develop an information-gathering and goals-clarification program in order to facilitate their planning for the suit of *Evans* v. *Buchanan*.

The school board and administration should increase their efforts to provide more effective communications to the school staff and to the community at large regarding their participation in the suit of *Evans* v. *Buchanan*.

Communication between the Wilmington public schools and the Wilmington community should be improved.

Community participation in school policymaking should be strengthened.

A major effort is needed to develop an entirely new middle-school curriculum.

A variety of alternative programs are needed to meet the curricular needs of Wilmington's high school students.

The administrative responsibilities for systemwide career education should be clarified and simplified.

The definition of career education as understood throughout the school system and the community must be divorced from the old notion of vocational education.

Current plans for the career center in Howard Educational Park must be changed in order to avoid the clear danger that they will result in a three-track school system, separate and not equal, for Wilmington high school students.

The reading program needs to be given full budgetary and administrative support immediately.

Certain specifics in the proposed reading program should be emphasized, given Wilmington's particular needs.

Certain specifics in the proposed reading program should be emphasized, given current research in reading.[70]

Jackson announced his decision to retire as of the conclusion of the 1974-75 school year in June. He felt that improvements had been made during his tenure, but that the system's problems and needs remained as formidable as ever. Four new members of the school board and Jackson's replacement, Thomas Minter, confronted a school system faced with serious financial and organizational problems. Minter, the system's second black superintendent, served less than two years, leaving Wilmington for a major appointment with the U.S. Office of Education. Joseph Johnson, a black, succeeded Minter. Johnson's tenure was short-lived. He holds the distinction of being the last school superintendent for the Wilmington School District as structured in 1975.

On May 19, 1976, the U.S. District Court for the District of Delaware issued its historic ruling in the case of *Evans* v. *Buchanan*. The court ordered the dissolvement of Wilmington public schools and eleven other school districts located in the northern area of New Castle County. By order of the court, these twelve school districts would be reconstituted into a single school district. In its desegregation order the court stated:

> . . . The exclusion of Wilmington from the process
> of reorganization by statute was an unconstitutional
> racial classification, and 'contributed to the
> separation of races by . . . redrawing district lines.'[71]
>
> Our duty is to order a remedy which will place
> the victims of the violation in substantially the
> position which they would have occupied had the
> violation not occurred.[72]
>
> The desegregation area which is required to
> remedy the effects of violation found in the instant
> case is that area comprised of the suburban districts
> of New Castle County north of the northern line of
> the Appoquinimink School District; and the District
> of Wilmington.[73]

The area of northern New Castle County covered in the court's desegregation ruling is some 251 square miles in area. In 1976 the area had a public school population of 80,678, of whom 63,370, or 78.5 percent, were white and 15,722, or 19.4 percent, were black.[74] Of the black students in this area 74.6 percent attended school in the Wilmington District, and the largest number of the remaining black students in the area attended school in the De La Warr District. The court held that any school whose enrollments in each grade range between 10 and 35 percent black constituted prima facie desegregation. Further, the court stressed that student assignment made by the local authority must remedy the existence of dual systems and must otherwise be designed to achieve the greatest possible degree of actual desegregation.

The court required that an interim school board be established to oversee the newly constituted school district. The State Board of Education would appoint the board until such time as the state adopted a change in the governance structure. But the interim board had to include a member from Wilmington. The interim board directed student assignments for fall 1977. The initial desegregatory assignments, especially in the high schools and intermediate schools, were to be completed by fall 1977. Full compliance on all grade levels was ordered completed by September 1978.

The court did not require all students in the new district to be reassigned. High school seniors in fall 1977 were not reassigned. Students in special education schools were exempted from reassignment for compliance with the desegregation order. Also exempted from reassignment were kindergarten students. The court did not mandate that teachers be transferred. The issue of racial balance among teachers in the schools was acknowledged by the court, but the court reserved its response to this concern until such time as the matter is brought before the court by petitioners seeking redress. The court's dissolvement of the Wilmington school system significantly increased the number of black students who attend more racially balanced schools and made the educational and financial problems of the former Wilmington school district the direct concern of a larger number of adult residents in New Castle County. For Joseph Johnson, the desegregation order resulted in a reduction in title and an increase in salary. He now serves as the deputy superintendent for the new district.

Wilmington has not been very receptive to the needs of black Americans. Economically, politically, socially, and educationally, blacks in Wilmington are being shortchanged. Wilmington lacks a potent black middle-class; the middle-class blacks in the city and surrounding suburbs are isolated from each other and are disenfranchised politically. Blacks are virtually powerless in city and state government, and do not have a leader who commands the attention and respect of powerful white elected officials.

Newark, New Jersey

The City

Newark is not an attractive city: "While the heart of the city's central business district is more open and attractive than many others, the city itself is regarded as unattractive and its approaches across the Hudson and Union County meadows are worse."[75] Newark's attempts to change its national image as a city that has succumbed to the diseases of insufficient resources and social disorganization have not been enhanced by the city's numerous unattractive physical features.

Mayor Kenneth Gibson once said that "wherever the central cities of America are going, Newark is going to get there first." Many Newark residents believe that the city could be salvaged by the appropriate commitment of human and financial resources. Mayor Gibson is Newark's most optimistic resident. His reelection both in May 1974 and 1978 indicated, in part, that his optimism was shared by many others in Newark.

In its May 1972 publication of *Newark* magazine the Greater Newark Chamber of Commerce focused on Mayor Gibson's first 1,000 days in office:

> No one knows better than Ken Gibson that the state of Newark's health is still critical. He is the first to admit his role as chief surgeon in Operation Reversal is sensitive and difficult. Getting the lumbering patient, with its many ailments, back on the road to recovery, restoring it to the vibrant center for business, industry, culture, and social life it once was, he knows, will require more than large doses of money, time, talent, and commitment. Patience must also be among the healing arts.[76]

With approximately 405,000 people and a land area of about twenty-four square miles, Newark is the most populous city in New Jersey. Newark's location at the center of an urbanized belt that extends from Boston to Washington makes it a natural hub for numerous railroads. Newark is also a port of entry for new-

comers to the United States because of the city's location on the
Atlantic Coast and its proximity to New York City. Although the
nation's third-oldest city, Newark has one of the smallest land
areas among the heavily populated cities. The problems posed
by the city's small land area are further compounded by the fact
that almost 24 percent of its land area is covered by the Newark
Airport, the Port of Newark, and the uninhabitable meadow-
lands. This land shortage has contributed to the limited number
of attractive residential areas in the city.

Prior to World War II, Italians, Irish, and Germans constituted
the most dominant groups in Newark, but since that time, and
particularly during the sixties, blacks and Puerto Ricans have
been replacing these groups. In the 1970 census blacks represented 56 percent of the population. Puerto Ricans and Cubans
formed the majority of a sizable Spanish-surnamed population.
In 1967 Rutgers University surveyed the various age groups in
Newark by race. The study reported the following:

> It showed that just over one-fifth (22 percent) of
> the city's whites were 15 years and under, while
> more than two-fifths (42.7 percent) of the city's
> blacks were of that age group. The survey showed
> that about one-third of both groups were in the
> 25-54 age group, with whites having 27 percent over
> 55 years old compared to 7.5 percent for blacks.[77]

Much of the available housing in Newark is more than fifty
years old. Many of the city's housing units are dilapidated. The
turnover in public and private housing units has been high. In
1974 Newark had more urban-renewal projects per capita than
any city in America, but deterioration in housing continued to
spread. Unemployment in Newark was higher than the national
average and was heaviest among the city's large number of
undereducated and unskilled residents, who were unqualified
for high-skill positions in business and industry. Newark experienced a steady exodus of light-manufacturing companies.

Apart from inadequate housing and the exodus of businesses,
other factors contributed to the city's difficulties. The following

conditions are described in demographic information provided
by the Newark public schools:

> There are, by conservative estimate, 20,000 drug
> addicts in the city, and only an estimated 7 percent
> of them are being treated. Newark, of cities of com-
> parable size, has the highest rate of venereal disease,
> new tuberculosis cases, and maternal mortality, a
> high rate of lead poisoning in young children, and is
> second in infant mortality.
> Newark has the highest crime rate of any city in
> the nation. In the Central Ward, perhaps the worst
> ghetto in the East, decent Black families live as vir-
> tual prisoners in housing-authority projects. . . .
> Like its cultural resources, the city's recreational
> opportunities also are limited. . . .
> A total of 46,545 children between the ages of five
> and seventeen were reported in 1973 to be receiving
> public assistance through the Aid for Dependent
> Children program (ADC). . . .
> Like most major American cities, Newark is lim-
> ited in the services and supports it can provide by
> inadequate revenues. Recent changes in the city's
> taxing powers have improved the situation some-
> what, but primary reliance remains on land-based
> taxes. The 1967 rate of $7.76 per $100 of assessed
> valuation with 100 percent valuation resulted in the
> city's having the highest per capita property tax
> burden in the nation for the year, and the rate has
> climbed since then. Under that situation, annual
> taxes on a $20,000 house amount to $1,536, and
> $2,328 on a $30,000 house. The 1970 rate was $8.44
> per $100. The 1971 rate was $9.19 per $100. And the
> 1972 and 1973 rate was $9.64 per $100.[78]

Newark's problems, like those of many other urban centers,
would be difficult for any single individual to rectify. If the city's
major problems are to be solved, Mayor Gibson will play a major
role. He must coordinate his efforts between dissident blacks

and fearful and uncommitted whites. Many improvements in city government and in living conditions have resulted from the efforts of his administration.

The mayor disagrees with those who claim that whites in their flight from the city of Newark also have taken most of the city's resources.

> This is certainly not true. When people looked at Newark in the late sixties, when I took office, they talked about the image of city hall and the mayor's office — indictments and trials and other things related to corruption. The resources in the city are not directed by the people who happen to be in city hall. This is a very rich city. The budget for the city of Newark is roughly $200 million. This does not even begin to talk about the budget for one of our major businessess — they still exist and have existed for many many years in the city. Prudential Insurance Company is right down the street. The world's largest insurance company. So this city certainly has not been milked dry. When you have milked insurance companies dry, then you have milked Newark.[79]

The mayor strongly feels that he did not inherit a well-administered city government.

> No! There is no question about it. It was not a well-administered city, and it existed for 300 years improperly administered. What we attempted to do was to improve the delivery of services. A good administration provides the people with the services as efficiently as possible within the economic and manpower resources available. That is what good administration is. I think we have come a long way in doing it. There are other things in a city which are important, but they are not controlled by the mayor's office. This means that you have to get involved in the coordination of other activities.[80]

Newark has all of the problems of New York City but few of its advantages. Black frustration and anger had reached a boiling point in July 1967 when riots broke out, resulting in 23 deaths and over 1,000 injuries. An estimated $10-$15 million in property was damaged or destroyed during the five days of rioting. Serious differences between certain groups of blacks continue to impede efforts to develop black solidarity. Some blacks in Newark feel that Mayor Gibson has moved too slowly and has not lived up to their expectations. One of the most vocal of Mayor Gibson's black critics is Imamu Amiri Baraka.

The mayor does not attempt to oversell his blackness. He recognizes that black people have established some very extensive expectations of him as mayor. He reflects on black consciousness and his relationship with blacks who are active in politics:

> Black consciousness, as such, is not new. It has been with us since there were black people, and there have been black people since the history of the world. The rhetoric surrounding black consciousness is relatively new. There probably was no person more conscious of being black than my father and grandfather, but they did not make speeches. The way I relate to black people is to relate to black people as I would relate to any other people. I think that blacks represent the same opinions as other people. They are looking for the same things — good education for their children; relative safety as they go to the store; they are looking for a job, and they are looking for a good place to stay.
>
> Therefore, when you improve the quality of life in these areas, you are doing something for black people. With a population that is 60 percent black, you do not have to go around talking about what you are going to do for black people. If you improve the educational system and if you improve housing in the city, you are improving things for black people.[81]

The School Board

The Newark Board of Education is composed of nine members, who are appointed by the mayor. Three members are appointed each year in June. Mayor Gibson once believed that the mayor ought not to have a direct political relationship to the day-to-day operations of the school system.

> I broke the pattern of the mayor attempting to control the school system. You do not get the best system by attempting to control from the mayor's office what goes on in the school system. This past practice is a part of the problem of the school system today.[82]

Acknowledging that he was pleased with some of his appointees, Mayor Gibson emphasized that he did not attempt to dictate to them. The mayor provided the following comments on his approach to the appointment of board members:

> I first look for an interest in education — an overriding interest in education. A person who gets involved without being stimulated is the person who will spend the time to remain interested and involved. You have to determine whether or not the person has the time. The various wards should be represented. You cannot have the board of education composed of one ethnic group. I appointed the first Puerto Rican in the history of the board of education. I made the first appointment of a young person. The input from the people served by the board has to be considered.[83]

On July 11, 1974, the following persons held seats on the board.

> Charles A. Bell (president) — engineer and acting director of the Newark Housing Commission (black).
> Michael A. Petti first vice-president — chiropractor (white).

Julie A. Quinones (second vice-president) — executive of a public employees program (Latino).

George Branch — community relations specialist with the Newark Housing Commission (black).

Robert V. Ciccolini — operates a furniture store in partnership with his brothers (white).

Vickie Donaldson — former employee of the Newark Housing Commission and a graduate student at Rutgers University (black).

Helen W. Fullilove — housewife (black).

Thomas Malanga — retired (white).

Fred E. Means — former principal and a lecturer in the Graduate School of Education, Rutgers University (black).

In July 1974, Bell began his third consecutive year as board president. Bell stated that he saw his role as nothing more than an expediter and as the person who tries to hold the board together.[84] According to Bell, the school system in 1971 was "an exact personification of the status of the city — the city was in turmoil, and the school system was a reflection of the city.[85] Bell identified his major problem with educators: "I have a problem getting educators to realize that they do not know everything."[86]

The board provided the community with the following assessment of Newark's efforts for self-renewal and the school system's role:

> Newark has survived the growing pains of transition; it has moved beyond its history of neglect. As a city, Newark has come further than most others in America. In Newark, black and white have already met head-on. They understand that mutual survival and collective growth are the only solution. The process of change has already begun and rebuilding and renewal of the city is underway. Educational development is an important part of that process. Mayor Gibson has said: 'The health and quality of life in a city are directly related to the effectiveness of its school system.'

> The board of education believes in the veracity of
> that observation. It intends that its role in the
> renewal of Newark will be one of leadership.[87]

In its 1973 superintendent recruitment brochure the school
board spoke of the responsibility of public education for social
consciousness:

> In conclusion, it is the responsibility of the
> Newark public schools to eradicate illiteracy in our
> city, and to prepare students sufficiently to cope
> effectively with problems, conditions, and
> responsibilities that they will confront as adults.
> Moreover, the quality of education provided poor
> people is a key not only to their mobility in society
> but to their survival. . . .[88]

Helen W. Fullilove was identified by a number of school
officers as the steadiest member of the school board. Fullilove
cited the following as the system's needs:

> I want to see some new schools in Newark because
> the system has some really terrible school buildings.
> I want to see our teachers involved, more and more
> committed to our black kids. There is a need for
> better training for principals. We need to help
> youngsters come out of school and function as
> decent human beings.[89]

Vickie Donaldson was the youngest member of the board at
the time of interview. She was articulate and expressed a commitment to preserving her integrity. Donaldson saw herself and
two other blacks on the board as constituting the liberal membership of the board; she was not interested in patronage or in
building a power base on the board. Both Donaldson and Fullilove regretted that the board did not function as an effective
unit.

Bell concurred that board-superintendent relations were not
what they ought to be, but he denied that any member of the
board was an adversary to the superintendent. He saw the source
superintendent as traceable to school officers who felt

threatened by a new superintendent. Some school officers courted school board members to prevent certain personnel actions that they believed were contemplated by the superintendent. Bell emphasized that some board members had sought to use the superintendent to take corrective actions against school officers who had gained their disfavor.

Bell noted that differences among board members and the superintendent were to be expected. He stated that the board had members who were very political.[90] He disagreed with those on the board who thought that he was involved too deeply in administrative matters. By maintaining the support of three white members and at least one of the two "swing" votes, Bell had been able to secure a majority vote on matters he supported or opposed.

The School System

By 1974 Newark's schools were severely overcrowded. About 70 percent of the students were black. Table 26 reveals that in school year 1973-74 the school system enrolled 76,887 students of whom 54,756 were black. The student enrollment included 12,505 students categorized as Spanish-surnamed or "other." The Spanish-surnamed students were mainly Puerto Ricans. The U.S. Census Bureau had made an analysis of the system:

> U.S. Census figures indicate that school-age children in 1970 totaled 101,125, the great bulk of whom attended the public schools. Adding to the low achievement and poor adjustment problems experienced by many of these children, and the overcrowding situation resulting from the overall increase during the past decade are other factors. These include a yearly pupil-turnover rate of nearly half (44 percent), a cumulative dropout rate in grades 0-12 of nearly one-third (32 percent), and the fact that one-third of the new pupils arriving in the schools each year are also new to the city. Included in this group are a number of children sent in from less educationally advanced areas to friends and relatives already residing in Newark.[91]

TABLE 26
Breakdown of Student Population by Race, School Years 1971-72 to 1973-74:
Newark Public Schools

School Year	Black	White	Other	Totals
1973-74	54,756	8,526	12,505	76,887
1972-73	56,102	9,605	12,022	77,729
1971-72	55,566	9,684	12,309	77,559

Source: Questionnaire completed by the Newark public schools, May 1974.

"Of 74 school buildings, 52 are more than fifty years old, 25 are over seventy-five years old, and 4 are over one hundred years old. Many have been extensively altered, but they nevertheless remain aged and costly to maintain."[92] Officials asserted that the physical state of the school buildings had had a deleterious effect on academic achievement and teacher morale. Academic achievement had declined for the past 15 years. Table 27 indicates that more than two-thirds of all first-through-sixth-grade students tested registered below the national norms in reading achievement. According to the school board, public education in Newark operated in a crisis situation:

> Education in Newark takes place in an atmosphere of crisis: an incessant state of alarm shared by a plethora of problems that are fiscal, political, moral, and administrative. These problems are reflective of the broader urban environment of Newark which fits the classic pattern of deterioration found in big-city public life.[93]

TABLE 27
Estimates of Percentages of Students in Grades One-Six Testing Below National Norms in Reading Achievement: Newark Public Schools

		Grades			
One	Two	Three	Four	Five	Six
69	73	86	90	88	89

Source: Questionnaire completed by the Newark public schools, May 1974.

TABLE 28
Minimum and Maximum Ranges of Salary Schedules for Teachers by Degree:
Newark Public Schools

Range	B.A.	M.A.	M.A. + 30
Minimum	$ 8,970	$ 9,600	$10,230
Maximum	14,350	14,980	15,610

Source: Questionnaire completed by the Newark public schools, May 1974.

White employees slightly outnumbered black employees. In school year 1973-74, the school system recorded 7,778 full-time employees paid from regular funds — 3,645 blacks and 3,856 whites. The racial breakdown of full-time employees from all funding sources numbered 4,089 blacks and 4,041 whites.

Newark's salaries are not competitive with those of the adjacent school districts, especially the New York City public schools. In 1970, a major issue in the bitter teachers' strike was the demand for a significant pay increase. Table 28 provides the salary schedule for teachers for school year 1973-74.

The board's approval of the following statement indicated that teacher militancy remained a concern:

Another important dimension of the educational system in Newark is the ongoing contest for power between least formally organized teachers' groups, the board of education, the central administration, and various community interests. The movement for militant professionalism among teachers involves encroachment into heretofore restricted areas of administrative policy and decision-making, attempts to reduce teacher responsibilities to pupils and their families, increased financial regards, and more job security. It is not that teacher groups oppose reform to the educational institution; rather the issue is that, within the context of increasing stress on the system and a scarcity of resources, the interests of the professional teacher are not to be diminished but on the contrary augmented. Thus, a clash has arisen

which confronts short- and long-run interests of the
black and Spanish-speaking communities, the board
of education, and the administrative structure,
thereby preparing the seedbed for continuing
struggles for power.[94]

TABLE 29
Financial Support from Regular Funds, School Years 1971-1972 to 1973-74:
Newark Public Schools

School Year	Amounts
1973-74	$104,161,662
1972-73	90,106,695
1971-72	83.598,418

Source: Questionnaire completed by the Newark public schools, May 1974.

Table 29 provides the levels of financial support from regular
funds for three consecutive school years. The financial plight of
the city and the school system are highlighted in the following
demographic data:

Newark's financial problems, like those of most
large cities, are staggering. Its property tax, of $9.19
per $100 valuation, is the highest in the state. Yet
the amount spent to educate pupils in Newark, as
compared to three other communities in New Jersey,
indicates that Newark is falling far behind its more
affluent neighbors in per capita educational
expenditures. For example, in 1967, Newark spent
$588.60 per student. Today, it spends $759.00.
Millburn, East Orange, and Montclair average $300
more per student, and Princeton, a wealthy suburb,
spends $1,740 annually, yet has a lower property tax
($7.82 and $7.93, in the borough and township
respectively). In Newark, $4.68 goes to the schools;
in Princeton $3.51 and $4.46 go to the school
system. Yet Princeton schools are modern and
spacious; Newark's are antiquated and literally
bursting at the seams.[95]

When Stanley Taylor accepted the position of superintendent on July 1, 1973 he was already well informed of the system's difficulties. The board did not attempt to tone down the system's problems and needs. The board declared:

> The central administrative structure of Newark's educational system suffers from two organizational characteristics which limit its ability to effectively deliver services to the children of the city. First, the structure lacks rational organization and an explicitly articulated purpose or mission. Currently there is confusion as to whether the superintendent's position is superior to the position of secretary to the board of education and business administrator. Second, the central administration has been used historically for patronage by local municipal government, the educational bureaucracy, and professional elite. A lack of instructional continuity and viability is the direct function of these internal problems with the central administration. Far ranging reforms are required to create an administrative organization that can effectively deliver relevant educational services to the children of Newark.[96]

Superintendent Taylor identified the most significant needs and problems confronting him as superintendent approximately ten months after he assumed the superintendency:

Significant Needs

Improvement of student achievement at all grade levels.

Attainment of adequate physical facilities.

Development of the teaching staff to a higher level of professionalism and involvement in the affairs of the community.

Development of management and managerial skills among the administrative personnel.

Differentiation of policymaking from administrative action.

Significant Problems

Resistance to change in organizational procedures on the part of the central office administrators.

Present union contract and its interpretation by involved personnel.

Relationship between the lay board and the administration.

Securing adequate fiscal resources and physical facilities to provide all of the programs desired for students.[97]

Reversal of the image of the school district.

In January 1974, the public schools received a $450,000 grant from the Rockefeller Foundation. The grant provided for a two-year program for the development of staff leadership, community leadership, and community resources. The grant enabled the superintendent to establish a task force to critically examine the system. The task force was to oversee an ambitious plan for retraining school personnel — particularly school administrators — and for developing community input. When the first grant director departed, Taylor assumed the day-to-day management of the grant. After the installation of the new grant director, Taylor continued his extensive direct involvement with the grant. A board member who was highly supportive of Taylor stated that despite the shortcomings of the new grant director, Taylor should not have given as much time as he did to the administration of the grant.

In 1970, prior to Taylor's appointment as superintendent, Mayor Gibson had appointed the Mayor's Educational Task Force. Mayor Gibson commented on the establishment of his educational task force:

> We created the Educational Task Force based on conditions that existed during the teachers' strike in Newark. The task force came about as a part of the agreement reached during the strike. There was a

lack of communication between the Newark
Teachers' Union, the Board of Education, and the
Office of the Mayor. As a way to deal with the
problems that we learned about during the strike,
with the lack of communication and with the need
for planning, the task force was created. The task
force deals with problems and conflicts before they
develop into strikes and demonstrations.[98]

Don Harris directed the mayor's task force. Harris was also the
mayor's chief advisor on matters related to public education in
Newark. The presence of the Mayor's Educational Task Force
and the superintendent's task force raised the concern of possible conflicts of interest. Harris did not believe that conflict
would develop:

Neither the members of the task force nor the staff of
the task force have any jurisdiction over a school, an
educational program, or anything that goes on in the
schools. The task force has a power connection to
the Office of the Mayor and has information and the
utilization of information. We are, in fact, the
mayor's educational staff. I can approach the board
of education and say that the task force says such
and such and be totally independent of the mayor.
On one hand, I represent the present task force and
on the other hand, I represent the present mayor.
The role of the members of the task force and the
staff of the task force is to help, in the most
constructive way, public education function
effectively. I cannot over-step my boundaries and
start doing something that the superintendent
should be doing. What I can do is to be a relatively
objective force in assisting all parties in the
resolution of problems and conflict.[99]

Mayor Gibson commented on his interpretation of the relationship of his office to the school superintendent:

The superintendent has a very critical role in the
city to develop and operate an efficient educational
system. The state law in New Jersey clearly separates
the educational function from the governmental
function. The superintendent has the responsibility
to respond to the policies of the school board. The
superintendent has a very difficult job. Whatever
relationships he has with the mayor should be
related purely to education. We either support or
complement each other or we do not.

I think that there ought to be a relationship
between the mayor and the superintendent that is
based on mutual respect. I have to respect his
position as superintendent of schools, and he has to
respect my position as mayor. He has to understand
the sensitive nature of education as a service being
provided in the city. Therefore, the decisions
surrounding education can create political problems.
Whatever controversy that surrounds education
becomes a political issue regardless of who is
superintendent. The mayor and the superintendent
have to remain attuned to each other. Even though
we may not agree on such issues, we ought to keep
in touch.[100]

Taylor wanted to make education in the Newark public schools
not only as human as he could make it but also as scientific and
objective as possible. He wanted to deal directly with principals
in his quest for educational accountability. He indicated that
most teachers in the system took the view that the system will
change me or I will change it. But Taylor believed that most
teachers did not like the way the system worked and wanted the
system to work more effectively. Most teachers, he emphasized,
wanted to have pride in what they did and did not work just for
money.

Superintendent Taylor gave full support to furthering the
implementation of a systemwide program of management by
objectives (MBO) that had been introduced into the system prior

to his appointment. He viewed MBO as a means to promote accountability. The commitment to MBO required the board and superintendent to develop districtwide goals with the other echelons developing goals.

Taylor believed that if major changes were to be introduced into the school system they had to be implemented within the first year of his superintendency. He was convinced that educational reform in the Newark public schools would be minimal unless he was able to improve the quality of his executive staff and to relocate certain principals, matching more appropriately their strengths and limitations with the scope of the challenges presented. He had inherited an executive staff that had conflicting educational philosophies as well as limited leadership competencies. Taylor's survival and success as superintendent would be highly dependent on his ability to transfer principals and to recruit competent persons to replace those on his executive staff who had deficient skills.

The executive staff members Taylor sought to remove had achieved their promotions, in no small measure, as a result of their solid political connections in Newark. Taylor was not prepared to "wheel and deal" with the school board to gain its support of his desire to improve the quality of his executive staff. He declared: "I am willing to compromise if I see where I am not compromising my principles or not giving the 'ball game' away."

Along with the need to effect personnel changes in key positions, Taylor knew that the system's antiquated organizational structure had to be changed to support a more efficient mobilization of the system's personnel and financial resources. He stated: "We are now presently organized to deal with the kind of school system that is needed if your organization is geared to 1927 or 1888."

In 1976 the state legislature reconstituted the organizational structure of the Newark public schools. Before the intervention of the legislature, the organizational structure of the school system separated the superintendent from essential management components. Under the legislature's mandate, the chief executive officer was designated as the executive superintendent. The position of secretary to the board was abolished. The business manager became a member of the staff of the executive superintendent. All school officers in the system under the legislature's plan were responsible to the executive superintendent. Taylor, after some hassle, received a new three-year contract, which was scheduled to expire on June 30, 1979. His $47,000 salary as executive superintendent made him the highest paid public official in Newark's history.

Taylor's strained relations with the board never allowed him to build the base of board support needed to accomplish the personnel changes he desired. The principals he sought to relocate were able to withstand his efforts to secure their transfers. He had accepted the superintendency without a commitment from the board to allow him to dismiss, demote or transfer members of his executive staff. Thus, Taylor was never able to build his team. He was to remain an outsider during his tenure as superintendent. His efforts to institute personnel changes alienated him from many of his executive officers and principals. These obstacles, combined with the inadequacy of Taylor's relations with the board's majority and a distant relationship with Mayor Gibson, proved to be insurmountable.

Taylor's strained relations with the board further deteriorated. Less than a year after receiving a restructured position and a new contract, Taylor was faced with a school board that sought his resignation. Board president Bell had left the board and had been replaced by Carl Dawson. In a May 1977 letter to Taylor, Dawson asked the superintendent to "recognize the crying needs of Newark students and step aside."[101]

On June 16, 1977, the board voted 6 to 3 to bring more than 100 administrative charges of malfeasance, nonfeasance, misfeasance and incompetence against Taylor; a week later the board suspended him. Many of the board's charges cited findings of a highly critical state evaluation of the Newark school system, which was prepared by the then acting Essex County Superintendent. The board's charges had been equally influenced by statements Taylor had made in response to Dawson's earlier demand for his resignation:

> I do not accept anyone's assumption that I should resign. In fact, I have no intention of resigning, particularly since the total state of the school system, the learning process, and the achievement of pupils have been greatly improved since my arrival in August 1973.[102]

On June 2, 1977 Dawson gave up the presidency but maintained his seat on the board. He vowed to continue to press for the removal of Taylor. In his May 1977 letter to Taylor calling for his resignation, Dawson had made his position very clear. He stated:

> I see no hope in the current direction of your leadership. It is not sufficiently aggressive, comprehensive or serious. My objective opinion is that you cannot lead this organization at this stage of its development.[103]

Helen Fullilove resigned her seat on the board "in utter contempt of the action and the conduct of the board over the past two years."[104] Her term on the board would have expired in two weeks. She had been one of Taylor's most ardent supporters. Fullilove accused her colleagues who had voted against Taylor of being selfish and dangerous to the well-being of children.[105] Vickie Donaldson and George Branch had served on the board during the full period of Taylor's superintendency and praised his performance. Donaldson declared that Taylor "has made contributions in his four years here."[106] Branch stated that "Taylor was a damned good superintendent who had a helluva job to do."[107] He categorized Taylor's forced departure as another sad example of blacks failing to support a strong black superintendent.

In a letter to Mayor Gibson, Fullilove stated that she had resigned from the board in order to demonstrate to the mayor and the community her contempt for the board's behavior in the Taylor matter. She took issue with the mayor for appointing his aide to the school board. Dawson is a member of the mayor's executive committee. Some observers viewed Dawson's appointment to the board as a clear act by Gibson to become directly involved in policy decisions of the board.

Taylor countered the board's attempt to dismiss him by securing the services of an attorney. Taylor's attorney and the board's attorney were able to work out a settlement. Taylor was reinstated as executive superintendent, after which he resigned. The board and Taylor reached agreement on a cash settlement of his contract.

Taylor had never received enthusiastic support from the board, his executive staff, the mayor, or the city council. He had entered the superintendency as an outsider and departed as such. Ironically, Taylor's successor was able to get the board to dismiss, demote, and transfer some members of the executive staff. Also, after Taylor's departure, the board supported the new superintendent's transfer of several principals.

Alonzo Kittrels, who had served as the director of personnel, replaced Taylor as executive superintendent. Kittrels is Newark's second black superintendent. As he confronts the system's many problems, he must cope with Mayor Gibson's expressed commitment to abolish the board of education and run the school system from City Hall. The following comments were attributed to Gibson by The *Star Ledger:*

> I would rather eliminate the board of education
> and have education as a department in the city of
> Newark with a superintendent as a department head.
> I think that it is important to get the state law
> changed. All I am saying now is: Either give it to me
> or take it away. I should not be held responsible for
> running a system that the law restricts me from
> running.[108]

Mayor Gibson's reelection (1974 and 1978) has not silenced his critics, but his return to office has solidified his position as the representative of the people of Newark. Under the Gibson administration, improvements in city government have been established. Yet Newark's problems are such that no short-term improvement programs can produce consequential improvements. Gibson is a cautious but capable administrator. He has become a stabilizing force in the city's efforts to establish a coexistence between the various black and white groups. The overall image of Newark remains negative, but Mayor Gibson deserves a large share of the credit for the increased optimism about the city's future.

Highland Park, Michigan

The City

Although totally surrounded by Detroit, Highland Park has managed to maintain its own identity. The residents of Highland Park have always exhibited pride in their community. Most residents, especially those who have resided in the city for decades, are quick to emphasize that Highland Park does not seek to become a miniature Detroit. Highland Park covers 2.9 square miles of concentrated residential area. With a population of 35,000, the city is the second most densely populated community in the state.

The city's population includes a relatively complete cross section of ethnic groups. The city is about 54 percent black. The majority of the city's whites are long-time residents. Despite a highly favorable employment market, Highland Park has a large number of low-income families. In comparison to forty other communities in Wayne County, excluding Detroit, Highland Park has the fourth largest social welfare caseload, the highest total public-assistance load, and the largest number of families receiving surplus-food commodities.[109]

Robert Blackwell made history when he was elected mayor in 1968. He was the first black Republican in America to be elected mayor. Blackwell was also the city's first full-time mayor. He inherited the difficult task of establishing authority guidelines for the office. Prior to his election, each of the city council members headed one of the municipal agencies. Therefore, the transfer of authority was hotly resisted. The mayor's first official appearance desegregated city hall. Blackwell recalls: "When I walked into my office in 1968, the day after my election, I was the only black person at city hall. I was the loneliest man in town at that time."[110]

In a later election, four of the five candidates receiving Blackwell's support were elected to the council, which included three blacks and two whites. Blackwell was supported by two council members, one white and one black. This impasse created a difficult situation for the mayor. He stated: "I operate by veto. It takes four votes to override a veto. It is a helluva way to run a government."[111]

Highland Park was in an enviable economic position. The city was operating in the black, and had increased employment fivefold. The city had about 35,000 residents but provided employment opportunities for about 100,000 persons. Highland Park is the site of a massive industrial complex, which consists of large and small manufacturers. The largest companies are the Chrysler Corporation, the Ford Motor Company and the Ex-cell-o Corporation. Industry provides 81 percent of the property-tax base. During Blackwell's first year as mayor, a rumor circulated that the Ford Motor Company was planning to leave the city. Through Mayor Blackwell's encouragement, the company expanded its operations.

Being surrounded by a major city causes both advantages and disadvantages. Mayor Blackwell sought to eliminate the disadvantages while gaining the optimum benefits from the advantages. With regard to the advantages, he said, "We can enjoy all of the services of a major city without many of the disadvantages of living in a large city."[112] Mayor Blackwell was concerned about Detroit's high crime rate spilling over into Highland Park. He was also concerned about the influx of Detroit's welfare and other low-income families. Mayor Blackwell attempted to discourage this influx by establishing more stringent policies governing housing in the city; he felt that poverty ought to be "spread out" in order that services could be adequately provided to the poor.

Mayor Blackwell identified the public schools as the city's most valuable resource. He did not advocate the placement of the schools under his authority; he did not see any merit in the school system coming under the jurisdiction of the mayor. Blackwell indicated that the system operated efficiently and effectively under the leadership of both the school board and the superintendent. He stressed that it is absolutely necessary for the school system and the mayor's office to work together to solve problems. He commended the board and superintendent for their efforts in promoting the revitalization of the school system after a period of decline during the previous superintendent's administration.

The School Board

Interviews for this section were conducted during January and July of 1974. In January the school board consisted of six members, five whites and one black. The black member served as board president. The six board members were not able to reach agreement on an appointee to fill the vacancy created by the departure of a black board member. The following constituted the membership of the Highland Park board of education in January 1974:

> Maria Willaims (president) — schoolteacher, Detroit public schools (black).
>
> Kenneth Griffin (vice president) — lieutenant, Highland Park fire department (white).
>
> Helen Field — retired schoolteacher, who had served on the school board for more than thirty consecutive years (white).
>
> George Cowing — middle-management employee, Chrysler Corporation, Highland Park (white).
>
> Lawrence Pike — community college teacher, Oakland, Michigan (white).
>
> Charles H. Novelli — attorney, Highland Park (white).

In June 1974, Cowing and Griffin did not choose to seek reelection. The following persons were elected to the school board in June:

> Elmer Treloar — retired, and a primary participant in the unsuccessful campaign to recall Mayor Blackwell (white).

> M. Lucille Jones — employed by the recreation department in Highland Park (black).
>
> Edna Baraky — employed by the Ford Motor Company (white).

Maria Williams was a candidate for the school board four times before she was elected. She stated that she could not gain the confidence of whites because she could not be a "yes person." Her active involvement in school board affairs began in 1959. Her eventual confrontation with the board centered around the pace and direction of desegregation in the city's schools. Mrs. Williams, along with other black residents, took the board to court to secure a comprehensive desegregation program. Viewed as too radical and too vocal, Williams' election was not greeted enthusiastically by some white members. She viewed herself as an active spokesperson for quality education and community involvement. Regarding Superintendent Mitchell, she said: "We felt that he had the agressiveness, the youth, and the stamina to do the job. He is making the system work."[113] Commenting on her role as a board member, Mrs. Williams stated that she refused to become an administrator: "This is why we hired a superintendent. This is sometimes called passing the buck by some community persons who want me to take more direct action."[114]

Prior to July 1, 1974, Superintendent Mitchell had had a reasonably liberal and exceptionally supportive school board. The three new members on the board produced a major shift in board-superintendent relations. Mrs. Williams was replaced by Ms. Field as board president; Ms. Field was believed to be in her eighties. Novelli had frequently been identified as the superintendent's major adversary; he had campaigned against increased millage for the public schools.

Before the three new members took office in July, the board offered Superintendent Mitchell a three-year contract. The board's vote on his contract was 6 to 0. In July the reconstituted board voted to reconsider the previous action. Mitchell believed, at the time, that his programs were too well entrenched to be significantly impeded by an overly conservative board. "I will have to be a super black to get new programs that are innovative and sorely needed."[115]

The School System

The school district has nine schools which serve students from preschool to senior high. Also included under the authority of the school board is a community college. Students in the regular schools are housed in one senior high school, three middle schools, and five elementary schools. Black students in school year 1973-74 constituted about 92 percent of the 7,230 student population. Table 30 provides a racial breakdown of the student population for three consecutive school years. About one third of the student body — 2,460 students — was identified in school year 1973-74 as recipients of a free lunch.

TABLE 30
Breakdown of Student Population by Race, School Years 1971-72 to 1973-74: Highland Park Public Schools

School Year	Black	White	Other	Totals
1973-74	6,656	530	44	7,230
1972-73	5,536	640	30	6,206
1971-72	6,677	844	30	7,551

Source: Questionnaire completed by Highland Park public schools, March 1974.

The student population in preschool through senior high school and community college was served by 755 employees funded from regular sources. Nearly two-thirds of all regularly funded employees were black. In July 1974, the superintendent's top staff was more integrated than the student population. The black-white breakdown of top staff was black superintendent; two black and two white assistant superintendents; a black senior high school principal; two black and one white middle school principals; and three white elementary principals. Two of the retiring white elementary principals were expected to be replaced by blacks.

In 1974 Highland Park Community College had a student body of slightly over 1,500. The president was black. He was assisted by five deans of whom two were black. Until recently, the community college had made money for the school system. The establishment of Wayne County Community College in the late 1960s reduced significantly the number of non-Highland Park residents enrolled in Highland Park Community College. At one time, Highland Park Community College stood alone in Wayne County as an economically viable and academically acceptable institution of higher education for low-income students. The school system was exploring the possibility of the community college becoming a part of Wayne County Community College.

Superintendent Mitchell identified the following as the most significant needs and problems confronting the school system:

> *Significant Needs*
>
> Further development of a systemwide accountability model that everyone understands, believes in, and implements for the betterment of student achievement in reading, math, science, and language arts.
>
> Effective alternative methods to educate junior and senior high school students in order to reduce/eliminate absenteeism and vandalism.
>
> Adequate full-funding support for education from the state of Michigan rather than from local taxpayers, i.e., yearly millages.
>
> Advanced funding notice for programs that are federally funded.
>
> Continued improvement in and updating of our management system and board of education policies.[116]
>
> *Significant Problems*
>
> A divided board of education.
>
> The unrelated political and social involvement that is demanded and requested by the community at large.[117]

Table 31 reveals declining academic achievement as a major problem in Highland Park public schools. Standardized reading achievement test results indicate that the majority of students in grades three through six tested below the national norms. Students in the second grade tested above the national norms. In contrast to the achievement estimates provided by other school officials, Superintendent Mitchell stated: "The majority of our elementary students are achieving at or above the national norms. The breakdown is at the middle-school level."[118] Mitchell was convinced that significant gains had been made in academic achievement in reading during school year 1973-74: "Three of the four elementary schools exceeded the state average in the Michigan Assessment Test."[119]

Dr. Louis Kocsis, in his capacity as Director of Compensatory Education for the State Department of Instruction, made the following comments on student progress in the Highland Park public schools in a letter addressed to Mitchell:

> I have reviewed the results and the evaluation materials which I have brought back with me. I am most pleased to note the tremendous improvement that has taken place, and is taking place, in your schools in the past two years. I realize that some of the youngsters in some of the programs are still below grade level; however, for the first time it appears they are making substantial gains in reading and math and this gives positive evidence of a breakthrough. You and your staff and your board of education should be commended for your dedication, your enthusiasm, and your objective approach in providing improved programs for educationally disadvantaged children. I could see the shift that has taken place in your program, that is, the concern with output and results rather than concern for input only. This is certainly consistent with the Accountability Model of the State Board of Education.[120]

TABLE 31
Estimates of Percentages of Students in Grades Two-Six Testing below National
Norms in Reading Achievement: Highland Park Public Schools

Two	Three	Grades Four	Five	Six
48.5	65.6	62.8	67.8	81.0

Source: Questionnaire completed by Highland Park public schools, March 1974.

Mitchell and his staff did not fall prey to inertia. He sought to document his assertion that the school system would someday be a model for the nation. He declared:

> Why all this sudden attention to what's going on in the classrooms of our town? It's the quality of education . . . particularly compensatory education . . . in Highland Park. Plain and simply, these programs are doing the job and, as a result, are receiving state and national recognition.[121]

> The entire curriculum — what our schools offer students — is being evaluated. It has meant taking a close look at what has been done, what was done right and what was done wrong, and what should be done. Taking that close look at education in Highland Park can be a slow, painful process. In the process of self-examination, decisions must be made. We're making those decisions — we're biting that bullet.[122]

The system has a taxable base sufficient to provide adequate financial support for public education in Highland Park. Voters in the city have continuously supported millage campaigns. For public education in Highland Park, "the financial picture continues to be a good one."[123] Mitchell indicated that during his superintendency the system had concluded two fiscal years with a surplus.

TABLE 32
Financial Support from Regular Funds, School Years 1971-72 to 1973-74:
Highland Park Public Schools

School Year	Amounts
1973-74	$10,295,919
1972-73	10,237,294
1971-72	9,715,639

Source: Questionnaire completed by Highland Park public schools, March 1974.

TABLE 33
Minimum and Maximum Ranges of Salary Schedules for Teachers by Degree:
Highland Park Public Schools

Range	B.A.	M.A.	M.A. + 30
Minimum	$ 9,000	$ 9,800	$10,200
Maximum	15,800	18,250	18,600

Source: Questionnaire completed by Highland Park public schools, March 1974.

The per-pupil rate of expenditures in school year 1973-74 was $1,324. (Table 32 provides the system's levels of financial support from regular funds for three consecutive school years.) Salaries for teachers in Highland Park were extremely competitive with those of most systems in the nation. Table 33 provides the salary schedules for teachers in school year 1973-74.

Mitchell emphasized that he had recruited and developed the best executive staff of any superintendent in the nation. With the application of sound principles of management, he believed that the creative talents of his executive staff had produced results and would demonstrate even greater productivity in the future. Mitchell, a former director of federal programs in Highland Park, sought to integrate compensatory educational programs with the system's regularly funded programs. "We have thrown away the former approach to the delivery of educational programs and services."[124] He attempted to implement federally funded compensatory educational programs with only the minimal extension of supervisory and administrative ranks. Teachers from all subject areas were involved in reading instruction programs. Every school was assigned a reading and mathematics specialist. The system's research and development unit thoroughly examined, not only federally funded programs, but also all programs in reading and mathematics. Reports on strengths and shortcomings of such programs were delivered annually to the superintendent and to program managers.

Progress in the improvement of adacemic achievement was made during Mitchell's superintendency. Prior to July 1, 1974, Mitchell was lavishly praised by his board for the success of innovative programs introduced under his leadership. But the school board election reshaped board-superintendent relations and the philosophical bent of the board. The newly constituted board was once again predominantly white and did not provide Mitchell with majority support. By not expressing their civic and social consciousness in the political process, black voters in Highland Park allowed a school board to be formed that was unrepresentative of the majority population in the city and that was unable to accept Mitchell as superintendent.

Mitchell's agressive style and penchant for "telling it like it is" had not caused him major difficulties with the board that appointed him. Mitchell and a majority of the members of his new board were incompatible. The new board failed to confirm the previous board's extension of Mitchell's three-year contract. On January 6, 1976, the board voted to terminate his contract. Mitchell went to court and was reinstated by the court. But on January 31, 1976, his contract was once again terminated. Mitchell again sought relief from the court. His suit has yet to be resolved by the court. Mitchell emphasized that the board had never presented him with any allegations, formal or informal.

A school administrator who served Mitchell and was highly supportive of him offered the opinion that Mitchell's termination had nothing to do with inefficiency:

> Mitchell was not removed because he was
> incompetent. The school board just could not get
> along with him. He was too smart for the school

board. The board could not accept a smart black
educator telling them what to do. Mitchell would
tell the board in no uncertain terms that some of its
proposals were stupid. He was a 'smart ass nigger'
who had to go.[125]

The board appointed a black superintendent to succeed
Mitchell. Donald Estill, who succeeded Mitchell, served for less
than two years. Thomas Lloyd, the present incumbent, is the
system's third black school superintendent. He serves a school
board that has six black and one white member.

Highland Park is no longer a predominantly white, middle-
class community. The city's percentage of black Americans and
low-income families has significantly expanded. The school
system is no longer listed among the finest in the state. Deterioration has left a negative impact on some neighborhoods. Yet, in
a period of American history in which urban deterioration and
social disorganization have made urban living almost intolera-
ble, Highland Park has managed to rebuild the city in a manner
that offers encouragement for other cities. Mayor Blackwell
gained the support of the business community and of a large
segment of the black community. His failure to win reelection in
1975 is attributed to a concerted effort by area Democrats to
remain in power in Highland Park. In 1979, Blackwell defeated
the black Democratic incumbent and returned as mayor of Highland Park.

6

The Commission of Black Superintendents

How do black superintendents coming into school systems previously headed by whites initiate reform at the top to mobilize their staffs and boards and influence external forces to support them? Black superintendents across the nation have encountered major problems directly related to their minority status and to the contemporary circumstances that surround the national efforts to desegregate public schools and to upgrade school systems that have suffered from decades of adverse discriminatory practices. The survival and success of black superintendents is greatly dependent on their ability to demonstrate conclusive evidence of professionalism in the discharge of their duties and responsibilities and to effect appropriate linkages with black-directed endeavors to resolve the problems and needs of black Americans in a racist society.

The availability of a well-trained and highly dedicated cadre of black educators for leadership positions in predominantly black and heavily black school systems is essential not only for improvements in the quality of life accorded blacks and other disadvantaged Americans, but also for the implementation of a viable concept of public education. Black superintendents have recognized that, through their own initiatives, they must develop the necessary structures through which they can meet, share ideas, and focus sharply on the unique problems that they confront as black educators.

In 1970 the enterprising nature of a former black superintendent and the empathy and financial support of a black-directed
organization provided the impetus needed to produce, in 1971,
the first national organization for black school superintendents,
the National Alliance of Black Superintendents. This organization was reconstituted in 1973 and became the National Alliance
of Black School Educators (NABSE). This chapter examines
NABSE's Commission of Superintendents with a review of its
past and current activities and the persons and circumstances
that contributed to the formulation of the Alliance and its commission of superintendents. The future of the Alliance and its
several commissions is also explored.

The Inception

Proper recognition must be given to Charles D. Moody, Sr. for
his efforts in the successful promotion of the first national meeting of the nation's black school superintendents. Dr. Moody had
two objectives: completing a dissertation on the emergence of
black superintendents and a national meeting of all black school
superintendents. His quests brought him to the Metropolitan
Applied Research Center (MARC) in New York City. Headed by
the distinguished educator Dr. Kenneth Clark, MARC offered
assistance well beyond financial support. MARC provided
Moody with the funds needed to complete the research for his
dissertation and gave the financial and technical assistance
needed to bring about the first national meeting of black school
superintendents.

Currently on the staff of the School of Education of the University of Michigan, Dr. Moody commented on his efforts to bring
about the first meeting of Black superintendents in a statement
before the newly formed National Alliance of Black Educators in
1973.

> As well as getting information for a dissertation, I
> was interested in seeing whether or not the other
> black superintendents were catching the same kind
> of hell that I was getting. You can say that misery

loves company, if you want to put it that way. I
really wanted to find out how the black
superintendents got their positions and what were
the conditions in the school districts in which they
served. I also wanted to find out how black
superintendents were handling their jobs.

I knew that I wanted to do this, but how I was
going to do it presented a problem. There were
about six or eight black superintendents at that time.
By the time of the first meeting of black
superintendents, there were about sixteen black
superintendents. When we met for the first time, in
1970, I was then a former black superintendent.[1]

More than twenty educators gathered for the first meeting of
black school superintendents in Chicago, Illinois, in 1970. Before the November 1970, meeting, Moody, his vigorous efforts in
the promotion of the meeting completed, had departed his
superintendency in Harvey, Illinois. MARC was represented by
Dr. Hyland Lewis and Mrs. Dixie Moon at that first meeting. Four
of the participants were acting superintendents. One black
superintendent, who is noted for his ability to coin a phrase,
reminded his colleagues of the "hostile winds" that the black
superintendents were encountering. Dr. James Lewis, then
superintendent in Wyandanch, New York, recalled: "For the
first time, I did not feel alone. I felt that there were other fellows
with me."[2]

The various sessions of the first national meeting were, by
design, kept informal. Dr. Russell Jackson, who served as the
chairman and later was elected president of the Alliance, commented on the participants and the agenda:

> The group that first met in Chicago in November
> 1970 was really a collection of individuals who
> obviously were going through many traumatic
> experiences and who expressed their trauma in their
> anxieties. The black superintendents were under a
> vast amount of pressure. Some were hesitant to
> become participants in a conference geared

exclusively for black superintendents.

The early sessions were devoted to therapeutic types of activities. Opportunities were provided for the superintendents to exchange ideas about their problems and needs. Time was also devoted to an exchange of ideas on how to cope with some of their problems. The superintendents shared the experiences of innovative programs in their respective systems that were having some degree of success. We talked basically about the specific educational matters that were prominent in those systems served by black superintendents.

These sessions involved not only open critiques of some of the programs in the systems represented, but also an assessment of the methods used to evaluate such programs. These critiques were very direct and pointed. I believe that in all instances the critiques were appreciated by the persons making the presentations.[3]

The superintendents generally agreed that the scope and complexity of the problems facing them and their communities necessitated establishing a national organization. The Miami, Florida meeting of August 1971 produced the decision to form the National Alliance of Black School Superintendents. Once the Alliance was officially established, MARC made adjustments in its financial support. Both parties agreed that it was now time for the membership of the Alliance to become more self-supportive.

Justifying Solidarity

There were some sharp differences of opinion among the black superintendents as to the determination of the most appropriate relationship for the Alliance with educational organizations that are dominated by whites. The majority of the membership indicated that while membership in predominantly white organizations would be maintained, the independence of the Alliance from the dictates of any other organization should be firmly established in the Alliance's official communications and in other relationships with white-dominated organizations. The membership stressed the point that no organization should in its contacts with the Alliance seek to place it in a subservient role or in a subordinate position, regardless of how new and thin the ranks. The following statement sets forth the purposes of the Alliance:

> The National Alliance of Black School Superintendents has set the systematic observation of public school systems composed of large percentages of ethnic-minority students and all of the problems inherent in their structures as its general goal and, subsequently, to attempt to analyze and share knowledge gained in methods of eradicating the problems which stand as obstructions to quality education for all children, particularly minority children. . . .
>
> The NABSS was developed primarily as an organizational means through which the problems of relevance in education as applied to the black ethnic minority in the United States could be adequately and systematically addressed. Its objectives do not include duplicating or supplementing programs and research engaged in by other education agencies which address themselves to the educational needs of public schools in general in the United States. The Alliance does focus attention, on the other hand, on those circumstances and problems unique to school systems whose student population is predominantly black and especially to systems which have a black superintendent as the chief school administrator.[4]

Simeon F. Moss, superintendent of schools in East Orange, New Jersey offered his rationale for the need of black school superintendents to meet and deliberate on the issues and problems that confront them.

Because the nature of the black superintendency is changing and is still a relatively new phenomenon in American education, it is, in my opinion, critical that we have a forum for meeting and establishing good relationships with one another. Regardless of whether we are members of urban school districts or suburban or rural ones, it is vitally important that we share our ideas and aspirations with each other. . . .

Social interaction at the professional level is important since all too often we find ourselves isolated from the mainstream of this activity within our current national administrative associations. It is at the social level where exchange of information on positions available can take place, where we can serve each other by disseminating information on relationships which normally are not available to us. Social gatherings also give us an opportunity to let our hair down and relax in an atmosphere of equality and with individuals who understand and appreciate us for what we are. . . .

Considering the current constraints put on black administrators, conferences of this type do much to 'charge his batteries' and give him an opportunity at regular intervals to exchange ideas with his peers on the firing line. At the same time it presents to him new concepts and approaches developed by experts who discuss educational problems from their specific areas of knowledge.[5]

Article II of the constitution and by-laws of the Alliance is presented in its entirety in order that the reasons established for this particular manifestation of black solidarity can be more completely comprehended:

ARTICLE II
Purposes and Functions of the Organization

The purposes of the organization shall be to make a strong commitment to the education of all children and to black children in particular; to provide a coalition of black educators; to create a forum for the exchange of ideas and techniques; to identify and develop black professionals who will assume leadership positions in the education of black children.

The functions of the organization shall be:

Section I

To work toward the elimination of and to rectify the effects of racism in education.

Section II

To significantly raise the academic achievement level of all students and to place particular emphasis on that type of learning which builds positive and realistic self-concepts among black students.

To establish and promote the degree of awareness, professional expertise, and commitment among black educators necessary to enhance and contribute to the efforts of other educators and community persons.

Section III

To provide an avenue for recruiting school personnel in general and qualified black personnel specifically.

To offer specialized training to prospective chief school officers via the development of courses for personnel through cooperative programs with institutions of higher education and school systems.

To seek to cultivate resource personnel equipped to assist the black educator in dealing with special problems, *e.g.*, deficit finance, integration, student concerns, decentralization, community involvement, teacher union, etc.

Section IV

To meet and share ideas, proven programs, and guaranteed techniques for demonstrating that black youth can achieve irrespective of socioeconomic conditions.

To provide resources and intelligence banks for black school educators on proven educational programs.

To exchange information on methods of obtaining
funds from federal, state, and private sources to support
educational programs in the schools.

Section V

To develop positions on key educational issues
which affect the education of youngsters.[6]

During the period the Alliance served solely as the organization for current and former black school superintendents, it
never had the full participation of all the identified black
superintendents. The majority of the known black superintendents had elected to become members of the Alliance, but a
small number had chosen, for various reasons, to remain apart
from membership in the Alliance. A very few totally ignored
invitations sent by the Alliance.

The Detroit Experience

The issue of the reluctance or refusal of some black school
administrators to become members of a black professional organization solely or primarily because of the racial factors at-
tached to membership is a matter that deserves further explora-
tion. A situation that I experienced while a school administrator
in Detroit is presented because of its relevance. In 1968 more
than sixty black school administrators in the Detroit public
schools felt the need to establish an organization of black school
administrators. Detroit had experienced a large increase in the
number of black school administrators. They were, in most
cases, relatively new to their assignments and, in all cases, easy
to identify. The black community in Detroit was demanding a
great deal from its black school administrators. The community
advocated its objectives to the black administrators often in
strong language and through unconventional methods.

Some of the school administrators voiced publicly and pri-
vately strong objections and opposition to forming an all black
organization for black school administrators. They believed it
was improper and undesirable for black school administrators to
segregate themselves. Nevertheless, the commitment was firm.
An interim executive body for the proposed organization was

established with the directive to prepare recommendations to the group for its preamble and by-laws. I served as chairman of the committee preparing the preamble and by-laws.

In wording similar to that used by the Alliance some three years later, the Metropolitan Detroit Society of Black Educational Administrators stated:

> The establishment of a society of black school administrators has evolved from the belief on the part of many black educators that because of their particular kinds of sociological and psychological experiences and sensitivities they must often . . . meet in order to examine and to determine what their proper and relevant individual and collective roles and responsibilities are prior to attempting to make an effective contribution to the entire profession and community.[7]

Some of the black school administrators in Detroit who opposed the establishment of the Society and who refused to join had very deep philosophical differences regarding the merits of such an activity. Others felt that membership would jeopardize their advancement within a white-controlled administrative structure. A courtesy visit with Detroit's superintendent, Dr. Norman Drachler, was arranged to inform him officially of the commitment to form an organization of black school administrators. As superintendent, Drachler, had been instrumental in appointing a majority of the black administrators in Detroit. In an interview more than five years after the establishment of the Society, Drachler commented on his perception of the role of the Society:

> I felt that it was not the role of the superintendent — particularly a white superintendent — to tell others that they had or had not a need to organize. My reason for encouragement was based primarily on discussions with black administrators. I sensed at the time that the black administrator was undergoing a tremendous intellectual soul-searching struggle. He

was constantly worried about how other blacks in the community, particularly critics of the establishment, were looking upon him. He was worried as to whether or not he was selling out his conscience and his values in behalf of a promotion. . . . But there was a unique need at the time, and that need may still exist, for black administrators to be able to come together in a more than haphazard way in order to hold hands with each other, to discuss issues that were facing the city, and to see whether these issues that they were responding to as administrators of a total city school system were in conflict with the interests of the black community and if so to possibly formulate a position. Basically, I felt that they needed to intellectualize their posture as black administrators in a so-called white establishment and at the same time be able to reassure themselves that they were not deserting their fellow blacks. . . .

There were some people who looked upon it as being a separatist movement and who were critical of me for participating officially in the formulation of the group. I frankly did not think that they saw the black administrator in the close range that I did. Such as when we met with a parent group and when we had gut issues to decide which had racial overtones or the possibility of being misinterpreted by whites or blacks. . . .

There was also a need for black administrators to meet with one another in order to assess jointly how they were being accepted or not accepted in their newly appointed positions. There were some strategies to be developed. How do you work your way into a school-community that is 80 percent white? How do you handle situations in an inner-city all-black community where you have everybody declaring that they speak for the community? The whole matter of community involvement was probably a much more active issue in a black community than it was in an all-white community.[8]

Realignment

Almost as soon as the date, time, and place were established for the first national meeting of black superintendents, requests began to come in from black educators who were not superintendents but who wanted access to the sessions. With the exception of a few, the superintendents were opposed to their sessions being opened to any other persons. On several occasions this practice contributed to incidents in which some black school administrators objected quite strongly to being excluded from a meeting of the "brothers." On the other hand, the black superintendents were firm in their conviction that their particular needs at the time were unique and that they needed to concentrate on communicating with each other without the presence of those who had not experienced the role paranoia and complications inherent in the position. Some strong statements and accusations were made at those closed sessions about people, conditions, organizations, and places which were not intended to be repeated outside the room. Later, modifications in this restrictive practice were made for black administrators whose attendance was cleared in advanced by the group's executive committee.

Even prior to the superintendents' decision in 1971 to establish a formal organization, the sentiment in favor of extending participation in meetings to other black school administrators was growing, but it was not the pervasive sentiment. In April 1973, the National Alliance of Black School Superintendents, after two years of existence, voted to reconstitute its membership. The debate on this issue was intense. Ulysses Byas served as the president of the Alliance during the period that realignment of the structure was being discussed and enacted. Byas commented:

> Several suggestions for possible expansions were turned down, and rightly so, by the membership . . .

knowing that when something is identified as a
problem there is an answer out there. Let's find the
proper mix. Fortunate for us, we did. An
organization with potential for an expanded
membership was structured within the framework of
a newly drafted constitution. Upon its approval, the
National Alliance of Black School Superintendents,
by its own action, went out of business. The
National Alliance of Black School Educators, in
April 1973, at Miami Beach, Florida, was born. The
constitution authorized the establishment of six
commissions and made it permissible within two
years to establish a commission of teachers. Thus the
potential solution as to how significant numbers of
persistent persons and resources could be brought
under one umbrella for seeking solutions to unique,
common and sometimes insidious problems
plaguing them.[9]

Many of the black superintendents who voted in favor of
reconstituting the Alliance expressed concerns about not being
able to maintain the unique identity and the desired camaraderie
within the structural confines of an alliance with six commissions. But the black superintendents were convinced that the
reasons for reorganization outweighed the reasons against it.
With some reluctance, the superintendents gave birth to an
organization so structured that their numerical dominance
would soon be transformed to a minority status.

Article III of the constitution and by-laws of the National
Alliance of Black School Educators delineates the essential
components of the six commissions:

    a. *Commission of Superintendents.* Any person who
       is employed by a local education agency on a
       regular basis as the chief administrative officer
       (usually called the superintendent of schools or
       education) of a school district and who is directly
       responsible only to a central board of education
       shall be eligible for membership in the National

Alliance of Black School Educators under this Commission. Persons who have occupied the chief administrative position on an acting basis for a period of twelve consecutive months or more; who are retired from the chief administrative position; who have previously held the permanent position; or who hold the office on a leave-of-absence status, are also eligible for membership in the National Alliance of Black School Educators under this Commission.

b. *Commission of General Administrators.* Any person who is employed by a local education agency in the capacity of deputy superintendent, associate superintendent, or assistant superintendent; or as an area, regional, district, or community superintendent, etc., shall be eligible for membership in the National Alliance of Black School Educators under this Commission.

c. *Commission of Local School Administrators.* Any person who is employed by a local education agency as the chief administrator of a local school (usually called a principal) or who holds a position in a local school as vice, deputy, or associate local-school administrator is eligible for membership in the National Alliance of Black School Educators under this Commission.

d. *Commission of Higher Education.* Any person who is employed as an administrator in a college or university; a department head or teacher of educational administration in such institution; or director or supervisor of special programs related to public school education is eligible for membership in the National Alliance of Black School Educators under this Commission.

e. *Commission of Supervisors.* Any person who is employed in a supervisory position with a local education agency and has responsibilities for directing other staff members in the accomplishment of some particular education function, program, or support service related to the local education agency's objectives is eligible for membership in the National Alliance of Black School Educators under this Commission.

f. *Commission of Directors*. Any person who is employed by a local education agency with responsibilities for directing or managing some educational function, program, or support service related to accomplishing the local education agency's objectives is eligible for membership in the National Alliance of Black School Educators under this Commission.

Two years from the adoption of this constitution and upon a major vote of the Executive Committee, a Commission of Teachers may be established.[10]

If the original and reconstituted Alliances are considered a single entity, five persons have served as president. The Alliance's first president was Dr. Russell Jackson, who was president for one year, 1971-72. His leadership provided the stability that the superintendents needed to move the group from a collection of individuals primarily interested in their particular needs to a group committed to the resolution of common problems. Dr. Ulysses Byas — 1972-73 — succeeded Jackson as president. Byas was extremely influential as president, and his leadership paved the way for the Alliance's interactions with predominantly white national organizations in education and for the restructuring of the Alliance. Dr. Charles Townsel was elected president of the Alliance in November 1973; his tenure as president coincided with the critical period of transition. Townsel was succeeded by Dr. Deborah C. Wolfe, who served as president until late 1977. Wolfe was a vigorous champion of the Alliance and traveled extensively in its behalf. Joseph Hill followed Wolfe in the presidency and was succeeded by Dr. Ernest Hartzog in November 1979.

During Townsel's presidency, the Alliance developed a membership of more than 500. He commented on the role and future of the Alliance:

> The future exploits of the Alliance in a large measure will be determined by the commitment and dedication of those black educators whose visions of taking in the slack bear on the nexus of the critical need for its existence. I see a viable organization capable of transforming our present dying educational systems into bastions of educational excellence. Educational leaders who manned these systems in the past have failed our youngsters — we must not, and cannot fail them! The future of a free and open society dictates our genuine commitment.[11]

The first meeting of the reconstituted Alliance, with its six commissions, was held in Detroit, Michigan in November 1973. (The commission of teachers was approved by the Alliance in 1975.) The major addresses presented at the conference were delivered by the dean of the College of Urban Affairs at Michigan State University, Dr. Robert Green, and by the only black state superintendent of instruction in Michigan's history, Dr. John Porter. The conference attracted more that 125 participants. A good segment of the conference was devoted to responding to those organizational matters that were related to the dissolution of one Alliance and the initiation of another. Each commission had representatives at their individual sessions.

Today's Challenges

Today, the Alliance has over 1,000 members. NABSE's fifth annual conference, held in Chicago in 1977, attracted the largest number of registered participants. The nearly 2,000 persons gathered in Chicago to explore the theme: "Challenges of the Next Five Years for Black Education." Major presentations were offered by Dr. Mary Berry, Assistant Secretary for Education of the U.S. Office of Education; Lerone Bennett, Jr., Senior Editor of Ebony Magazine; Dr. Ruth Love, Superintendent of Schools in

Oakland, California; Honorable William L. Clay, First Congressional District in St. Louis, Missouri; Reverend Jessie Jackson, National President of People United to Save Humanity (PUSH); Dr. Thomas Minter, Deputy Commissioner, Bureau of Elementary and Secondary Education of the U.S. Office of Education; Dr. Kofi Asare Opoku, Professor of Philosophy and Religion at the Institute of African Studies of the University of Ghana; Dr. Thelma Davidson, Professor of Education at Queens College in New York City; and Dr. John Porter, State Superintendent of Instruction in Michigan.

The seventh annual conference of the Alliance convened in Detroit in November 1979. Dr. Marvin L. Greene was the coordinator for the Detroit conference. The conference theme for 1979 was "International Year of the Child: Focus on Black Youth." Detroit has the largest base of membership and the most active local affiliate of NABSE. The 1979 conference was the best attended in the history of NABSE.

In his speech accepting the presidency of NABSE in 1977, Joseph Hill was highly enthusiastic about the Alliance's potential for service and urged the membership to work for the fulfillment of this potential. In a December 1977 letter to the membership Hill reminded his colleagues that the efforts of the Alliance must be continuous and presented the following as the Alliance's major thrusts for 1978:

1. To form local chapters across this nation so that our total membership can become active in helping NABSE to achieve its goals at the local, state and national levels.

2. To impact on educational legislation in Washington, D.C., and in every state capital in America.

3. To secure 200 life members and to increase our overall membership by at least 2,000 members.

4. To take public positions on those vital issues that impact on the education of black students. NABSE must be the voice for excellence across this nation.

5. To expand and strengthen our relationship with the Urban League, the NAACP, Operation PUSH, SCLC, the Martin Luther King, Jr. Center for Social Change, and all others who are in our struggle for total freedom.

6. To continue our mid-year regional conferences across the nation and also to conduct drive-in workshops to share the expertise of NABSE with our membership.

7. To open a national office in Washington, D.C., by July 1, 1978, with a director and staff on board doing the job for our organization that can only be accomplished with this kind of solid paid staff.

While progress has been made toward the realization of these objectives, Hill's hopes for NABSE were too ambitious in scope. The expansion of the Alliance's membership has not kept pace with the projected goals. The absence of a full-time support staff for NABSE has significantly minimized efforts to coordinate NABSE's resources into a well-planned and executed response to major educational issues and problems. But despite numerous obstacles, the Alliance opened its national headquarters in Washington, D.C. on October 2, 1978.[12]

NABSE is governed by an executive board which is formed from the elected general officers and the elected heads of the seven commissions. In November 1977, the executive board, upon completion of a national search, selected the Alliance's first executive director. The executive director is responsible for directing the administrative, fiscal, clerical, and program operations of the Alliance and is accountable to the executive board of NABSE through the president. The name of the executive director is not revealed because negotiations for his contract have not been finalized. The executive director designate believes NABSE should be able to provide assurances that it has sufficient funding to finance the directorship for a period of not less than two years. Pending the resolution of this matter by the executive board, the services of an interim administrator have been secured. Ms. Dorothy Moore, on leave of absence from the Detroit public schools, supervises the operations of the national office of NABSE. Since Moore's salary is paid from grant funds, it is not certain that such funds will again be available to finance this position.

As an emerging organization representing an array of black educators, who are committed to the insertion of black consciousness into the content and intent of public education for black Americans, NABSE has the potential to make a significant contribution to the advancement of the concepts of equal educational opportunity and quality education. There exists a rich and relatively untapped reservoir of black educators to be recruited and utilized by NABSE. By its very name, the Alliance must represent and serve a membership that is constituted from several disciplines and from various regional areas of the nation. The path to the realization of the service potential of the Alliance has some formidable external and internal roadblocks. Factionalism within each commission and among the seven commissions has to be minimized and appropriately handled. Competition as well as opposition from the entrenched majority-white power groups in education must be successfully engaged. The Alliance must survive its growing pains, and its current members must be willing to invest in a commitment to the future potential of the Alliance.

Focusing primarily on the needs of black school superintendents, the Alliance, with its seven co-equal commissions, has some operational problems that have yet to be resolved. While the Alliance must serve as an effective format for the black superintendents to confront needs that are unique to them in their positions, it must also serve as an effective mechanism for black superintendents to effect a satisfactory organizational relationship with the members of the six other commissions. Currently, the preference among the black superintendents is to spend the greater portion of their time at the meetings of the Alliance in sessions that are devoted to the needs of the Commission of Superintendents. Nevertheless, the membership of the National Alliance of Black Superintendents knew that twenty-nine members could not sustain a viable national organization.

In the end, the black superintendents accepted the fact that the financial gain and the need to communicate with other black educators outweighed their probable loss of influence within the reconstituted Alliance.

The Alliance must effect a disciplined militancy in the discharge of its responsibilities to its members, in particular, and to black Americans, in general. Black communities have been waiting a long time for powerful and responsible black educators to organize an effective force capable of championing, on a national scale, the fundamental right of equal education.

The very nature of power and influence precludes expectations on the part of reformers that those to be reformed will contribute — without pressure being applied — to their own demise or departure. Power has to be extricated by those unwilling to settle for anything less. Neither the black superintendents nor other members of NABSE should permit insignificant issues to divide them in their pursuit of legitimate goals. In the quest for power and influence, the Alliance must guard against the bureaucratic inflictions that often cripple many organizations. The Alliance must not become overly self-protective and operate as an entrenched entity that lobbies primarily for the self-serving interest of its members.

7

The Future of Black School Superintendents

Lowell Thomas, in an article entitled "What About the Future?" said that "to attempt to predict the future is presumptuous, at best — and at worst, an exercise in sheer fantasy."[1] The essential elements of future events and circumstances are shaped by many factors. The factors that will shape the future of public education for black Americans are not all known, and some known factors are not completely understood. The future might hold the following speculations on matters relevant to black superintendents.

> Unless a significant national effort is launched to confront the problem of societal deterioration and institutionalized socioeconomic deprivation, life in America will become progressively worse.

> The student population of many urban school districts will become predominantly black and will represent a greater percentage of students from low-income families.

> As the percentage of students from low-income families increases in urban school districts, a proportionate decline in academic achievement test results in reading and mathematics will occur.

In urban school districts with a high concentration of disadvantaged students, school officials and other school personnel will not have the resources to improve the quality of life and the level of academic achievement without more assistance from other essential service institutions.

Significant increases in the number of black superintendents will reflect continued societal deterioration and increased racial isolation rather than decisions by school boards to comply with the principle of equal employment opportunity.

Blacks and Public Education

Historically, black-directed efforts to improve public education have been aimed at the attitudes and professional competencies of school personnel and at effecting broad reforms in curricular materials. Many people believed the preeminent causes of performance deficiencies among black students could be traced to irrelevant curricular materials, the racist attitudes of boards and school personnel, and inept teachers and administrators. Many blacks believed significant improvements in educational services would not come about until blacks gained a more potent voice in determining the nature of public education.

Because of the efforts of blacks, there have been improvements. The improvements, although limited, did not come easily. Demonstrations and disruptions were frequently the only means of communication left open to blacks seeking redress of grievances. Since the *Brown* decision of the U.S. Supreme Court, lower courts have been forced to impose court-mandated formulas to effect educational opportunity. White-dominated educational organizations were not among those groups supporting affirmative responses by the courts. Often, the education establishment was in the vanguard of the most fierce campaigns of resistance to extending equal educational opportunity.

Many of the overt racist policies and practices that were once an integral part of public education have been eradicated or modified. The increase in the number of black superintendents at all levels is directly attributable to black demands for greater black representation in instructional, supervisory and administrative positions. Textbooks and other curricular materials have shown improvements in the treatment of blacks. Publishing companies now compete to provide the most acceptable materials on the "black experience." Yet these steps, although progressive, have not forged advancements in upgrading the basic learning skills of large numbers of black students.

History provides no support for those who assume that schools can singularly salvage masses of people who have been severely victimized by societal forces designed to ensure their disenfranchisement and deprivation. Deprivation and disenfranchisement are not societal conditions that germinate solely or primarily in the schools. But the institutionalization of deprivation and disenfranchisement has permitted race and socioeconomic status to function as the chief determinants of success or failure in the schools.

Too often in discussions centered around the issue of educational problems and needs of black children from depressed homes, a great deal of time is expended answering the question: Are the majority of black children from the most deprived circumstances innately capable of functioning adequately in a highly technological and scientific society? Such a question is steeped in the myths and half-truths of the doctrine of racism. The legitimate question is: Can black children who are victims of the most severely deprived environments achieve in the schools in proportionate numbers and levels with children from middle- and upper-income families? As long as society permits millions of black children to grow up in environments that impede growth and development, the answer is no.

The inadequacies of socioeconomic support — not poor instructional and related services — put high numbers of black students into the low percentiles on reading and mathematics achievement tests. The alarming deficiencies exhibited by some school personnel in urban schools are not the primary reasons that large numbers of black students are not acquiring the basic skills. What school systems are responding adequately to the educational needs of large concentrations of black and white children from deprived conditions? None! Those school systems that are lauded across the nation for the high quality of their educational services and products either do not serve any meaningful percentage of children from deprived backgrounds or serve them poorly. Public education has never been able to respond adequately to the most disadvantaged of this nation's population. The public schools are not the preeminent infliction of the deprived and the disadvantaged, but the public schools do represent an integration of society's most crippling diseases — indifference, injustice and inequity.

Black Americans learn early that if white Americans were totally free to exercise choice the overwhelming majority would desire neither to live near nor to attend school with blacks. Similarly, low-income black families know that middle-class blacks would prefer to be completely separated from them. In a widely heterogeneous society, schools are remarkably socioeconomically and/or racially homogeneous. Even though low-income black and white families are not satisfied with the public schools, alternatives are practically nonexistent. If middle-class black and white families continue to leave public schools in urban centers at the present rate, public education will become synonymous with poverty.

For the first time in the history of public education, students with serious development problems that stem from their environments constitute the majority of the urban school population. Students from disadvantaged circumstances are staying in school longer. The effects of discrimination and deprivation on growth and development in the schools are not necessarily permanent or beyond remedy. Yet some school systems are almost completely overpowered by the demands upon financial resources and professional expertise needed to provide equal educational opportunity for students afflicted by societal malevolence.

The future of education for the disadvantaged does not indicate any significant improvements. Even in systems that do desire to educate distinctly disadvantaged students the results of their efforts offer little hope for the future. In homogeneous enclaves, the disadvantaged apparently present an unmanageable situation. Politically, busing is not viable. Reducing classes to eight or ten students to minimize professional mediocrity and other modifications seem impractical because of taxpayers' unwillingness to support public education.

Effective educational leadership and "good teaching" will save an undetermined percentage of disadvantaged students from experiencing twelve or thirteen years of inconsequential public education. But public education will be the most productive when the environments for both living and learning are mutually supportive of human growth and development. Black superintendents must extract benefits for their students from the existing circumstances and simultaneously establish a better society.

Black Superintendents

In the future black superintendents can expect to fill positions in school districts with the most demanding challenges. They will inherit little that is worth preserving and much that needs to be changed. Upon acceptance of the responsibilities of executive leadership, superintendents will encounter few people who will publicly support either many of the system's past efforts or many of their proposed recommendations and programs. Black superintendents must engineer improvements at a time when school personnel are well organized and resist change.

With regard to their school boards, black superintendents will often enter a house divided. Differences between black and white factions on school boards and disputes among black members will present serious difficulties to a superintendent looking for a cohesive board-superintendent relationship. Superintendents must produce improvements that curb the imprudent and impetuous whims of some board members. They must maintain the respect of their board while each learns how best to respond to the peculiarities of the relationship and the difficulties of the tasks.

Even though the number of black superintendents will never be as large as the number of white superintendents, there will be an increase. However, this increase will not be linked to any assertive affirmative action program in the education establishment. The expansion in the ranks of black superintendents will be related to whites not wanting to deal with the engrossing problems of cities. Black superintendents will inherit the effects of increased societal deterioration, unabated decline in academic achievement, defficient financial resources, higher percentages of black students and students from low-income families, a black majority or activist blacks on the school board, large numbers of blacks in the community, and demands from vocal blacks in the community.

School districts serving a student population that is at least 40 percent black are confronting weighty problems. When black students constitute less than 50 percent but more than 40 percent, the chance of a black becoming superintendent depends on the level of declining white interest in the schools. Where blacks constitute the majority of the student body and the community, the best opportunity exists for the board's appointment of a black superintendent. In those school systems in which blacks constitute a heavy majority of the student population but the minority in the school district, a black's appointment depends on pressures exerted by the black and white communities. The selection of a black superintendent is often a symbolic assertion of the political strength of blacks in the community. Successful white resistance to demands for a black superintendent symbolizes the continued dominance of white power.

Increases in the number of black superintendents within the next five years should more than double the March 1974 total of 44. Since 1974, black superintendents have been appointed in Detroit, Miami, Kansas City, Memphis, and Richmond. The smaller school systems will constitute the principle source for the expansion in the number of black superintendents. Black superintendents will take the helm in many if not all predominantly black communities.

Regardless of how much public education needs miracle workers, black superintendents are not miracle workers. The blackness of a superintendent will not eradicate deep-rooted problems. Of all the lonely positions in public service, the black superintendent's is the most isolated. Only a few of his or her colleagues are black. The black superintendent cannot expect to gain much in the manner of constructive advice and counsel from his or her white counterparts. To them the very presence of a black superintendent represents a white's displacement. Until demonstrated actions support the contrary, the black superintendent must assume the precautionary position and view white superintendents as willing or unwilling agents in the process of maintaining the subjugation of black Americans.

The black superintendent must effectively confront and construct. His or her efforts must extend well beyond the boundaries of traditional operational areas of the school superintendent. The black superintendent is potentially one of the most influential social forces in a community. Black superintendents must unite with other black leaders in shaping the best possible options for their people. The problems presented are monstrous. Many will fall victim to their own inadequacies and the ingratitude and injustice of those they serve.

The contradictions, conflicts, and calamities that beset school superintendents took their toll on five of the seven black superintendents who were the subjects of this study's capsule examinations. Patterson and Sizemore were terminated following lengthy and expensive public hearings. Byas and Taylor obtained cash settlements from their boards prior to their early departures. Mitchell's termination was imposed without benefit of a dismissal hearing or a financial settlement.

Where are the seven black superintendents today? Sizemore is an associate professor at the University of Pittsburgh in the department of Black Community Education, Research and Development. Patterson is the district superintendent for Community School District Number Nine in the Bronx, New York. Byas is superintendent of schools in Roosevelt, New York. Mitchell is the interim director for Governmental Relations and Grantsmanship in the Oakland Unified School District in Oakland, California. Taylor is completing his doctoral studies at Fordham University. Jackson is retired and still residing in Wilmington, Delaware. Crim is completing his sixth year as superintendent in Atlanta, Georgia.

The experiences of the seven black superintendents, as well as those of others, constitute valuable vignettes of black history. Their strengths and limitations provide future black superintendents with a rich source from which to gain insight and inspiration. Black superintendents are almost exclusively admitted to practice in school systems with well-developed reputations for being reservoirs of unmet needs. White Americans have a capacity for not relating causes to effects when the connection presents a contradiction to an espoused principle of our democracy. As blacks secure superintendencies in other large urban school districts such as New York, New Orleans, Chicago, Cleveland and Philadelphia, they will be cited as the perpetrators of widespread deficiencies in students' basic skills and for their failure to remedy, in mass, the ravages of an uncaring society. Possession of the problem will be grounds for blaming the victim for not being able to salvage the victimized.

As the public forms its judgments regarding the efforts of black superintendents, the black superintendent may receive some comfort from Robert Hutchins' observation about the school administrator's greatest satisfaction. The black superintendent's satisfaction will come "even if he fails from having seen and attempted one of the most difficult works of the mind and one of the most challenging of human tasks."[2]

APPENDICES
NOTES
INDEX

Appendix A

Profiles of
Seven Black
Superintendents

The seven black school superintendents highlighted in these profiles graciously agreed to participate in this very personal and time-consuming endeavor. The superintendents were probed on matters related to their family background, educational preparation, professional experiences, aspirations, hopes, beliefs, and concerns. In their similar and dissimilar ways, each serves as an advocate for the have-nots of this society. Recorded in these profiles is the synthesis of my impressions and interpretations of what was said and written by and about the seven superintendents.

As an educator in a prominent administrative position, the school superintendent makes a great number of decisions that have a significant impact on the quality and scope of public education in the school district. Often these decisions are influenced by the superintendent's sociological values and understandings of the problems and needs of his or her constituency. The superintendent's philosophy of education also influences his or her decisions and actions, but this is greatly shaped by how the superintendent sees society and the people who constitute it. The profiles, it is hoped, will assist efforts to understand more completely the emergence of each of the superintendents and to gain insights into the motivating forces behind their commitments and actions as school superintendents.

ULYSSES BYAS
Macon County, Alabama

In the cluttered and unpretentious office of Ulysses Byas sat a small plaque on the window ledge directly behind his desk with an inscription that is frequently quoted by Byas: "We have done so much with so little for so long we think that we could do anything at all in no time flat." Byas has set for himself a very demanding code of professional standards and integrity. He is not a large man physically, but he has an intellectual capacity and curiosity that produce an extraordinary impression of energy. His dress is conservative, with the accent placed on small bow ties. He discouraged any ceremonial difference that might be accorded to him as superintendent. At times, he can be very blunt with friends and foes. Among black superintendents, he is highly respected and well liked.

Byas conveys a spirit of self-assurance. This self-confidence has been developed from years of successfully confronting demanding responsibilities and difficult circumstances. His colleagues have repeatedly selected him for leadership positions in education at the local, state, and national levels. Byas served for two very important years as the president of the National Alliance of Black School Superintendents. Few persons can match his skill at producing intellectually stimulating — and witty — statements. His usage of the English language emphasizes purpose and perception while adhering to the universal guidelines for proper grammar. He stated:

> Some people do not like my speech. I have experienced a lot of intolerance in systems in which I have worked because people did not like my speech. I tell people that they are probably more responsible for how I talk than I am. Growing up in the society in which I was raised, you talked like most of the folk around you talked. And I talked like most of the folk around me talked. If anyone is displeased over that, then they have to stand in front of a mirror and work with what they see. I do not violate the rules of the King's English as far as subject and verb are concerned. How it comes out otherwise is someone else's problem.[1]

As with many black Americans born in 1924, Byas was born in the South and in extreme poverty. He was born in Macon, Georgia, the second child in a family of eight children. For most of his early life, there was no man in the home: "I owe my existence to my mother, who had seven years of schooling." His mother constantly reminded the children of the importance of education. During his first year in high school, his mother remarried. "My stepfather is still living and strong in his eighties, and he is one of the finest men that I have ever had the pleasure of knowing."

His public school experiences can best be described as up and down. He made the honor roll repeatedly in elementary school. He missed one year when his mother withdrew him from school after viewing the bruises that he had received from a beating inflicted by a teacher. Later, he dropped out of high school because of his desire to contribute to the family's limited financial resources, and because of his struggle with Latin. He took a job in a drugstore. Regarding his bout with Latin, he recalled:

> My first year at Hudson High School, an industrial school, I dropped out. My very first day in school is one that I shall never forget. I was assigned to the Latin teacher as a homeroom class. She had the book opened to the first Latin lesson. She announced that first day that since we didn't know any Latin we didn't have anything to talk about. She proceeded to conjugate the verb *amo*. Frankly, I didn't give a damn whether or not the verb ever got conjugated.

Delivering packages each day at the drugstore, for fifteen hours a day, did not prove either financially rewarding or occupationally stimulating. Of the $4.50 that he earned each week, his mother took $2.50 and the rest was consumed in the purchase of various items of "junk." "I learned from that lesson that there was something tougher than Latin." He returned to school only to drop out once again to enlist in the Army. The Army turned him down for allegedly being physically unfit for service. He returned to Hudson High School to get his diploma. He perceived high school as a place where one ought to learn something that would help one get a job. His favorite subject was industrial arts. In the shop class, he developed his skills as a carpenter. Upon his graduation, he had hoped that he would be able to pursue a successful career as a carpenter. After graduation in 1943, he was drafted into the Navy and served honorably as an officer's cook for two and one-half years. Somehow the advent of a war had reconciled the previous physical unreadiness that the Army had discovered in him when he sought to enlist.

Leaving the Navy in 1946, he headed for "up South," to New York City, to get one of those "good jobs" in the East. In search of employment as a carpenter, he found people nice, but the answer to his job inquiries was usually no. The work he did get paid less than he was able to earn in the South. Frustrated, he decided to head back to the South because "the promise of the promised land was unpromising." Upon his return to the South, he learned that several of his friends were enrolling at Fort Valley State College, twenty-five miles south of Ma-

con, Georgia. Utilizing the G.I. Bill and his skills as a carpenter and cook
to finance his education and living expenses, he entered Fort Valley in
March 1947. Carpentry, not college, had been the focus of his career
plans, but unemployment made college an alternative.

He had never developed any strong interest in going to college because he saw no practical way of overcoming the financial burden of a
college education. College was now a good choice, since there was no
promising employment possibility. At Fort Valley, he majored in social
studies. He was a good student, making the honor roll most semesters.
In the summer of 1950 he graduated from college. The student body
elected him the president of his senior class.

A superintendent from a nearby school district offered him a job as a
principal. Practice teaching had been his only prior experience in the
education profession. Always quick to assess an opportunity, he decided that, if he were good enough to be offered a principalship without
any prior professional experience, then he ought to secure some professional training in educational administration. Also, the principalship
would have netted him less than that which he had received from the
G.I. Bill and his part-time carpentry work. He sent out numerous appli-
cations to various colleges of education for admission to their master's
degree programs in education administration.

Columbia University responded positively to his application for admission. He moved to New York City once again and began work on his
master's in educational administration at Teachers College. Some of his
friends had cautioned him not to go to Teachers College. They felt that
his lack of experience in educational administration — and the fact that
he was a black from the South — would be used unjustly against him.
But Byas' confidence was intact. He stated:

> I don't doubt myself. I know in my own mind's eye that a major
> part of the solution to any problem is the identification of the
> problem. Once one is able to identify the problem, he has part of
> the solution because the identification process points to the
> direction of the solution. There is no problem without a solution.
> When we don't come up with a solution, it means that we have
> not looked at the right mix. The responsibility for coming up
> with the right mix rests with the persons faced most immediately
> with the problem.

At Teachers College, he was admitted with a stipulation that a certain
number of deficiency points be assigned to him to fill the gaps in his
prior preparation. He accepted the deficiency points with the notion

that, if his academic work were good, a number of the deficiency points would be dropped. While at Teachers College, he committed himself almost totally to two forms of work: academic work and gainful employment. He recalled:

> I lived studying for five and one-half days per week. I immediately got a job baking breakfast pastries at the cafeteria at Columbia University. I opened that facility at 4:30 A.M. in the morning, and I did not leave until the library closed at night at 10:30 P.M.
>
> From Monday morning at 4:30 A.M. to Saturday at 12:00 P.M. schooling was the only thing that I participated in — schooling and working to support the schooling. I had a most profitable year. Incidentally, I was an honor-roll student in undergraduate school and my grades at Teachers College were better than in my undergraduate major.

Upon completion of the master's in education administration at Teachers College, he had an offer to go to Elberton, Georgia to teach. His friends in the North could not understand why he would want to return to the South. He responded, in typical fashion: "I would go to hell for $5,000." He did not quite get his $5,000, but the professional experience was a thoroughly enjoyable one with a special fringe benefit:

> Also coming to work in that town for the first time was a young lady who had a couple of degrees in music and who had studied at Julliard. She was employed to teach public school music. I carried my students up to her for music lessons, and I started dating the music teacher. In a few months we solidified the relationship. At the end of the first year, we got married.
>
> Our principal had sort of a paternalistic, fatherly image and he encouraged me to go up and take that lady out. Later, he confessed that he was concerned about keeping her in the community. If she did not have an adequate male escort, he was afraid that she might leave him. He said he did the wrong thing because after two years I left him and took his music teacher away.

With his bride, he moved to Douglasville, Georgia, to assume a principalship. He remained in Douglasville until 1957. His next position was to hold him longer than any other. In 1957, he accepted the principalship of E. E. Butler Senior High in Gainesville, Georgia. At Butler he developed a statewide reputation as an outstanding school administrator. The desegregation movement in the South was to cost him his principalship. During this tenure, he served for two years as state president of the High School Principals' Organization. After eleven years of distinguished service to the Gainesville community he resigned. Byas had been informed that he was not to be named principal of the desegregated and consolidated black and white high schools. His resignation was a protest against what he considered to be an injustice. The school system was prepared to offer him the token position of assistant superintendent rather than place an exceptionally qualified black principal in a desegregated high school.

An editorial in the *Daily Times* of Gainesville in 1968 commended Byas' expertise and contribution, but it did not give him a clear-cut endorsement for the principalship of the desegregated high school. In part, the editorial stated:

> So Mr. Byas, who has played a leading role in race-relations improvement, has served his people and his town well and who is now about to join in eliminating two other segregated institutions, isn't sure of his own future. We hope the Gainesville school system continues to use his talents effectively, although the decision as to exactly how to do so is some eighteen months away.[2]

For Byas, this incident remains a bitter recollection. Commenting on the counter-offer made to him by the superintendent of schools in Gainesville, Byas stated:

> He came to me and informed me that two years hence they were going to put the two high schools together. There were only two high schools in the system. He was thinking about recommending that I be named an assistant superintendent. Well, I had enough sense to know that our school system had only nine schools. We already had an assistant superintendent and a superintendent. We did not need a superintendent for every three schools.
>
> I said to him that I was a high-school principal, and that I thought that I was the damn best high-school principal in the state. In answer to his statement that this would be a promotion, I had to say to him that a promotion was how the worker perceived it. Since he was thinking like the rest of the people, as soon as I could write him an acceptable letter of resignation he would have it on his desk. My only regret is that it took me six seconds to tell him that.

After his resignation as principal, he became the assistant executive secretary for the 12,000 members of the Georgia Teachers and Education Association, the all-black component of the state's National Education Association affiliate. Prior to his appointment, Byas had served as the organization's president. He admits that the organization demonstrated its empathy for his situation when it created a position for him. About two years later, Georgia's all-white and all-black NEA affiliates merged. He played a major role in making certain that the black affiliate would gain as much as it would lose in the merger. In 1970, he became the director of Administration and Special Services for the newly formed and racially integrated 30,000-member Georgia Association of Educators. Shortly after he assumed his new duties and responsibilities, his name was sent to the Macon County, Alabama Board of Education as an educator deserving serious consideration for the vacant superintendency. In July 1970, he departed Atlanta for Macon County and the superintendency.

He took the superintendency because he believed that if one had some ideas and opinions about where a school system ought to go then one should try to put them into practice. The superintendency offered the only vehicle for the implementation of some of his beliefs. He reflected on how his name came before the Macon County Board of Education and why he agreed to accept the position:

> The dean of the School of Education had introduced my name to some board members. The dean and I had served on the board of directors of an educational corporation — a private corporation. As a result of his introduction of my name, the board contacted me in Atlanta and it invited me to come down for an interview. I spent two hours talking with the board. I went back to Atlanta. They offered me the position. I decided to take it without looking at the problems. In retrospect, it was the best damn decision that I ever made. No one in his right mind would have come to Macon County school system knowing the scope of the problem.

Opposition to Byas' appointment was presented by an undetermined number of school employees. Just prior to his appointment, he received a telegram that urged him not to accept the appointment because of the strong support for the acting superintendent. The telegram declared that the acting superintendent "is doing an admirable job as acting superintendent, although he was exploited to assume the role. He has come through the ranks, and he is the man our people really want and pledge to support as superintendent."[3]

The telegram was signed: all teachers, principals, central-office personnel, bus drivers. Byas, of course, did not heed the advice that was so
generously given. He was not disturbed by the contents of the telegram.
Since the persons sending the telegram did not know him as an individual, he felt that their recommendation was not based on personal
knowledge of his qualifications. He stated:

> This was a statement in support of another person, and that's
> all. For anyone to read into it that some other person would not be
> supported, if selected, I knew would be a mistake. Time and
> circumstances have proven this to be correct. Rapport and
> leadership are the responsibility of those in supervisory
> positions. When persons do not cooperate, then the leadership
> did not appropriately initiate such cooperation. I must say that to
> the extent that I have really wanted cooperation our personnel
> have been real professionals. The many innovations and changes
> which have been generated during the past four years could not
> have been accomplished without the help of some of the very fine
> people in the system. In the months and years ahead we will be
> expecting even more as we get deeper into the problems of low
> achievement plaguing many of our students. To say the least, I
> am encouraged!

ALONZO CRIM
Atlanta, Georgia

Born in Chicago, Illinois on October 1, 1928, Alonzo Crim was the
youngest of three children. Crim believes that his family experiences
during the formative years of his life lacked some essential ingredients.
He is an intensely private individual who at times exhibits a stubborn
independence and an uncompromising personal pride. The following
comments by Crim provide critical insights into his impressions of
childhood:

> My first recollection as a child was kneeling at my mother's
> bed praying because we all thought that she was going to die.
>   Strangely enough, I felt a sense of happiness with my
> childhood; yet I also felt a sense of rejection. Because of my
> mother's illnesses, my brother was more or less responsible
> for raising me.
>   My father was a very rigid person. He worked nights most
> of my early years. So I did not get to know him very well. He

represented that guy that was going to punish me — which
he did with great regularity. I have come to know and to
appreciate my father more as an adult than I did as a child.
My father is a very fine man. I love him dearly now, but I did
not love him as a boy.[4]

Dissatisfied with the quality of his personal relationships with his
family, he sought companionship outside the family to compensate for
the perceived inadequacies of his family relationships. During his high
school days, he became active in the first black Hi-Y Club in Chicago.
This experience and his personal contact with the adult leader of the
club left an unforgettable impression on him.

> I joined the first black Hi-Y Club in Chicago. A group of
> young fellows — all of whom have become successful in one
> way or the other. It was just one of those unusual collections
> of young men. We worked with an exceptional YMCA
> secretary, Lawrence Burr. He moved us to do a lot of things.
> It was sort of a surrogate father-son relationship that I had
> never experienced. He saw that he had a talented group of
> young men and he pushed us all to higher academic
> achievement and athletic excellence. We became a very
> exclusive group of all poor boys.
> Girls were attracted to us. A different kind of attention was
> showered on me at that time. I had nothing to do with girls
> up to this point, but I now had four girl friends. It all came
> together. I did not need family. This was the period in which
> my family turned to me, but the relationship, at that time,
> had not been established as it has subsequent to that period.

He worked during high school and established economic independence from his parents. Crim emphasizes the fact that he has worked
hard for everything that he has received: "Nothing was ever given to
me." Yet, when he was offered a scholarship to attend Harvard, he
refused the scholarship. He viewed it as a black scholarship, and thus it
was unacceptable to him. Crim has always felt the need to prove that he
could compete successfully with anyone. His brother and sister were
excellent students in high school, and they provided the academic
achievement models for him. He believes that he was never given
appropriate recognition within the family for his own quality performance in school: "I was smart and highly motivated. My mother frequently compared me with my brother and sister, both of whom were

exceptionally bright in terms of school. They could do school work with such great ease. I was always dragging in the rear. But with my own peers, I was at the top of the class."

Crim received a bachelor's degree in sociology and history from Roosevelt University in Chicago. He had intended to use the degree to launch a career in social work; for monetary reasons, however, he passed up these career aspirations. He became, in his words, " a very successful insurance salesman." Seeking a change of environment, he and his wife left for Los Angeles. Once in Los Angeles, he again found employment as an insurance salesman. His wife's dislike for Los Angeles brought him back to Chicago. At this time, he decided to enter the education profession. Working as a "cracker jack" vacuum cleaner salesman and at other jobs, he financed his course of study at Chicago Teachers College. In 1954, he received his teaching certificate. From 1954 to 1963, Crim taught math and science in the seventh and eighth grades. In 1958, he received his master's degree in education — and twin daughters.

In 1961, he took the principal's examination, which he passed. His first principalship came in 1963, when he was appointed principal of the Whittier Elementary School. From Whittier, he was promoted to principal for the Adult Education Center in 1965. In September 1965, Crim was appointed principal of Wendell Phillips High School. He remained in this position until he took a leave of absence, in 1967, to attend Harvard University. Crim had made up his mind when he got his master's that he was going to get a doctorate in education. His academic work at Harvard marked the first time he had ever attended school on a full-time basis without being employed full-time. His home was sold to provide part of his living and educational expenses. The refusal to accept the scholarship because it was judged to be a "black" scholarship might have helped his pride, but it did not reduce his financial needs.

Crim credits his academic success at Harvard as a key factor in the elimination of many of his agonizing doubts about his ability to respond in an above-average manner to rigorous intellectual demands. He reflected:

> I had great doubts about my academic ability prior to going to Harvard. By gaining the academic credentials at Harvard, I knew that I could compete with some of the brightest guys on the scene and compete effectively. The experience and success at Harvard turned my life around.
>
> The experience at Harvard was the most dramatic in my life

and the most critical period of my life. They saw things in me at Harvard that I did not see in myself.

Just before he completed his course work at Harvard, he was promoted to district superintendent in Chicago. He feels that his doctoral advisor, Dr. Herold Hunt, played a strong role in his obtaining the promotion. Hunt had been the former superintendent of schools in Chicago, and his executive assistant at the time was James Redmond. Redmond promoted Crim to district superintendent; he remained in this position for less than a year. In 1969, he accepted the superintendency of the Compton Union High School District in Compton, California. This school district was merged with the Compton Unified School District in 1970. At Compton he developed a reputation for his involvement of the community in school affairs. He remained at Compton as superintendent four years, before his move to Atlanta, Georgia.

Crim, while a very complex individual, is a relatively easy person with whom to interact. He cannot be categorized as either a radical or a conservative. His quiet demeanor provides a deceptive cover for an individual who, on some matters, can be intensely militant. The more one observes him in action the greater the respect one gains for Crim the superintendent. The following observation by a colleague illustrates this point:

> He is tough. . . . You do not get that impression from looking at him. You get the impression that his mind is racing ahead, but he is listening. When he has gotten enough input, the decision is his.
>
> Dr. Crim is not a flamboyant man, a table pounder. . . . He is not an outstanding orator, but he is articulate and direct — an easy man to communicate with.[5]

Crim's greatest struggle through the years has been an internal affair involving the two Alonzo Crims — the Crim who preferred the more introverted life and who constantly conducted an extensive program of self-criticism and the Crim who sought a more extroverted approach to life and who had full confidence in his abilities and his future. Today Crim is not an extrovert, but he is also not an abnormally introverted individual. While he still yearns for more periods of solitude to engage in meaningful self-exploration, he responds well to large groups in public meetings. His personality is tranformed as he moves from small- to large-group settings and from private to public meetings. In his presentations before large groups, he is much more animated. He admits that the large-group sessions tend to bring out the best in him.

Crim is confident that the board selected the right person. He is also confident that he will be successful as an educational leader in Atlanta. He came to Atlanta to be interviewed for the vacant superintendency with the knowledge that his contract as superintendent of schools in Compton, California was going to be renewed by his board of education and with the confidence that he had the necessary professional skills and personality to effect a coalition of citizens and professionals behind his administration of the schools in Atlanta. "I knew that I was good. The board of education was so open that I was able to conduct the interview myself. I gave them the questions during the interview to ask me." With regard to his chances for survival and success as a superintendent in Atlanta, Crim offered the following comments:

> I know that we can deliver. I must express gratitude to my predecessor. He had put together a good school system. What needs to be done now is to effect a good management system in order to bring all of the components together.
>
> Some people in Atlanta call me an optimist; they feel that I ought to give up because they feel that the problems are too severe. What they cannot see or feel is that the people down on Auburn Avenue are still hopeful. That is my edge. That to me is the black consciousness of being a superintendent. That I can relate to that glimmer of hope. I hope I can maximize that hope by bringing visible evidence of accomplishments for them.

Barbara Sizemore, former superintendent of the Washington, D.C. public schools, and Alonzo Crim are very close friends. Yet they are in some important ways as dissimilar as two good friends and prominent educators can be. His comments on Sizemore document his deep admiration for a friend, but they also reveal some valuable insights into both Sizemore and Crim. He observed:

> Barbara and I were appointed on the very same day as principals. When I went to the Adult School she remained at the elementary school. Then we were appointed secondary-school principals at the same time to schools which were only a few blocks from each other. We used to hold one another's hands with regard to the kinds of problems that we confronted.
>
> We are very different personalities but complementary ones. Professionally, Barbara gave me courage, and I gave her insights and patience. Barbara and I have spent many hours together. We are really very close friends. We can cry together as well as laugh together.

> One of the reasons that I have found Barbara so intriguing is her all-encompassing concern for people. The role that Barbra Streisand plays in the movie *The Way We Were* is Barbara.
> Barbara impresses me as being one of the most secure persons that I have ever known. She never really worries about herself. Barbara in her way is brilliant. She has an intuition in terms of people that is just astonishing. She was always being knocked around and coming back like a terrier, constantly focusing on a problem and coming back with creative solutions.
> Barbara is just as articulate with a small group as she is with a large group.

Crim believes that he has reached that state in life in which most of the inner conflicts that used to disturb him have been resolved or arrested. He accepted the superintendency in Atlanta with quiet but firm confidence in his professional capacity to make a contribution. Crim is not a radical educator, but he did not come to Atlanta just for the purpose of adding another superintendency to his résumé. In his pursuit of educational progress in Atlanta, he resists being manipulated unduly by either his board of education or by groups of citizens. His commitment is to be his own man in the presentation of recommendations to the board and to exercise his best professional judgment in the assessment and resolution of needs.

BARBARA SIZEMORE
Washington, D.C.

"Barbara is ready for Washington, but is Washington ready for Barbara?" This statement was made by a person who knew Mrs. Sizemore in Chicago. In response to this statement, she observed: "I think that they were taking the political postures which were exhibited at the termination of the Woodlawn Project and saying that the political structure in Washington will not tolerate that kind of controversy."[6] Mrs. Sizemore's activities while in Chicago had generated too much controversy for her arrival in Washington not to be greeted by some local controversy. She is unique, not only as a personality but as a superintendent. As a result of a 7-to-3 vote and one abstention by the D.C. Board of Education, Sizemore became the only black female superintendent. The three votes not in her favor were cast by three of the four white members of the board. The one abstention was from a black board member. Two board members felt so strongly about their votes that they issued rather lengthy statements to their predominantly black constituencies, providing a rationale for their opposing votes. The local newspapers placed a disproportionate emphasis on negative comments about the new superintendent. A reporter was even dispatched to Chicago to dig up information on Sizemore. The overall response to her appointment was positive, especially among those blacks who were in the most desperate need of the benefits of educational reform.

Alonzo Crim offered the following comment about Sizemore: "Barbara has always been brilliant and controversial."[7]

Did she modify her behavior after becoming superintendent? Sizemore believed that she had:

> My behavior has been modified by my experiences in the Woodlawn Experimental School Project so that the kind of behavior that I exhibited in Chicago would not be the kind of behavior that I would do here. I would not even do it again in Chicago. I think that rhetoric is unnecessary if it forewarns because then when you come up the pike, everybody knows that you are coming.
>
> If you put your hand on a stove that is hot, and you take it off and it hurts, you don't do it again. You learn different ways of doing things. If I want something to do with that hot stove, I do it in a different way. I would put something between my hand and that stove. It does not mean that I don't continue using the stove to try to accomplish my objectives. I just do it in a different way. I do not intend to make certain mistakes again, but I do intend to pursue the same objectives.

When she speaks, her words flow steadily and quite often very eloquently. In conversation, she quickly organizes her responses, and they are delivered in a manner that reveals her skill at giving sequentially ordered statements on or explorations of a topic or an issue. Sizemore has a full reservoir of views and opinions on many matters. The shock of some of her statements is reduced significantly when her supportive definitions and clarifications are provided. In response to the inquiry as to whether or not she thinks that she is often misunderstood, Sizemore replied:

> I think that it happens often. It happens often because if I take a position, it is usually an analytical position which means that I go to the definition. I take the definition and say that if you are saying this, what you are really saying is X, Y, and Z. It seems to

me that what we should do is A, B, and C. But people bring up X, Y, and Z.

I think that on some issues I am controversial. I am controversial on the issue of women's participation in the society. I am controversial on the issue of integration. I think that I am radical on the issue of education. I am asking for a great change in the structure of education. I would say that this is radical if you are using the political definition of a radical. I am not talking about communism or socialism or anything like that. I am talking about using change as the important variable.

Sizemore is an advocacy-motivated individual: "I have always been an activist. That is the kind of person my mother is. I would say that I have been a good student of my mother's behavior." Despite the steady flow of concepts that readily emerge when she speaks, Sizemore zealously guards her private life. She has a reputation — well earned — as an extremely outgoing individual who has a ready response on almost any subject. A much deeper look suggests that she meets people very well but relates closely to very few people. She is quick to initiate efforts to extend the personal contact of Barbara Sizemore, the advocate, but there is a resistance on her part to any attempts by outsiders to penetrate the protective shield to her inner self. One staff member in the school system stated with some degree of puzzlement: "I do not know the lady yet!" Sizemore admits that she is a loner: "I belong to me. I am a loner. My confidant is my mother. My mother is the only person living who really knows me. As much of me as anybody is going to know."

Sizemore was born in Chicago, Illinois during the Depression, on December 17, 1927. She was the only child in a family that was economically poor but intellectually stimulating. Her mother and father had both attended college, but they were not able to secure employment in their professional areas of preparation. With her parents unable to find employment, the family returned to Terre Haute, Indiana when she was six months old. They remained in Terre Haute until she was in third grade. Again in search of employment, the family moved, this time to Evanston, Illinois, for a short stay. The period between fourth grade and her senior year in high school was spent in Terre Haute. Both parents secured employment in 1943 at the Great Lakes Naval Training Station, near Chicago. The family relocated once again in Evanston. When she was eight, her father died. Her mother remained single for four years.

Her recollections of childhood are pleasant for the most part, but there was a period in her formative years which she would just as soon forget:

I was the only child in a family of adults. Looking at the interim period when my mother was single — from eight to twelve years old — I lived with my mother, my grandmother, her other brother, and his wife. I lived with a family of adults, and I was the only child there. Everybody taught me all of the time. I was their preoccupation.

I remember my childhood as pleasant until age twelve. I think that if anyone was to ask me if I would want to relive my life, I would say yes, but you can skip the period from age twelve to nineteen. The sexist nature of the society imposed all kinds of stringent rules on the behavior of women that strained their creativity and stifled their individuality.

In January 1944 she graduated from high school and enrolled at Northwestern University. A classical-language scholar in college, she wanted to be a translator at the United Nations. Sizemore was an exceptional student both in the public schools and in college. She commented:

I have always been a very good student. I was number one in my high school graduating class.

My mother was a school teacher who was denied the right to teach school because of the sexist policies of the Depression years which said that if you were married you could not teach, but she continued to teach me.

Her pursuit of employment with the United Nations was not successful, so she began her teaching career as a substitute teacher in Chicago in 1947. At that time the Chicago system gave exclusive direct entrance for full-time employment only to graduates of the Chicago Teachers College. She passed the teachers' examination and was given her first regular teaching assignment in 1950. This assignment was filled with unpleasantries and confrontations. In her view, the principal was "...a racist from Texas who was determined that she was going to show niggers their place. One obsession that she had was that black people were not patriotic."

The principal directed that there were to be daily marches around the school: "A march around the school with drums and bugles and a return to the room to sing the Star Spangled Banner." Sizemore reluctantly complied with this directive, but after four or five days of compliance, she refused. This refusal led to a series of efforts to have her marked unsatisfactory during her probationary period. She survived the attempts to give her an unsatisfactory rating, but the struggle between principal and teacher continued. "I applied for a transfer. The pressure from this principal was so great that I found myself spending my time and energy responding to her rather than to the students." The situation deteriorated to the point that the personnel department was informed that she was teaching Communism: "They investigated me for two and one-half years, but they did not find anything. There was nothing to find out."

The desired transfer finally came through. The experience of her next teaching assignment was just the opposite of that of her previous assignment. The assignment at Gillespie Elementary School was a "thrilling" experience that was terminated when she was bumped from the staff because of a personnel reduction. She was transferred to Drew Elementary School, where Byron Minor was the principal. Minor, according to Mrs. Sizemore, provided the kind of leadership that resulted in the development of an excellent staff and a quality educational program. He encouraged her to pursue a career as a school administrator. Sizemore recalls: "He was just an ideal principal. He was the kind of principal that everybody wishes that they had. It was the happiest period in my career as a teacher."

Sizemore took the principal's examination and passed it in 1961. Her promotion to principal came in 1963. This first principalship was to have a great impact on her thinking: "Most of the things that I think should be done started in that school." Reluctantly she departed the Anton Dvorak School, but she had been offered the opportunity to become a secondary school principal. She viewed a secondary school principalship as a stepping stone to eventual promotion to district superintendent. The secondary school facility was a converted elementary school put into service to appease certain community protests. She departed this principalship in 1967 to enroll full time at the University of Chicago; from 1967 to 1969, she directed her efforts to her doctoral program. Sizemore has not yet completed the final requirement for her doctorate, the dissertation. She commented:

> Those people want to help me to get my Ph.D. so bad that they don't know what to do. Those people would give it to me if I would complete the requirement. I cannot get worked up about it because there is really nothing that a Ph.D. can do for me. I am going to do it, but I can do it when I retire.

She returned to the Chicago public schools as the director of the Woodlawn Experimental Schools Project. The Woodlawn Project was a highly innovative education program which sought to bring the community and the school together to form a partnership in the decision-making process in public education. "I was selected by the people and not the Chicago public schools." It was her directorship of this project that lifted her name into the national scene. Sizemore's efforts at Woodlawn also escalated the resentment against her, the controversial advocate of the community. Sizemore believed her role as director of the project was to bring parents, staff, and the rest of the community together to promote change for the betterment of the community. She believed the school personnel ought to be advocates for the community rather than the community's adversaries. She remained in this assignment until the funding period terminated. After a short period as a proposal development officer in the central office, she left Chicago. Sizemore came to Washington, D.C. in February 1973 as the associate secretary for the American Association of School Administrators (AASA). She became the highest-ranking black in the most prestigious organization for school administrators in the nation. Her tenure with the AASA was also limited. Sizemore then took on the greatest challenge of her career, the superintendency of the D.C. public schools.

Asked why she sought and accepted the superintendency in the District, which has a national reputation among professional school administrators as being one of the most complex and difficult systems to manage in America, she declared:

> The student populations of urban school systems most
> accurately reflect the cultural and ethnic diversity of our
> bigger society. If it could but be demonstrated that an
> institution is capable of being responsible to all individuals
> while respecting their differences, then bigger strides can be
> made toward making our society a more just one. This system
> is without a doubt complex.

The management of the D.C. public schools was certainly complex. Between 1967 and 1973, four superintendents and two interim superintendents had provided the tenuous executive leadership for the system. The school system is the largest of the predominantly black systems in America. Sizemore came equipped with an exceptional mind, some very definite ideas about how public education should work, and an unquestionable commitment to improving the quality of living in a community through change in the conduct of public education. The following comments by Sizemore provide further insight into this dynamic activist, who sat in one of the hottest seats in public school administration:

I think that all black people are militant. I defined militant as meaning resistant to oppressive forces. Now, people fight back in different ways. I believe that Booker T. Washington was a militant.

At a time when most blacks were talking about integration, I was talking about separatism. At a time when most blacks were trying to fit into the white capitalistic structure, by becoming a part of the pieces, I was advocating that they build a route for themselves like other people do.

I want to find out why we cannot educate poor people, and why we cannot educate black people who are poor. I want to know why we cannot do that. I have a better sense of my priorities now than I did in Chicago. I had a number of things that I was trying to liberate all the black people from in Chicago. I was trying to get them to see Mayor Daley for what he really was. I was trying to get the churches responsive to the black community. I had a whole repertory of goals. I am concentrating on a single area while in Washington — public education. Our future as a people and nation is in the future of our children. If there is a solution, that is where it rests.

I think that what I am arguing educationally is good for all kids. Multi-age and multi-level grouping is good for anybody's kids. Multi-cultural and multi-lingual education is good for anybody's kids. The restructuring of the age-graded process so that kids can grow according to their own rates is good for anybody's kids. Changing the structure of history so that it accommodates the child's understanding that all people started at year X and that all people are here at year Y and that all people have cultures and accomplishments is good for anybody's kids. The things that I am arguing for are good for all children and nobody has been able to say that they are not.

ROLAND PATTERSON
Baltimore, Maryland

Of Roland Patterson, one may say that he is a "big man" for whom nature has seen fit to house exceptional skills and relentless drive in a rather diminutive physical structure. At five feet four inches, he looks more like a classical scholar in one of the nation's prestigious universities than the extremely forceful school superintendent he was in one of the nation's largest school systems. Patterson does not relax often, and his manner tends to give a much sterner impression than is truly representative of the man. When he took on the massive responsibility of Baltimore's schools he frequently became so engulfed with the burdens of the tasks inherent in his office that he was often viewed by others as a distant person or an extremely intense individual. Even those who were his most fierce supporters were concerned about the false perceptions that circulated widely about him. The comment that follows is a good illustration of the respect — and bewilderment — that he stimulates:

> He is an intense person. He is work-oriented. I feel comfortable with him, but I hold him in awe. He is all business during business hours, but he has a sense of humor. I am proud to work with that man. He is a helluva taskmaster.[8]

Patterson is sensitive to the fact that some people find him distant, even difficult, in the area of human relations, but while recognizing that he is not necessarily the easiest person with whom to relate, he does not consider himself to be a negative person. He offered the following self-analysis:

> It is not that I do not intend to extend myself. But I am not the kind of man who finds it very comfortable to call another on the phone and ask him out for a drink because I want him to do something for me. If that is negative or introverted, then in that sense, I am an introvert.
>
> In some situations, I can be very easygoing, but I am at the same time a driving kind of person. I tend more to extroversion than to introversion. I expect that in the opinion of some, I am a little difficult to meet and to get close to, yet there are many people who find it fairly easy to relate to me.
>
> I really do not get overly annoyed at people. However, it irritates me when people become dogmatic and make concrete statements which they profess to be facts when I know that such are opinions resulting from a lack of knowledge. But, frankly speaking, I really do not get angered easily.[9]

Patterson rejects being confined to descriptive labels such as militant, conservative, or extremist. "What do militant and conservative mean?

In some instances, I am militant and in some instances people would call me a moderate and in others a conservative. My reactions and actions are determined by the parameters of a situation." On the subject of the delivery of educational programs and services to the students of the Baltimore City public schools, Patterson was militant in his persistence that the have-nots of that community could learn. "If young people receive the kind of respect and treatment that adults demand for themselves, then many things about how and what students learn can be changed. Much depends on changing attitudes in the adult population."

Patterson did not spare himself in his quest to make equality of educational opportunity a reality in Baltimore City. He stated:

> People know that what I say I am going to do, I have done. Most people know that I have never backed off a major issue irrespective of the effect it might have on my tenure in the superintendency. I have attempted never to put myself in a position in which I might be compromised, that is, never to give up my principles for personal gain. This is a kind of commitment on my part which is difficult for many people to appreciate.
>
> I believe that there is only a short period of time in which to solve a lot of problems, problems which can be solved. The mistake which has been made in the past is that we have listened to a lot of theory and pursued many hypotheses which have been printed in books, most of which are based on a purely theoretical framework developed out of any real context. I just don't think that the hypotheses are practical or applicable in so many instances.
>
> I believe that if one persevered and understood where he was going, he could change public education so that it would become meaningful for everybody. Right now, it is not so good for blacks. I think that in a big school system like this there is no reason for the majority of black youngsters to have deficiencies in reading and math. It has something to do with the availability of resources, but a great deal to do with techniques, skills, and understandings on the part of adults.

When asked to respond to the implications of black consciousness in his administration of the schools in Baltimore City, Patterson said:

> Equality of educational opportunity is a goal more often given lip service than positive action. We in the school

system must understand the inequalities in order to eradicate them. This demands a black consciousness as well as a white, red, brown, or yellow consciousness.

This consciousness also helps in responding to many of the issues with which the community confronts us. Insights into the motivating forces behind partisan demands are a part of this.

I refuse to preside over a system that continues to do disservice to any group. I know that I am the superintendent for *all* of the students in our schools.

Roland Patterson was born on September 22, 1928 in the Anacostia section of Washington, D.C. His was a large family — three girls and eight boys. His father worked part time for himself and full time as a machinist for the Washington Navy Yard. "We did not realize it then, but each of us would say now that our father had a tremendous impact on our lives in the sense of being task oriented." His father completed the eighth grade. "He was what we think of as a self-educated man. We looked upon our father as the best-educated person in the family." By most standards the family was poor, but not destitute. "As a family, we were reasonably close, but as each member grew older, we were close when one of us got into trouble. I think that each person in our family was rather aggressive and independent. That militated against our being a very close-knit family."

With regard to city planning, the Anacostia section of Washington has historically received inadequate treatment. At the time of Patterson's birth, Washington was one of the most segregated communities in America. The city had a small, locked-in black community surrounded by hostile whites. Patterson continues: "You had to fight as a youngster growing up in Anacostia. You constantly had to fight whites because at that time whites were on top and we were powerless." The elder Patterson disciplined his youngsters against succumbing to hatred as a retaliation against racism. Patterson recalled his father's words:

'You don't hate people, because hate destroys you. What you do is learn to overcome. You do this by developing yourselves to the fullest, but without letting yourselves be caught in the role of taking advantage of others.'

My father felt that what had happened to blacks in this country was that whites had learned to discriminate against them because they saw them as threats. Many white people did not know how to handle that. His constant reminder to

his children was that we could not relax. We had to continue
to develop, to develop, and to develop. The more
development that took place, the less likely we were to
remain in a subjugated position.

School life in Washington was relatively uneventful and undistin-
guished. Patterson suspects that he was a little better than an average
student in high school. His major interest was music. Playing his
trumpet and having fun were his major objectives at the time. Satisfying
the academic requirements of Cardozo High School was not difficult for
him. "I am glad that I was not pushed. I enjoyed it more." He did not
have the money to enter the Julliard School of Music or Howard University, and he did not want to go to Miner Teachers College in the District
of Columbia. (Miner was the segregated college established for blacks in
the nation's capital.)

Patterson joined the Army in 1945 and spent a good portion of his
service time in Japan. Upon returning from the service, he settled in
Washington and enrolled at Miner Teachers College. The next school
year he enrolled at New York University, with a major in music. Later he
was to change to a double major in elementary education and English.
The G.I. Bill and a part-time job financed his college days at NYU.

Upon graduation from NYU in 1951, Patterson obtained a position in
the Seattle public schools as an elementary teanher. He enrolled in the
graduate school at the University of Washington. Subsequently, he
decided to study at Teachers College, Columbia University. In 1955,
Patterson married a young lady from Seattle. He and his wife settled
temporarily in New York City, where he was a teacher for the Department of Corrections, an exciting as well as satisfying position. After
receiving his master's degree in 1957, he decided to pursue his doctorate in education at Columbia. He then entered the New York City
public schools as a teacher.

In 1960, he received his doctorate in education from Teachers College. In planning his future, he realized that promotional opportunities
were not promising in New York. He accepted an assistant principalship in Montclair, New Jersey, and later, in 1964, was promoted to a
junior high principalship in Montclair. Motivated by his father's ad-
monition to develop, he never abandoned his quest for education. In
1967, the superintendent in Seattle requested that he return to his
former school system as a junior high school principal. This meant a
lateral transfer, but one that was very enticing, because he would
become the first black secondary school principal in Seattle and he
would be returning to his wife's hometown. He remained the principal

of Meany Junior High School in Seattle from 1967 to 1969. From 1969 to 1971 he served as assistant superintendent of schools with the administrative responsibility for a number of schools from kindergarten through twelfth grade. This position provided him with the opportunity to put into practice some of his ideas about quality education.

On October 1, 1971, he became the second black superintendent to head a system in one of the major cities of America. Patterson initialty viewed the process of applying for the superintendency in Baltimore in 1971 as a means of securing an invaluable personal learning experience. He did not apply with any conviction that he was going to be among the top candidates or that he would even accept the superintendency if offered. There was no great urgency on his part to leave Seattle, but circumstances often have a way of upsetting plans and priorities.

Patterson does not seek to be controversial, but he was deeply committed to the resolution of the tasks that he accepted when he became the superintendent. His intensity at times is perceived as aloofness. His honesty often shocks; he says what he believes. During the interview for the superintendency, he responded to an inquiry as to whether or not he believed that improved educational programs and services would reduce significantly the prison population. Patterson declared: "A large number of those persons who are in prison and who are black are there for no other reason than political reasons." Much was made of this statement in the media and detailed explanations were demanded.

The job took its toll on him. The long hours, the frustrations, and the setbacks far outweighed the pleasures of the job. He believed that sooner or later one of his decisions would cost him his job, because he wanted to turn the school system around — a massive revitalization of the entire system to benefit all of its students. Patterson refused to preside over a system that continued to do a disservice to any of its students:

> I know that I am the superintendent for all the students of Baltimore City. I also know that if I do a good job of delivering educational programs and services to the most deprived of the youngsters in Baltimore City, I will have been instructive in providing a good education for all others.

EARL C. JACKSON
Wilmington, Delaware

Time almost ran out on Earl C. Jackson. He was appointed to the position of superintendent in Wilmington, Delaware at an age when most educators have either retired or given up any thoughts of taking on a new and extremely demanding assignment. At sixty-two, he became superintendent. His eventual appointment and the board's initial reluctance to appoint him provoked one of the most extraordinary series of events ever to surround any superintendent's selection. The predominantly black Wilmington school board had passed over Jackson's name and selected a black woman as its new superintendent. The newly appointed superintendent, an assistant professor of urban teacher education at Rutgers University, received her appointment on a Monday and was notified by the board that the appointment had been rescinded by the board on Thursday of the same week.

Pressure from black students and parents — who threatened to disrupt the city — the mayor, and the governor persuaded the board to meet for the purpose of rescinding its previous recommendation. The *Evening Journal* commented on the pressures put on the board and presented remarks by the board president:

> The board's decision this morning followed nearly ten hours of meeting yesterday. One meeting with city, state, and police officials lasted until after midnight. . . .
> 'We were under tremendous pressure to change our decision,' Casson said, 'both political and public safety.'
> '. . . Dr. Jackson, although you were not our first choice, you are now our first choice. You are now our superintendent and you have the unqualified support and we expect yours and I'm sure we'll get it.'[10]

Before the board's official vote to rescind its previous appointment, Jackson was notified of the board's intentions and given some time to think about them. After five minutes of deliberation, Jackson informed the board that he would accept the appointment. He felt that the community had made its choice obvious to the board and that he had to support the community. He is quoted in the newspaper as offering the following comment on the board's appointment: "The board has reluctantly decided to rescind its decision and I have reluctantly decided to accept the position."[11] Thus began the superintendency of Earl C. Jackson — at the age of sixty-two.

Pride played a major role in Dr. Jackson's acceptance of the board's delayed appointment. He had been encouraged by friends and many others in the community — black and white — to submit his name as a candidate. Jackson was prepared to be gracefully received but passed over, not because of any lack of confidence in his ability to do the job but because of his age. From his deep respect for the desires of a large segment of the Wilmington community, he did not discourage the efforts from the community to gain him the appointment even after the board had officially declared its appointee. As the local favorite with large community support but very limited support from the board, he stated:

> The school system was trying to find a black superintendent. They asked parents to give them input about this. The parents gave them input and a part of that input was in my favor. The board realized that the community was putting considerable pressure on them not to hire a black superintendent, but to hire a particular black. The board felt that the community was putting too much pressure on them. They got more input than they wanted.
>
> I had made up my mind that I was not going to make excuses for the wrongdoings of the Wilmington school system.
>
> I felt that I was prepared and that the community was behind me, so I decided to stay in the fight for the superintendency.[12]

The board that finally appointed Jackson had seven members, four black and three white. The Wilmington Board of Education is appointed by both the governor of the state and the mayor of the city. The governor appoints four members and the mayor appoints three. These two political leaders both made their strong support of Jackson known to the board by direct intervention into the deliberations of the board, which followed the protests and demonstrations in the streets of Wilmington when Jackson was initially passed over. The opposition to Jackson on the board crossed the racial line. He had only one supporter on the board who urged his appointment. It is doubtful that there exists any other example of the community so influencing a board of education to go against its preference in the selection of the chief executive for a school system.

Jackson has had an unusual life. He was born in Knoxville, Tennessee, in 1910, into a family that was not just poor but poverty-stricken. Before Jackson was born, one of his father's legs had been amputated. There were seven children in the family. Jackson left junior high school in the eighth grade to go to work when he was eleven years old. He was not old enough to quit school legally, but as he states, "in the Deep South no one really cared." The interim period between his dropping out of school and his return lasted eleven years. He returned because he had an intellectual curiosity that could not be satisfied without continuing his formal education. When he left the eighth grade, he went to work in a railroad station. He later became a bellhop and then a bell captain in the John Sevier Hotel in Johnson City, Tennessee. In 1927, he married Mildred Silvers. Their first child, Norma Jewel, was born in 1931. She is now an attorney at law working in Delaware. His son, Earl C. Jackson, Jr., was born in 1933. He died in 1972 just after receiving a very prominent appointment as a manager of a business concern.

Jackson returned to the eighth grade and began a long trek that was to culminate in his receiving a high school diploma at age twenty-eight. In 1934, Jackson obtained special permission from the Tennessee legislature to permit him as a married man to attend regular high school; he was graduated from Langston High School in Johnson City in 1936. Upon completion of high school, Jackson felt more compelled than ever to pursue his education. He enrolled at Morgan State College in Baltimore in 1936. His first choice had been Morehouse College in Atlanta, Georgia, but he was unable to secure a job in Atlanta, so he went to college where he could combine education and employment. Jackson worked from 11:00 P.M. to 7:00 A.M. each day in a hotel to finance his education and to maintain his family. He went directly to college from work each morning because of the tightness of his schedule. In 1940, he graduated *magna cum laude.*

A dean at Morgan State College helped him to secure employment as a teaching principal at Stephen Long Elementary School in Worcester County, Maryland, in 1941. Later, Jackson became principal of Worcester Senior High School, a position he held from 1942 to 1949. While in Worcester, Jackson began his graduate studies in education. Admission to the University of Maryland was denied because the university did not accept black students. Unable to attend the University of Maryland, Jackson enrolled at the University of Pennsylvania. He made the decision to transfer his graduate studies to Harvard because he was impressed with the quality of books by several authors who were professors at Harvard. Jackson financed his summer sessions at Harvard by working as a waiter during the free periods at the close of the schools in Worcester and at the close of the summer session at Harvard. Jackson reminisced:

> Each summer, when I would leave the little school where I was principal, I would go to Baltimore and work in a seafood restaurant until it was time to go to Harvard. When I finished my summer work at Harvard, I would work until it was time to be a principal again. I only made $810 per year as a principal.

Jackson completed the requirements for the master's degree in education in 1947. He decided to continue his academic efforts at Harvard and began work on the doctorate in education, which was completed in 1951. He was never really comfortable at Harvard, but expresses gratitude to Harvard for a $4,500 fellowship, which enabled him to take a leave of absence from his principalship and bring his family to Harvard while he completed the academic year on campus. In the completion of his pursuit of the master's and the doctorate, Jackson had maintained an "A" average. But he posed a problem for the prestigious national reputation of the Harvard placement office. Harvard could find many opportunities for its white graduates, but a black graduate presented a challenge beyond its capabilities. "Harvard couldn't do anything for me, but they had a record of turning out ten superintendents for every doctorate they gave out. They couldn't do a thing for a black."

Jackson, upon receiving his doctorate from Harvard in 1951, returned to Morgan State College as its director of student teaching. He held this position for two years. In 1953, he became principal of the Bancroft Junior High School in Wilmington, Delaware. Jackson remained in this position for almost twenty years. When asked why he permitted so many years to pass without advancing his professional career as an educational administrator, Jackson replied:

I did not apply for any other position. I felt that they knew my credentials and my experiences. I told everyone that I was not going to get on my knees to get a job as an administrator. They knew my credentials.

I would always manage to get assignments on the selection committees for central-office positions. This would keep you from applying. I was offered the position of acting director of secondary schools on an interim basis. I held this position while maintaining my secondary principalship.

I now realize that I should have applied several years ago for promotional positions. But I did feel that they should promote me to a position rather than for me to have to beg for one. I have considerable pride or I would have been in there fighting for a position a long time ago.

"I started out in 1941. I have spent about thirty-three years getting to a point that I deserved several years ago." In reflecting on his career, Jackson is not bitter, but he does not want to see what has happened to him happen to other qualified blacks:

Time has caught up with me in terms of age. I sometimes rationalize that maybe I was born at the wrong time in history.

I am reaching a point where the demands physically and otherwise may be such that I may not have the energy that I had earlier. I do not feel too badly that I am reaching the point where I will be forced to retire in about a year and a half. I do feel that I have not contributed to the extent that I was capable of at a high level of administration. I feel that with my training I have never had to stretch myself to the extent that I would have liked. You can get caught into a situation where you are larger than the situation itself, and it prevents you from growing.

Jackson does not consider himself a militant, but he emphasizes that he is most certainly not a conservative. While stressing that he has always been engaged in efforts directed to the improvement of the plight of blacks in any community in which he has worked, he admits, "I am an even-tempered person. Probably, I have been too much in that direction. People sometimes take this as a sign of weakness." Prejudice and pride have been important factors in shaping the life and career of Jackson. Prejudice made his life a greater struggle than it would have been if he had been white and impeded his professional advancement once he had prepared himself far beyond the accepted standards for his particular professional aspirations. Pride prevented him from more vigorously pursuing his professional advancement, and it was this same pride that motivated his decision to accept a superintendency at a late age and in spite of the fact that his board had passed him over.

Jackson retired from the superintendency in 1975. He wanted to devote a significant part of his activities during retirement to helping other black educators avoid some of the pitfalls that he encountered during his career. Jackson accomplished far more than most educators — black or white — during his professional career, a career filled with many disappointments:

I have felt that I had the responsibility to do the best possible job and to carry myself in a certain way. I have always thought about the race. I do not think you can help from being concerned that you have the race on your shoulders. I always tried to do the best that I could.

STANLEY TAYLOR
Newark, New Jersey

The executive office of the superintendent of schools in Newark is located in the downtown section of the city. Stanley Taylor occupied an office located in facilities that had quite some time ago lost their adequacy and attractiveness. Fortunately, plans were under way for a new facility. In the lobby of the antiquated and dingy administrative center for the public schools of Newark were pictures of nine members of the board of education and a picture of Taylor, the superintendent.

In high school and in college, Taylor was a punishing blocker and runner who used the old-style single-wing formation to launch attacks on his opponents. Except for a very slight paunch, he has maintained the stocky frame that once terrorized those who confronted him on the football field and on the basketball court. He is an extremely easy person to meet and relax with. Taylor did not often deviate from the calm but firm manner that he projects in his conversations with staff and others. His generally mild manner has developed from the obvious maturity that he exhibits. Yet he quickly points out, "I can be rough. I will kick back if kicked."[13]

He was patiently aggressive in his sessions with his executive cabinet members. With his board of education, he deliberately avoided any unnecessary confrontations. Taylor rationalized that, with a predominantly black board, he had a responsibility to promote as much unity and constructive effort as possible within the constraints imposed by his personal sense of integrity and his professional code of ethics. His three years as a region superintendent in Brooklyn, New York, working with a decentralized community board, helped him to develop the patience that he believes is necessary in working with a board of education.

For many years, the role of the superintendent in Newark was diluted by the direct activities of members of the board and by the involvement of city hall in the administration of public education. Also, the structural, organizational relationship of certain key school officials called for their reporting, not to the superintendent, but to the board. Politics and education in Newark had been very intimately commingled prior to the arrival of Mayor Kenneth Gibson. Taylor moved in a very disciplined manner to effect the organizational changes needed to establish the appropriate administrative coverage for the office of the superintendent.

His working relationship with the board early during his tenure was good. His most aggressive sessions with his board were usually confined to closed conferences. He admitted that from time to time he forgot his own guidelines and took over a board meeting. He was reminded by the president of the board at one meeting: "You are in the chair with me."

His aggressiveness with his staff in executive cabinet sessions was not an abusive form of aggression. Taylor is an exceptional exponent of the Socratic method of problem-solving. He projected both clarity and conviction in his discussions with members of his staff. Taylor is adept at thinking on his feet. In his leadership style he imposed on his staff in a subtle but effective manner the need to produce justifications or recommendations or be confronted with an exposure of their lack of readiness or indecisiveness. He is good at highlighting an issue while illustrating the possible alternatives. His tone and manner in group discussions encouraged rather than discouraged conflicting points of view. Frequently, he began his remarks with an indirect approach to the basic issues inherent in the topic being reviewed. At the appropriate time, there was the insertion of questions or comments that either elicited a more complete response or accentuated the fact that the parties assembled were ill-prepared to deal adequately with the subjects under scrunity. He often looks directly at a person when he is making a point and says: "See what I mean?"[14]

Taylor sees himself as the kind of person who has always wanted to get things done, a person not satisfied with the status quo. He considers himself an empathic human being, but he admits: "I used to be a lot more considerate of imperfections than I am now. I have a tendency now to say let's perform; let's do it." He gives credit to his two daughters for his improved view of life and for helping him to see that things can and do change for the better. "I do not think that we should take ourselves too seriously."

Taylor classifed himself as an extrovert, but emphasized that his personality manifestations are conditioned by the occasion:

> I like to spend some time by myself relaxing, but I like people. People fascinate me. I am very interested in people. I enjoy it here in Newark. It is challenging. I am not a brooder. I try not to worry about what I cannot do. I tend to fight for something very hard — forget it — and do everything that I can to prevent something from happening which I think should not happen. Once it takes place, I do not worry about it. Let's go on to the next thing. Maybe we can come back to that and do it later.

Taylor was born in Philadelphia, Pennsylvania on January 10, 1926. His father was steadily employed as a mechanic. Neither he nor his two brothers and a sister were ever afflicted by economic deprivation. He recalls his family as a very industrious group. In school, his first love was sports; he was a four-letter winner in high school sports. The academic aspect of school life was not given serious attention until his senior year in high school, but he recalls with pride that he did quite well in mathematics. He received what he calls a "fair education" at Overbrook High School, which had a predominantly Jewish student body. Taylor notes that many of the problems that confront students today in school also plagued his days in high school.

Upon graduation from Overbrook High School, in 1944, he wanted to pursue his athletic interests and see more of the world. He enrolled at the University of Nevada on an athletic scholarship. Football and basketball were his major concentrations during his brief stay in Nevada. He found the social environment in Nevada lacking. The college had too few blacks and the political atmosphere was Republican dominated. One semester was the length of his stay in Nevada. He was drafted into the Army in 1944, and he served as a first lieutenant in the Pacific combat zone. While in the Army, he received something from the black experience that had eluded him previously. He recalls: "It gave me a self-identification and pride that I never had before. It gave me the experience of the evils of segregation as well as a pride in knowing what black people could do."

When Taylor received his discharge from the Army in 1947, he gave himself a six-month vacation before resuming his academic pursuits. He enrolled at New York University with majors in physical education and science. After his degree was granted by NYU in 1951, he taught science and physical education at Public School 93 in Brooklyn. Later he transferred to Junior High School 258 in Brooklyn, where he remained for ten years. In 1955, he obtained his master of arts in secondary school administration. With a Ford Foundation Fellowship for the training of administrative interns, in 1969 he received a professional diploma in instructional administration from Fordham University. His appointment to principal of Junior High School 294 in the Bedford-Stuyvesant section of Brooklyn came in 1969. Less than two years later, he was selected by the Community Board of Education of Bedford-Stuyvesant as its region superintendent.

Three years later, on July 1, 1973, Taylor became Newark's first black superintendent. At forty-seven, he assumed one of the more challenging superintendencies in urban education. Six months later, when I first interviewed him, he was enjoying the experience. With regard to the challenges he stated:

> It takes five to seven years to do the job well, and I came here to do it well. I came here to change the system and to make it a school system of which we all can be proud. . . . I do not think that you can be successful if you consider failure. I do not like to fail.

Throughout most of his adult life Taylor has been an active participant in improving the quality of life for black Americans and other minority groups that are placed in a disadvantaged status in this country. He has a long history of involvement with the NAACP, and he served as a member of the Roosevelt, Long Island board of education while carrying out the demanding responsibilities of his professional position of region superintendent in the New York public schools. Taylor is an activist who expresses a strong commitment to be directly involved in the process of making change. Some years ago, he had a career decision to make:

> [I had to decide] whether to really go out and be an elected official in government or to concentrate in education. I concentrated in education because I believed that education was the place where we had the biggest clout.

Taylor views himself as a militant with a proven record of relevance and commitment to the improvement of the lives of black Americans and other disadvantaged Americans. "I do not know if I come across to people as a militant in my role as a school administrator. Perhaps that is because I think that many of the things that people now take for granted or are fighting for, I came to grips with as things that we must have a long time ago. He does not see himself as supportive of any form of extremism. "I do not think that any extremist is safe to himself because he cannot see the other side." In a reference to a young militant board member, Taylor recalled a conference in which he reflected: "I often tell Mr. Chunga that some of the things that he attempts to do and that he talks about are mild in comparison to some things that I have done."

Taylor seeks to condition his militancy with a purpose and a program. His participation in civil rights struggles has convinced him that it takes more than rhetoric to conduct an effective campaign:

> If you do not have a program, if you do not organize, and if you do not get troops, you may go ten miles, but you can get pushed back twenty miles because you cannot consolidate.

This has been my approach here in Newark. Not to come in saying, 'Change this, this, and this.' Unless we can move that mile and keep it, I have a tendency to wait for the best moment. But this is not to say that I will wait forever.

While considering himself a militant black with a proven record in the civil rights movement, he does not give license to the manifestation of all forms of militant behavior in behalf of the "movement." As a member of the Roosevelt, Long Island, board of education, he joined with his colleagues in support of the denial of tenure to a black-militant teacher whom they viewed as having violated the tolerated boundaries of activism in the schools. He maintained his support of the black superintendent's recommendation for the denial of the teacher's tenure because he felt that the documentation presented justified such a decision on his part:

> This board has the courage to do what someone else should have done. This young lady was never in the schools. It was not a matter of her being singled out for being a militant. She just was never where she was supposed to be. She was not teaching. She was out preaching, at any school, at any place, and at any time.
>
> My belief is that as a board member you really have to look at the issues and to make decisions. I do not think that a board member should make rash decisions, but I do feel that to slide into decisions or to back out and not stand up for what you really believe is the most dangerous thing that you can do as a board member.

CHARLES MITCHELL, JR
Highland Park, Michigan

Charles Mitchell is an unusual individual. If an award were given to the school superintendent who had experienced the most unusual first day in office, Mitchell would win uncontested. He arrived at his office around 8:00 A.M. While taking his coat off, he was informed by his secretary that two parents and a student wanted to see him. Although somewhat surprised that he would be getting visitors so early in the morning on his first day on the job, he told the secretary to send them in. He recognized immediately the two adults and the student. The man pulled out a snub-nosed .38 revolver and pointed it directly in the superintendent's face. Not knowing anything else to say, Mitchell responded: "Is there anything that I can do for you?"[15] While still keeping his gun on the superintendent, the parent informed him that his son — who was an honor student in high school — was a quarter of an hour short of graduation. The gun was his means of persuading the superintendent to intercede and to authorize his son's graduation. Mitchell informed the father that there was nothing that he could do since the boy had not completed his required number of semester hours. He and the boy's mother finally convinced the father to put the gun away. Things were later worked out to the satisfaction of all parties.

Mitchell today presents an almost exact physical replica of the Mitchell who was an all-state and all-city basketball player for Cass Technical High School in Detroit. The athletic physique and the quickness of movement that once served him well on the basketball court and in the high-jumping pit have not been lost. His words come out in a rapid flow. He is a man possessed with a great deal of nervous energy; his colleagues frequently refer to his drive as amazing. But nature has a way of warning us all to slow down when the pace exceeds the maximum capacity of the body. Late in 1973, he collapsed. At first, it was thought that he had suffered a heart attack; fortunately, it was simply physical exhaustion catching up with him. After several weeks of recuperation, he was back on the job. He said his pace slowed down some, but it was difficult to measure the difference.

He was not a desk superintendent. Somehow the paper that crosses a superintendent's desk gets moved, but one quickly got the impression after a few hours with him that sitting at his desk was not his preference for the best way to run a school system. A good deal of his time by choice was spent away from the office. He was always on the move. Mitchell believed that he had one of the finest executive staffs of any superintendent in the country, and he delegated to this staff the full measure of the responsibility for the direct implementation of those duties that came under the organizational units that they headed. He was a stern taskmaster, and found good people and gave them authority sufficient to carry out their assigned tasks. This basic administrative philosophy governed his relationship with his executive staff. He was just as quick in praising a staff member for a job well done as he was in reminding him or her that much remained to be done.

When one entered his office, one could not miss a printed statement of philosophy which sat on the wall behind his desk. The statement read: "Black is beautiful, but business is business." This statement is open to a number of interpretations, but Mitchell feels quite strongly that blacks must move from the production of rhetoric that is emotionally inspiring to the development of programs and practices that enhance meaningful improvements in the lives of black Americans. His statement (he copyrighted it) was a declaration to all who sought employment with and who were then employed by the Highland Park public schools that high standards would prevail. Mitchell is good at coining or adopting phrases that he believes effectively illustrate a point. He frequently reminded students: "Get some info under your Afro." Those who sought to win Mitchell's support by selling their blackness were headed for a disappointment and a possible strong rebuke — unless that blackness also carried with it a demonstrated expertise and a commitment to make the Highland Park schools a model for the nation.

At thirty-five, Mitchell was younger than most of the members of his executive staff. He is an extremely affable person who thoroughly enjoys being with people. "I am gregarious. I like people. Not all people, but most people." He did socialize with members of his executive staff. Yet he and they had been able to maintain that fine line generally accorded to an executive — without his being overbearing and his staff's feeling uncomfortable in the quick changes often made between social and professional relationships. As long as school personnel took care of business, Mitchell paid scant attention to their manner of dress or to most particularities of behavior. He was interested, first and foremost, in performance. He saw himself as a different kind of superintendent: "I am a 'way-out dude,' as they say. I am far from being a conservative."

The terms go-getter and wheeler and dealer are often used by those who know Mitchell. His personality supports immeasurably his professional skills. He is a likable individual who is an excellent conversationalist. He dresses very much in fashion but not to an extreme. His connections were extraordinary. Few individuals — white or black — could lay claim to lunching frequently with Lynn Townsend of Chrysler Motor Company and Henry Ford of Ford Motor Company. While not necessarily boasting of his friendship with these two giants of the automobile industry, he was justifiably proud of the fact that he could list these gentlemen among his personal friends. Also, he had good connections with a number of the members of both houses of the Congress. Within the state of Michigan, he traveled often to the state capital to maintain his contacts with members of the state legislature. Mitchell is a man who has achieved success within the education profession at a relatively early age, but he is the kind of person for whom one feels things were just beginning.

Mitchell personalizes almost everything with which he becomes involved. "I have always had the ability to get along well with people. I have always been the kind of person who would get into a fight only if I had to." This very personal approach to much of what he does can produce an emotional drain that can overtax even what he considers to be a low frustration point. He reflected:

> I think that I have a very low frustration tolerance. I taught mentally retarded children in Detroit for five years.
> One shortcoming that I know that I have is that I tend to personalize things that are dear to me. When board members and/or community people attack the kind of job that I know that we are doing, my first reaction was to respond almost violently. 'How dare you challenge me?' Now with more experience behind me, I just give them the data. I do not get emotional about it.

There was an occasion during a closed conference with his board of education that his emotions got the best of him. A new board member had been giving him a hard time. Mitchell felt that much of what the board member was saying was personal and thus inappropriate and unacceptable. Earlier, another member of his board had given him a gift of a can of "Bullshit Repellent" which she had purchased during a trip to New Orleans. Knowing what superintendents have to endure, she felt that it would make a nice humorous gift for her favorite superintendent. The discussion became more intense between Mitchell and the new board member. Finally, he decided that he had had enough. He went to his desk, which was just a few feet from the conference table, and got his can of "Bullshit Repellent." He calmly returned to the conference table, sat down, and pointed the can in the face of his antagonist on the board and sprayed. Some words were exchanged, but afterwards the two had a better understanding of each other. Mitchell is not one to maintain a passive role when he feels he is being unjustly criticized or abused.

Mitchell has lived most of his life in the Detroit area. He was born in Detroit, Michigan on April 21, 1938. He has three sisters, one older and two younger. "There was always plenty of love in the family. Both parents were very religious. They took us to church every Sunday." His father has worked steadily for the Ford Motor Company for more than forty years. His parents encouraged him to push himself and to go as far in school as possible. He commented on his parents:

> My father taught me all of those good all-American virtues and values. Work hard, be honest, get along with people

regardless of race or creed, and go to church every Sunday. In my opinion he did a damn good job of supporting us. He is very frugal. He works hard. He misses very few days from work. My father taught me how to work. My mother kind of taught me how to enjoy life.

I was about fifteen when I began to rebel against my dad dragging us to church every Sunday.

Mitchell attended Sampson Elementary School in Detroit. This school is located in one of the most consistently stable lower-middle-class black communities in Detroit. He recalls being double promoted twice in elementary school, but admits that he just "goofed off" in junior high school. His admission to Cass Technical High School is in itself an indication that his grades in junior high school were above average. This high school for years has been Detroit's best academic high schools and one of the outstanding high schools in the nation. In high school, his grades were average. He devoted most of his time to sports and to having fun. As he advanced through high school, he became more concerned about his grades. His grades and his athletic abilities combined to gain him admission to Western Michigan University in Kalamazoo, Michigan.

He entered college with the hope of getting a teaching certificate. He felt a teaching position would assist him in earning a yearly income of $10,000 — a sum that he thought would settle his financial needs for the rest of his life. He came to Western Michigan University on a basketball scholarship; later he received an academic scholarship. In 1959, he received his bachelor of science degree in education with a major in physical education. Upon graduation, he taught in Kalamazoo for one year. He returned to Detroit in 1960 as a teacher of the mentally handicapped. Because he considered the classroom too confining, Mitchell left the Detroit schools and took a position with the Highland Park schools as school-community coordinator. This job gave him plenty of opportunity to move about the community; this new position required that he report directly to the superintendent.

In 1965 he received a master of education degree with a major in special education from Wayne State University in Detroit. In 1967, he became the director of special projects for the Highland Park schools. This new position gave him the responsibility for the procurement and monitoring of all federal grants. He earned a reputation as a hustler while serving as the director of special projects. With the long-range view of advancing his administrative career, Mitchell returned to Wayne State University in 1968 and obtained an education-specialist certificate with a major in administration and supervision. Mitchell cites Dr. Charlotte Junge, retired professor of education at Wayne State University, and Lynn Townsend, president of Chrysler Motors, as the two most influential persons in shaping his professional career and his approach to school administration. Junge was a no-nonsense educator who was feared by most students. She was an exceptionally difficult taskmaster who had, rightly or wrongly, earned a reputation as being not particularly supportive of black educators. Mitchell found her extremely helpful. She encouraged him to make good use of his expertise and to enter a doctoral program. Through the direct effort of Townsend, Mitchell was awarded one of the coveted Sloan Fellowships. He spent one academic year at the Massachusetts Institute of Technology in a specialized program for promising business executives. Not only did Townsend go outside the personnel of Chrysler for his selection, but he selected a black. The experience at MIT provided Mitchell with opportunities to travel to Europe and a number of American cities. He left MIT with a master of business administration degree, some invaluable contacts, and a host of unforgettable experiences.

Mitchell returned to Highland Park from MIT in 1970 and was promoted to assistant superintendent for personnel. He also resumed work on his doctorate at Wayne State University. For two years, he served as the administrative head of the personnel department for the Highland Park schools. In 1972, he received his doctorate in education and a superintendency. The news in 1972 was not all good. His wife divorced him. He feels that they are still good friends, but "I just did not spend enough time at home."

He approached the formulation of his contract as superintendent of schools with the same boldness that had characterized his career. "You tell me what you want, and I tell you what I can do. I want that in writing." He did not get it in writing, but he established an extremely good working relationship with his board. Mitchell feels that "blackness" has always been equated with "brokeness" and he wanted it emphasized that the Highland Park schools were not bankrupt. Of his superintendency he stated:

> Having worked in the school system for eight years, I thought that I knew what the problems were. I had no idea until I sat in the superintendent's chair what the real problems were. Things had been kept so quiet and hidden.
> We want to make this a model school district. I think that we are well on our way.

Appendix B

Significant Problems
and Needs of Twenty-one
Black School
Superintendents

ROLAND PATTERSON, Baltimore, Maryland

Significant Needs

Improve achievement levels in reading, writing, and mathematics.
Continue the necessary planning for greater accountability on the part of all concerned with schools, including students, administrators, and parents.
Improve human relations.
Develop procedures for increased community participation.
Develop programs that improve student-adjustment behaviors.

Significant Problems

Public image of department of education.
Relationship with city government.
Availability of financial resources.
Integration of public schools.
Retention of a high-quality staff.

BARBARA SIZEMORE, Washington, D.C.

Significant Needs

Reorganization of prekindergarten-to-grade-twelve-multi-age, multi-level group practice.

Decentralization mechanism.
Allocation-of-resources formula.
Special-education-services continuum.
Staff development.

Significant Problems

Moving staff where needed.
Changing structure.
Board relations.
Student and community involvement expansion.

ALONZO CRIM, Atlanta, Georgia

Significant Needs

Improved student achievement in basic skills.
Organization of appropriate staff-development programs on system-wide basis.
Stabilization of student mobility — particularly white students.
Increased community involvement.
Organized management program.

Significant Problems

Public distrust of the public schools.
Communication channels not yet established.
Change of leadership style — not yet understood by staff and community.
Management team not yet moving by design.
My own impatience.

EDWARD FORT, Sacramento, California

Significant Needs

Increased state aid.
Increased teacher (staff) retraining.
Long-range building plan.
Total district desegregation.
Increased achievement for disadvantaged students.

Significant Problems

Developing viable models of teacher accountability.
Developing viable models for administrative accountability.
Completing elementary school construction plan.
Completing district-wide secondary school construction plan.
Completing implementation of early childhood master plan already
developed.

ORTHA PORTER, East Orange, New Jersey

Significant Needs

More teaching expertise.
Improved facilities.
Long-range planning.
Stable staff.
Funds.

Significant Problems

Adequate staff.
Stable board.
Outside political influences.
Lack of central office control — traditional in this district.
Low tax base.

RUSSELL JACKSON, Phoenix, Arizona

Significant Needs

New school facilities to relieve large class sizes.
Upgrading of existing school facilities.
Additional funds to expand educational opportunities of children.
Updating of administrative staff to improve professional compe-
tence.
Program for parent involvement.

Significant Problems

Negative attitudes on the part of key black administrative personnel.
Lack of sufficient funds for flexibility in making expenditures for
program requirements.

Complacency on the part of some principals.
Legislative restrictions related to expenditures of funds for capital improvement.

ULYSSES BYAS, Macon County, Alabama

Significant Needs

Financial support for the schools.
Funds for the recruitment of specialized personnel.
Massive improvements in the physical conditions of the schools.
Construction of a vocational education and continuing education facility.

Significant Problems

Improving student achievement.
Effecting the superintendent's role as that of a change agent.
Motivating key personnel to produce improvements and to do such with enthusiasm.
Keeping the public informed of the system's problems and needs.
Improving the management of the system's resources.
Developing more adequate school facilities.
Developing proposals.

CHARLES MITCHELL, Highland Park, Michigan

Significant Needs

Further development of a systemwide accountability model that everyone understands, believes in, and implements for the betterment of student achievement in reading, math, science, and language arts.

Effective alternative methods to educate junior high and senior high school students in order to reduce/eliminate absenteeism and vandalism.

Adequate full-funding support for education from the state of Michigan rather than from local taxpayers, i.e., yearly millages.

Advanced funding notice for programs that are federally funded.

Continued improvement and updating of our management system and board of education policies.

Significant Problems

A divided board of education.

The unrelated political and social involvement that is demanded and requested by the community at large.

ALBERT WARD, Inkster, Michigan

Significant Needs

Adequate finances.

Improvement of basic skills.

Staff unity.

Community unity.

Assistance for youngsters with multiple problems from homes with multiple problems.

Significant Problems

Lack of finances (we have a loan from 1968 that costs us $100,000 a year).

Lack of administrative staffs (there are three central administrators).

Negotiations and contract administration (we had a five-week teacher strike this year).

Board relationships (irresponsible boardmanship and interference with administration).

Militant and uncompromising individuals and groups.

JOHN SYDNOR, Muskegon Heights, Michigan

Significant Needs

Curriculum relevance.

Achievement deficits in cognitive skills.

Personnel development and adequacy.

Building expansion.

Significant Problems

Fiscal and monetary solvency.

Teacher and personnel dedication, enthusiasm, and commitment.

Labor constraints imposed by collective bargaining agreements.

Parental involvement.

Lack of trained, high-level administrative technicians.
Apathy, indifference, and motivational elusiveness.
Massive employment needs of fifteen-to-eighteen-year-olds.

HERMAN BROWN, Jefferson Township, Dayton, Ohio

Significant Needs

Curriculum program in math and language arts with kindergarten-through-twelfth-grade continuity.

Higher tax base or more state and/or federal funds to increase the average expenditure per pupil.

Remodeling and repairs to existing facilities and grounds.

Improved community participation in school activities and promotion of school-community relations.

Improved academic achievement for all students as a result of improved teaching techniques and the utilization of instructional materials designed to meet individual student needs.

Significant Problems

Board interference with administrative matters.

Lack of sufficient administrative assistance.

Insufficient funds to implement educational programs needed to improve academic achievement and improve buildings and grounds.

Recruitment of competent professional staff personnel (this is directly related to the low salary schedules for the district).

CHARLES TOWNSEL, Del Paso Heights/Sacramento, California

Significant Needs

Delivery systems designed to enhance the academic achievement of boys and girls.

Support basis for the above — fundings at the state, local, and federal levels.

Complete transformation of what is and what ought to be regarding the education of kids in this district.

Continued staff development to accommodate the above-mentioned three needs.

Reorganization of all schools in the county in order to provide a better chance of educational survival for youngsters in the district.

Significant Problems

Improving the academic achievement of boys and girls in the district.
Improving the delivery systems of skills.
Creating additional community involvement as that involvement impacts on the lives of youngsters.
Budget.
Additional hands to accommodate the above needs and problems.

EDDIE COLLINS, Wabbaseka, Arkansas

Significant Needs

Finance.
A good public-relations system that will coordinate the ideas of the school and community.
A reading program for grades seven through nine.
Equipment.
New buildings.

Significant Problems

Because of past unfortunate experiences with the school board and superintendent, it is difficult to establish trust and confidence.
Recommendations in the best interest of the school district are not always accepted (because of item 1).
Low morale of teachers.
Confidential information leaks.

PETER FAISON, Menifee, Arkansas

Significant Needs

Additional funds.
Specialized facilities to provide further projects of individualized learning.
Teachers, especially in the fields of art and foreign languages, counselors, etc.
Better transportation facilities.
Improved science room with all of the latest equipment.

Significant Problems

An uninformed board without the ability to function totally as school directors.

A staff indifferent to change.

Patterns preset by the former administrator during a long tenure, before compulsory retirement.

School desegregation suit involving the six school districts of the entire county.

Pressures of board members to hire relatives or favorites in non-professional and professional positions.

PETER DANIELS, Moscow, Arkansas

Significant Needs

Upgrading of library.

Fine arts program (upgrading music department and adding art).

Expansion of campus for outdoor activities.

Renovation of elementary school, or replacement.

Repairing gym on high school campus.

Significant Problems

Public awareness of the importance of the public school to the extent of majority participation.

Financial problems (salaries and buildings).

W.B. MOSS, Magnolia, Arkansas

Significant Needs

Finances.

New facilities.

Special education.

Counselors.

Significant Problems

Meeting the needs of community and satisfying the general public.

Decisions that are affected by various technicalities of the law.

EARL C. JACKSON, Wilmington, Delaware

Significant Needs

Administrative staff to design and implement the middle-school concept.
Adequate funds for staff development and curriculum improvement.
Administrative reorganization and role definition.
Change in staff perception of the worth and dignity of all students.
Articulation between levels of administration and the community.

Significant Problems

Board members who confuse their role as policymakers with administration.
Local politicians who appear to be in opposition to the identified needs of the school district.
A state department of public instruction that has been identified by the Civil Rights Commission as a party to racism in hiring and establishing state policy.
A board of education that appears to be split along racial lines.
Administrative insecurity in line and staff administrators.

STANLEY TAYLOR, Newark, New Jersey

Significant Needs

Improvement of student achievement at all grade levels.
Attainment of adequate physical facilities.
Development of the teaching staff to a higher level of professionalism and involvement in the community.
Development of management and managerial skills among the administrative personnel.
Differentiation of policymaking from administrative action.

Significant Problems

Resistance to change in organizational procedures on the part of the central office administrators.
Present union contract and its interpretations by involved personnel.
Relationship between the lay board and the administration.
Securing adequate fiscal resources and physical facilities to provide all of the programs desired for students.
Reversal of the image of the school district.

MARVIN LEWIS, Hancock County, Georgia

Significant Needs

Adequate staff-development program.
Adequate financial resources.
Physical facilities including construction of school plant.
Parental involvement.

Significant Problems

Inadequacy of staff — finding competent personnel to fill positions.
Low academic achievement of pupils in reading and mathematics.
Funding the educational programs.
Developing on the part of school personnel a sense of dedication,
responsibility, duties, and authorities.
Communicating with the white power structure at the local level.
Freeing black minds from an imprisoning feeling and fear that a black
man cannot do the job and that the white man has been doing a good job
for the past two hundred years.
Motivating black people to want to improve efficiency.

ROBERT PEGUES, Youngstown, Ohio

Significant Needs

Rebuild an atmosphere of trust and confidence in the public schools.
Improve the financial support of the school system.
Strengthen the educational program.
Improve race relations.
Develop a strong, effective administrative team.

Significant Problems

Suspicious nature of people (public) in today's society.
Lack of funds to meet all of the needs.
Poor race relations in the community.
Lack of a strong, interested staff which works as a team.
Problems in the open society.

ROBERT BROWN, Greene County, Alabama

Significant Needs

Finance.
Additional classrooms.
Instructional equipment and supplies.
Libraries and gymnasiums.
More competent teachers and support personnel.

Significant Problems

Insufficient funds to operate a first-class school system.
Lack of trained or competent personnel (all categories).
Uninformed agitators in the community (black and white).
Indifference toward public education among black and white community leaders and local parents.
Poor attendance and low aspiration among black children.

Notes

CHAPTER 1

1. Martin P. Deutsch, "The Disadvantaged Child and the Learning Process," *Education in Depressed Areas,* A. Harry Passow, ed. (New York: Columbia University Press, 1963), p. 168.

CHAPTER 2

1. Task Force on Urban Education, *Schools of the Urban Crisis* (Washington, D.C. National Education Association of the United States, 1969), p. 3.

2. Luvern L. Cunningham, "A Tribute to Norm." Speech delivered in Detroit, Michigan, June 7, 1971.

3. Harold J. McNally, "Golden Age for Education: Promise or Illusion?" *Wisconsin Elementary Principals Association Bulletin,* Vol. 35 (1970): 4.

4. Frederic C. Neff, "Education and Freedom of Choice," *Graduate Comment – Wayne State University* (Detroit, Michigan, April 1971), p. 19.

5. Ernest Melby, "The Community School and Its Administration." Speech delivered at the Community School Educators Conference in Miami, Florida, November 1967.

6. Raymond H. Muessig, "Change — The Only Constant," *Education Leadership,* Vol. 26, No. 6 (1969): 1.

7. W.W. Charters, Jr., "Social Class Analysis and the Control of Public Education," *Harvard Educational Review,* Vol. 23 (1953): 268.

8. W.L. Warner, Marchia Meeker, and Kenneth Ells, "Social Status in Education," *Phi Delta Kappan,* Vol. 30 (1948): 117.

9. Kenneth B. Clark, "Educational Stimulations of Racially Disadvantaged Children," *Education in Depressed Areas,* A. Harry Passow, ed. (New York: Columbia University Press, 1962), p. 144.

10. James W. Guthrie and James A. Kelly, "Compensatory Education — Some Answers for a Skeptic," *Phi Delta Kappan,* Vol. 47 (October 1965): 74.

11. *Brown* v. *Board of Education,* 347 U.S. 483, 74 S. Ct. 686, 98 L.Ed. 873 (1954).

12. James Olsen, "The Challenges of the Poor to the Schools," *Phi Delta Kappan,* Vol. 47 (1965): 84.

13. Bayard Rustin, "Equal Opportunity and the Liberal Will," in "Outlook" section of the editorial page of the *Washington Post,* October 15, 1972.

14. Charles A. Asbury, "Yesterday's Failure," in "Outlook" section of the editorial page of the *Washington Post,* October 15, 1972.

15. George S. Counts et al., The Social Foundations of Education (New York: Charles Scribner's Sons, 1934), p. 533.

16. Earl C. Kelley, In Defense of Youth (Englewood Cliffs, New Jersey: Prentice-Hall, 1962), p. 144.

17. Henry M. Levin, "The Effect of Different Levels of Expenditures on Output," Economic Factors Affecting the Financing of Education, ed. Johns, Goffman, Alexander, and Stollar (Gainesville, Florida: National Educational Finance Project, 1970), p. 201.

18. Urie Bronfenbrenner, "The Psychological Costs of Quality and Equality in Education." Speech delivered at the Conference on Psychological Factors in Poverty in Madison, Wisconsin, June 22-24, 1967.

19. Richard A. Rossmiller, "Fiscal Capacity and Educational Finance," Economic Factors Affecting the Financing of Education, p. 361.

20. Norman Drachler, Arthur J. Levin, and John Silard, "Equity for Cities in School Finance Reform" (Washington, D.C.: The Potomac Institute, 1973), pp. 2-3.

21. Public School Finance Study (Jefferson City, Missouri: State Department of Education, 1972), p. 48.

CHAPTER 3

1. Dan Dodson, quoted in The Principal in the New World. Conference report of Chicago Urban League, May 28-30, 1968, p. 5.

2. Luvern L. Cunningham, "A Tribute to Norm." Speech delivered in Detroit, Michigan, June 7, 1971, at a testimonial dinner for Dr. Norm Drachler, former superintendent of public schools in Detroit, Michigan.

3. Statement by Dr. James Redmond, former superintendent of public schools in Chicago, Illinois, taken from a recorded interview, January 31, 1974.

4. Statement by Dr. Richard Gousha, superintendent of public schools in Milwaukee, Wisconsin, taken from a recorded interview, December 5, 1973.

5. Statement by Dr. Norman Drachler, former superintendent of public schools in Detroit, Michigan, taken from a recorded interview, February 12, 1974.

6. Statement by Dr. Gene Geisert, superintendent of public schools in New Orleans, Louisiana, taken from a recorded interview, January 3, 1974.

7. Marcus A. Foster, "Oakland's Time Is Now." Statement delivered to the certificated staff of the Oakland Unified School District on September 10, 1970, p. 10.

8. Gousha, interview.

9. Geisert, interview.

10. Statement by Dr. E.L. Whigham, superintendent of public schools in Dade County, Florida, taken from a recorded interview, October 26, 1973.

11. Statement by Dr. Thomas Goodman, superintendent of public schools of the San Diego Unified Public Schools, taken from a recorded interview, October 26, 1973.

12. Whigham, interview.

13. Geisert, interview.

14. Goodman, interview.

15. Geisert, interview.
16. Statement by Dr. Roland Patterson, former superintendent of public schools in Baltimore, Maryland, taken from a recorded interview, January 29, 1974.
17. Whigham, interview.
18. Redmond, interview.
19. Drachler, interview.
20. Wolfe, interview.

CHAPTER 4

1. Charles David Moody, Sr., "Black Superintendents in Public Schools: Trends and Conditions." Ph.D. dissertation, Northwestern University, 1971. p. 16.
2. From a statement by Edward Fort, superintendent of public schools in Sacramento, California, to the Commission of Superintendents of the National Alliance of Black School Educators in Atlanta, Georgia, July 14, 1973.
3. From a statement by Charles H. Durant III, superintendent of public schools in New Brunswick, New Jersey, to the Commission of Superintendents of the National Alliance of Black School Educators in Atlanta, Georgia, July 13, 1973.
4. From a statement by John Minor, associate superintendent of public schools in Atlanta, to the Commission of Superintendents of the National Alliance of Black School Educators in Atlanta, Georgia, July 13, 1973.
5. From the author's interview with Alonzo Crim, superintendent of public schools in Atlanta, Georgia, on January 10, 1974.
6. From a written statement on the black school superintendent submitted to the author on July 9, 1974, by John Dobbs, special assistant to the state superintendent in Michigan.
7. From a statement on the black school superintendent submitted to the author in July 1974 by Solomon E. Bonds, Jr., superintendent of public schools in Ridgeland, South Carolina.
8. From a statement on the black school superintendent submitted to the author in July 1974 by Albert Ward, superintendent of public schools in Inkster, Michigan.
9. From a statement on the black school superintendent submitted to the author in April 1974 by Russell Jackson, superintendent of public schools of Roosevelt School District in Phoenix, Arizona.

CHAPTER 5

1. Blue Ribbon Citizens' Committee, "Final Report: Study of the Macon County School System" (Tuskegee, Alabama, May 1, 1973), p. ix.
2. Ibid.
3. From the author's interview with Mayor Johnny Ford of Tuskegee, Alabama, December 10, 1973.
4. Blue Ribbon Citizens' Committee, "Final Report," pp. 57-58.
5. Mayor Johnny Ford, interview.
6. Ibid.
7. Based on information obtained from a copy of an agreement reached between Byas and the Macon County Board of Education, dated December 1, 1976.

8. Jim Fain, "The Go-Go Cities — No. 11," *Atlanta Journal* (January 17, 1974), p. 17A.

9. Edgar and Patricia Cheatham, "Atlanta," *Mainliner,* Vol. 12, No. 2 (February 1974): 49.

10. "Ten Best Cities For Blacks," *Ebony* (November 1973), p. 152.

11. "New Politics in Atlanta," *New Yorker* (December 31, 1973), p. 32.

12. Jim Fain, "Go-Go Cities — No. 11," p. 17A.

13. From an interview with Benjamin Mays, president of the Atlanta board of education, Atlanta, Georgia, May 24, 1974.

14. *Calhoun* v. *Cook,* Civil Action No. 6298 in the United States District Court for the Northern District of Georgia (February 22, 1973), p. 16.

15. Research Atlanta, "School Finance in Atlanta" (December 1973), p. iii. Research Atlanta is an independent, nonprofit organization which studies public policy issues that affect the metropolitan Atlanta area.

16. Information extracted from Dr. Alonzo Crim's responses to the author's questionnaire, returned March 1974.

17. From an interview with Alonzo Crim, Atlanta, Georgia, February 17, 1979.

18. *Ibid.*

19. *Ibid.*

20. *Ibid.*

21. "The People of the District of Columbia" (Washington, D.C.: Government of the District of Columbia, Office of Planning and Management, December 1973), pp. 18-36.

22. *Ibid.,* p. 33.

23. Barbara A. Sizemore, "Superintendent's 120-Day Report," p. 2. Submitted to the board of education of the District of Columbia, March 1974.

24. "People of the District of Columbia," p. 71.

25. *Ibid.,* pp. 71-72.

26. From a presentation made by Virginia Morris, president of the D.C. board of education at the time of her installation as president, July 15, 1974. Her statement is entitled "Statement of Virginia Morris, President, Board of Education."

27. Quoted by Tom Littlewood in an article in the *Chicago Sun Times* (March 5, 1974).

28. "Superintendent's 120-Day Report," p. 19.

29. From "Official Report of the Administrative Hearing Officer in *Board of Education of District of Columbia* v. *Barbara A. Sizemore, Superintendent of Schools for the District of Columbia"* (October 8, 1975), pp. 1-2.

30. *Ibid.,* pp. 2-8.

31. *Ibid.,* p. 32.

32. The *Washington Post,* editorial, "What Next for the Schools?" (October 11, 1975).

33. *Ibid.*

34. From "Respondents Answer in the Matter of *Board of Education* v. *Barbara A. Sizemore, Superintendent of Schools for the District of Columbia,"* p. 113.

35. Figures for 1970 are from "A Statistical Profile of Baltimore City and Its

Metropolitan Area" (Baltimore, Maryland: Department of Housing and Community Development), p. 3.

36. From the author's interview with John Walton, president of the board of school commissioners in Baltimore, Maryland, January 28, 1974.

37. *Ibid.*

38. From the author's interview with William Sykes, special assistant to the mayor and director of the mayor's Office of Human Resources in Baltimore, Maryland, August 1, 1974.

39. *Ibid.*

40. *Ibid.*

41. Figures are from a questionnaire completed by school officials in the Baltimore City public schools, March 1974.

42. Statement attributed to Roland Patterson in the *Staff Newsletter* of the Baltimore City public schools, September 7, 1971.

43. Baltimore public schools, completed questionnaire.

44. Office of the Superintendent, "Reorganization Fact Sheet No. 1, Baltimore City Public Schools" (Baltimore, Maryland: Baltimore City Public Schools, January 1973).

45. Office of the Superintendent, "Reorganization Plan for Baltimore City Public Schools" (Baltimore, Maryland: Baltimore City Public Schools, 1972), p. 2.

46. *Ibid.,* p. 10.

47. Board of School Commissioners, "Desegregation Plan for Baltimore City Public Schools, p. iii. Submitted to the Office for Civil Rights of the U.S. Department of Health, Education and Welfare, 1974.

48. Richard Ben Cramer and Antero Pietila, "Board's Whites Try To Fire Patterson," the *Baltimore Sun* (August 9, 1974), p. CL.

49. *Ibid.*

50. *Ibid.*

51. *Baltimore Afro-American,* August 13, 1974.

52. Richard Ben Cramer and Antero Pietila, the *Baltimore Sun.*

53. *Patterson* v. *Ramsey* 413 F. Supp. 523 (1976), p. 525.

54. *Ibid.,* p. 534.

55. *Ibid.*

56. *Patterson* v. *Ramsey,* 552 F. 2d 117 (1977).

57. *Patterson* v. *Ramsey* (1976), p. 523.

58. From an interview with Roland Patterson in New Orleans, Louisiana, February 17, 1979.

59. *Ibid.*

60. Wilmington public schools, teachers-recruitment brochure 1973.

61. Harvard Graduate School of Education, "The Wilmington Public Schools: A Preliminary Needs Assessment" (April 1973), p. 5.

62. Wilmington public schools, "School Desegregation Suit *Evans et al.* v. *Buchanan et al.*" Fact sheet distributed in November 1973.

63. *Ibid.*

64. *Ibid.*

65. *Ibid.*

66. Figures are for school year 1973-74 and are derived from a questionnaire completed by school officials.

67. Wilmington public schools, "Budget: 1973-74" (Wilmington, Delaware).

68. From a questionnaire completed by Earl C. Jackson, superintendent of schools, Wilmington, Delaware, April 1974.

69. *Ibid.*

70. Harvard Graduate School of Education, "Wilmington Public Schools," pp. 3-4.

71. *Evans* v. *Buchanan,* U.S. District Court for the District of Delaware, Civil Action Nos. 1816-1822 (May 19, 1976), p. 8.

72. *Ibid.,* p. 20.

73. *Ibid.,* p. 59.

74. *Ibid.,* p. 5.

75. Newark public schools, demographic data on Newark, January 28, 1974.

76. From an article by Pat Lauber in the May 1972 issue of *Newark,* a magazine published by the Greater Newark Chamber of Commerce. Reprinted in the "Third Annual Report: Mayor Kenneth Gibson Reports to the Citizens of Newark," Newark Public Information Office (1973).

77. Newark public schools, demographic data on Newark.

78. *Ibid.*

79. From the author's interview with Mayor Kenneth Gibson, Newark, New Jersey, January 23, 1974.

80. *Ibid.*

81. *Ibid.*

82. *Ibid.*

83. *Ibid.*

84. From the author's interview with Charles Bell, president of the Newark board of education, July 11, 1974.

85. *Ibid.*

86. *Ibid.*

87. Newark Board of Education, "Superintendent Search: Can You Meet the Challenge?" (Newark, New Jersey, 1973), p. 3.

88. *Ibid.,* p. 12.

89. From an interview with Helen W. Fullilove, member of the Newark board of education, July 11, 1974.

90. Charles Bell, interview.

91. Newark public schools, demographic data on Newark.

92. Newark Board of Education, "Superintendent Search," p. 4.

93. Newark public schools, demographic data on Newark.

94. Newark Board of Education, "Superintendent Search," p. 9.

95. Newark public schools, demographic data on Newark.

96. Newark Board of Education, "Superintendent Search," p. 9.

97. From a questionnaire completed by Stanley Taylor, superintendent of schools, Newark, New Jersey, May 1974.

98. Mayor Kenneth Gibson, interview.

99. From the author's interview with Donald Harris, director of the mayor's Educational Task Force, Newark, New Jersey, January 23, 1974.

100. Mayor Kenneth Gibson, interview.

101. As quoted by Sandra King, the *Star Ledger*, June 3, 1977.

102. As quoted by Sandra King, the *Star Ledger*, May 5, 1977.

103. As quoted by Sandra King, the *Star Ledger*, May 11, 1977.

104. As quoted by Stanley E. Terrell, the *Star Ledger*, June 22, 1977.

105. *Ibid.*

106. As quoted by James Harney, Jr., the *Star Ledger*, July 1, 1977.

107. From the author's interview with George Branch, member of the Newark board of education, in New Orleans, Louisiana, February 17, 1979.

108. Based on Mayor Kenneth Gibson's comments during the taping of *Dateline: New Jersey*, which were reported by Tex Novellino and Guy Baehr in the *Star Ledger*, July 8, 1977.

109. Highland Park public schools, untitled demographic information on Highland Park, Michigan. Delivered to the author March 1974.

110. From the author's interview with Robert Blackwell, mayor of Highland Park, Michigan, January 16, 1974.

111. *Ibid.*

112. *Ibid.*

113. From the author's interview with Maria Williams, January 16, 1974. At the time of the interview, Williams was president of the Highland Park board of education.

114. *Ibid.*

115. From the author's interview with Charles Mitchell, Jr., superintendent of schools, Highland Park, Michigan, July 8, 1974.

116. *Ibid.*

117. *Ibid.*

118. *Ibid.*

119. *Ibid.*

120. From a letter written by Dr. Louis Kocsis, director of compensatory education for the state of Michigan, to Charles Mitchell, Jr., dated March 19, 1974.

121. Charles Mitchell, Jr., "Keeping in Touch," *Your Schools in Highland Park* (published periodically by the school district of Highland Park in cooperation with students, teachers, and the community, June 1973).

122. Charles Mitchell, Jr., "Keeping in Touch," *Your Schools in Highland Park* (November 1972).

123. Charles Mitchell, Jr., interview.

124. *Ibid.*

125. Identity of school official is withheld because individual remains in the employment of the Highland Park public schools.

CHAPTER 6

1. From a tape recording of a statement made by Dr. Charles Moody, Sr. before the first national meeting of the National Alliance of Black School Educators in Detroit, Michigan, November 26, 1973.

2. From the author's taped interview with Dr. James Lewis on November 11, 1973 in Oakland, California. Dr. Lewis is the former superintendent of schools in Wyandanch, New York. At the time of the interview, Lewis served as the chairman of the Department of Teacher Education at Medgar Evers College in New York City.

3. These statements were received by the author from Dr. Russell Jackson on April 16, 1974 in response to a request for his reflections on past and future activities of the Alliance. In April 1974 Dr. Jackson served as superintendent of schools in School District Number 66, Phoenix, Arizona.

4. National Alliance of Black School Superintendents, "Comparative Intercultural Social Concepts Development For Use in K-12 Public School Curricula." Proposal submitted to the U.S. Department of Health, Education and Welfare: Office of Education, Institute of International Studies in 1973, p. 1.

5. From a statement submitted by Simeon F. Moss to the National Alliance of Black School Educators at their conference on "Politics and Education" held in Atlanta, Georgia, July 12-14, 1973.

6. National Alliance of Black School Educators, "Constitution and By-Laws." Approved at the annual spring meeting, April 12, 1973, pp.1-2.

7. From the Preamble and By-Laws of the Metropolitan Detroit Society of Black Educational Administrators (September 1969), p. 2.

8. From the author's interview with Dr. Drachler in his office at the Leadership Training Institute of George Washington University, taped on December 7, 1973.

9. In response to the author's request that he submit a statement providing his views of past activities and his hopes for the Alliance, Mr. Byas responded with a previously prepared statement, "Some Major Problems Faced By Black School Superintendents," prepared in 1974. Excerpts from that statement are quoted.

10. National Alliance of Black School Educators, "Constitution and By-Laws," pp. 3-4.

11. From a letter to the author from Dr. Charles Townsel, dated March 19, 1974.

12. The office is located in the Carter G. Woodson Center for the Study of Afro-American Life and History, Washington, D.C.

CHAPTER 7

1. Lowell Thomas, "What About the Future?" Mainliner, Vol. 12, No. 1 (January 1974), p. 30.

2. Robert Hutchins, "The Administrator," Journal of Higher Education, November 1946. Reprinted in Phi Delta Kappan, Vol. 49, No. 6 (February 1968).

APPENDIX A

1. Unless otherwise noted, all quotations in this profile are from the author's interview with Ulysses Byas, December 10, 1973.

2. From an editorial in the *Gainesville* (Georgia) *Daily Times,* April 18, 1974.

3. From a telegram delivered to Ulysses Byas in Atlanta, Georgia, May 29, 1970.

4. Unless otherwise noted, all quotations in this profile are from the author's interview with Dr. Alonzo Crim, January 10, 1974.

5. Statements attributed to unnamed associates of Crim in Bruce Galphin, "The Education of Dr. Crim," *Atlanta,* Vol. 13, No. 7 (November 1973).

6. Unless otherwise noted, all quotations in this profile are from the author's interview with Barbara Sizemore, February 13, 1974.

7. Alonzo Crim, interview.

8. Statement made by one of Roland Patterson's cabinet officers.

9. Unless otherwise noted, all quotations in this profile are from the author's interview with Roland Patterson, January 29, 1974.

10. *Wilmington Evening Journal,* April 27, 1972, p. 3.

11. *Wilmington Morning News,* April 27, 1972, p. 2.

12. Unless otherwise noted, all quotations in this profile are from the author's interview with Earl C. Jackson, January 14, 1974.

13. Unless otherwise noted, all quotations in this profile are from the author's interview with Stanley Taylor, January 23, 1974.

14. "See what I mean?" is a comment Taylor frequently offered when he had made an observation or a point.

15. Unless otherwise noted, all quotations in this profile are from the author's interview with Charles Mitchell, Jr., January 16, 1974.

Index